Controlling Industrial Pollution

Studies in the Regulation of Economic Activity

TITLES PUBLISHED

Studies in the Regulation of Economic Activity

Controlling Industrial Pollution

The Economics and Politics of Clean Air

ROBERT W. CRANDALL

THE BROOKINGS INSTITUTION
Washington, D.C.

Copyright © 1983 by

THE BROOKINGS INSTITUTION

1775 Massachusetts Avenue, N.W., Washington, D.C. 20036

Library of Congress Cataloging in Publication data:

Crandall, Robert W.
   Controlling industrial pollution.

   (Studies in wage-price policy)
   Includes bibliographical references and index.
   1. Air—Pollution—Government policy—United
States—Cost effectiveness. 2. Air quality management—
Government policy—United States—Cost effectiveness.
I. Brookings Institution. II. Title. III. Series.
HC110.A4C7 1983   363.7'31   82-45982
   ISBN 0-8157-1604-4
   ISBN 0-8157-1603-6 (pbk.)

1 2 3 4 5 6 7 8 9

THE BROOKINGS INSTITUTION is an independent organization devoted to nonpartisan research, education, and publication in economics, government, foreign policy, and the social sciences generally. Its principal purposes are to aid in the development of sound public policies and to promote public understanding of issues of national importance.

The Institution was founded on December 8, 1927, to merge the activities of the Institute for Government Research, founded in 1916, the Institute of Economics, founded in 1922, and the Robert Brookings Graduate School of Economics and Government, founded in 1924.

The Board of Trustees is responsible for the general administration of the Institution, while the immediate direction of the policies, program, and staff is vested in the President, assisted by an advisory committee of the officers and staff. The by-laws of the Institution state: "It is the function of the Trustees to make possible the conduct of scientific research, and publication, under the most favorable conditions, and to safeguard the independence of the research staff in the pursuit of their studies and in the publication of the results of such studies. It is not a part of their function to determine, control, or influence the conduct of particular investigations or the conclusions reached."

The President bears final responsibility for the decision to publish a manuscript as a Brookings book. In reaching his judgment on the competence, accuracy, and objectivity of each study, the President is advised by the director of the appropriate research program and weighs the views of a panel of expert outside readers who report to him in confidence on the quality of the work. Publication of a work signifies that it is deemed a competent treatment worthy of public consideration but does not imply endorsement of conclusions or recommendations.

The Institution maintains its position of neutrality on issues of public policy in order to safeguard the intellectual freedom of the staff. Hence interpretations or conclusions in Brookings publications should be understood to be solely those of the authors and should not be attributed to the Institution, to its trustees, officers, or other staff members, or to the organizations that support its research.

Foreword

Federal environmental policies have proliferated since 1970 as the Environmental Protection Agency has assumed increasing responsibilities for reducing air and water pollution, controlling the quality of drinking water, supervising the management of hazardous wastes, registering toxic substances and pesticides, and even cleaning up old hazardous waste sites. But evidence on the effectiveness or the efficiency of most of these programs is scarce. In this book Robert W. Crandall examines one part of one of these programs—the regulation of public utility and other industrial sources of air pollution.

Controlling such sources of air pollution has cost between $15 billion and $20 billion a year. Yet the control program and these large expenditures do not seem to have been the cause of reduced concentrations of air pollutants such as particulates and sulfur oxides. Though these concentrations appear to have fallen in the 1970s, progress in that decade may have been slower than that achieved in the 1960s, before the EPA was established.

The present system for controlling air pollution relies on technology-based standards and reflects a legislated bias against new sources. Crandall argues that it is inherently inefficient. In his view, recent attempts by the EPA to improve efficiency by moving toward a system of marketable pollution rights are steps in the right direction. He emphasizes that the deliberate bias against new sources that Congress wrote into law to impede the movement of industry from the North and Northeast to the South and West constitutes a barrier to the establishment of a truly efficient system of marketable rights.

After calling for improvements in monitoring and enforcement as prerequisites to any successful modification of the air pollution control program, Crandall concludes with a plea for abandoning different standards for new and old sources and replacing them with a two-part pollution fee. Polluting emissions would be allowed up to a specified level; above that a pollution fee would be levied. Firms could avail themselves of these pollution rights or trade them to other firms with higher pollution-control costs. In Crandall's view, this would permit a general reduction in pollution at lower cost than the present control program entails—and it would remove the bias against new sources.

Robert W. Crandall is a senior fellow in the Brookings Economic Studies program. He is grateful to Gordon Brady, Roy Gamse, Robert Hahn, David Harrison, Lester B. Lave, Richard Liroff, Roger G. Noll, William F. Pedersen, and Paul R. Portney for comments and suggestions. Gregory Call, Elliot L. Birnbaum, and James D. Kole provided valuable research assistance; Penelope Harpold checked the factual content of the manuscript; Anne Petty edited it; Florence Robinson prepared the index; and Lisa Saunders and Anita G. Whitlock provided secretarial and typing services.

This is the twenty-second in the Brookings series of Studies in the Regulation of Economic Activity. The research was supported by grants from the Alfred P. Sloan Foundation, the Ford Foundation, the Alex C. Walker Educational and Charitable Foundation, and the Andrew W. Mellon Foundation.

The views expressed here are those of the author and should not be ascribed to the foundations whose assistance is acknowledged above, or to the trustees, officers, or staff members of the Brookings Institution.

BRUCE K. MACLAURY
President

May 1983
Washington, D.C.

Contents

Text Tables

Appendix Tables

Figures

Abbreviations and Glossary

AQCR
Air quality control region; the Environmental Protection Agency has designated 247 such regions throughout the country

Attainment
Compliance with ambient air quality standards

BACT
Best available control technology

BART
Best available retrofit technology

Banking
Stored emission reductions available for future growth

BAT
Best available technology

BCT
Best conventional technology

BOF
Basic oxygen furnace

BPT
Best practicable technology

Bubble policy
An existing plant is allowed to trade pollution among sources of emission as if the plant were under a bubble

CEQ
Council on Environmental Quality

Criteria pollutant
A pollutant for which the EPA has set a national air quality standard

Emission
Pollutant discharged from a source

Emission standard
Maximum emissions of a given pollutant for an individual source

Exceedance
Specific time when an ambient air quality standard is exceeded

Increment
Amount of additional pollution allowed in a given area

LAER
Lowest achievable emission rate

LCV
League of Conservation Voters

NAAQS
National ambient air quality standard; the maximum allowed concentration of a criteria pollutant

NCAQ
National Commission on Air Quality

Netting
Policy of increased emissions from one source being offset by reductions elsewhere within that plant

Nonattainment
Not in compliance with ambient air quality standards

NSPS
New-source performance standards

Offsets
Reductions in emissions from older sources to offset emissions from new sources in nonattainment areas

PSD
Prevention of significant deterioration; refers to a policy designed to prevent areas with above-average quality of air from being degraded

PSI
Pollutant standard index; a measure of air quality based on the pollutant with the highest concentration relative to its NAAQS

RACT	Reasonably available control technology
SIP	State implementation plan; plan of a state to meet federal air quality standards
SMSA	Standard metropolitan statistical area
Technology forcing	Strict standards for new sources designed to stimulate improved pollution control technology
TERA	Transferable emission reduction assessment
TSP	Total suspended particulates
VOC	Volatile organic compounds

Introduction

Thirteen years have passed since the federal role in air pollution policy was greatly expanded by Congress. The 1970 Clean Air Act Amendments gave the Environmental Protection Agency (EPA) far-reaching powers to set air quality goals, oversee state policies for reaching these goals, establish specific standards for new sources, address interstate pollution problems, and identify and regulate hazardous pollutants. Congress also legislated emission standards for new automobiles and provided EPA with a variety of responsibilities in enforcing these standards.

How has the new air pollution policy fared? Can the impact of this regulatory structure on the quality of the nation's air be assessed? What has the policy cost in terms of a reduction of private goods and services? Could these costs have been reduced without an effect on the quality of the air? Surprisingly little effort has been devoted to answering most of these questions. While the 1970 legislation has been amended once and is being debated again, these legislative processes have not been accompanied by much inquiry into the effectiveness or efficiency of the overall policy. Some academic research has been completed on a number of important issues, but it is limited by the inadequacy of data on air quality, emissions, and costs. The federal government has mandated the expenditure of billions of dollars in control costs, but it has not constructed a data retrieval system that would facilitate evaluations of its efforts.

In this book, I review the evidence on the efficiency and effectiveness of air pollution policy. Particular emphasis is given to the control of industrial sources and to the recent attempts to streamline this policy. I ignore automobile emissions, not because they are unimportant but because mobile sources present a different array of regulatory problems.[1] My approach is decidedly that of an economist; the control of pollution is a subject for which economic analysis provides valuable insights. Whether economic incentives can or should work in this area is, however,

---

1. For an excellent analysis of the mobile source program, see Lawrence J. White, *The Regulation of Air Pollutant Emissions from Motor Vehicles* (Washington, D.C.: American Enterprise Institute for Public Policy Research, 1982).

1

quite a different matter. Not surprisingly, much of this book is devoted
to the appropriateness of economic incentives in air pollution control
and the political constraints that limit their use.

Economists have long pressed for the use of market incentives—
particularly pollution taxes or fees—as a method of simplifying environmental policy and greatly improving its efficiency. Their suggestions
have largely been ignored until recently by the zealous protagonists and
the powerful antagonists of environmental policy. The former group
feared that allowing firms to pay for the right to pollute would increase
product prices without reducing pollution while clearly polluting the
country's moral values.[2] The latter group is obviously disinclined to
submit to an array of new indirect business taxes that are not likely to
be offset by other business tax reductions.

Some opposition to pollution taxes or other market approaches to
controlling pollution has reflected an ignorance of the contributions of
microeconomics to an important policy problem. On the other hand,
economists and policymakers have devoted too little attention to the
problems of implementing these schemes and to the political repercussions of the resulting income transfers. In recent years, however,
experience with a limited array of market mechanisms—involving transfers of pollution rights (or pollution *reduction* responsibilities)—and
frustration with the bureaucratic enforcement of traditional antipollution
regulations have generated new hope that economic rationality may
increasingly invade policy formation in this area. Indeed, there has never
been a better time to offer the economists' prescription to legislators and
policymakers concerned with the problem. A movement to reform
environmental policies is gathering momentum, particularly in the regulation of air pollution. This movement derives its succor from a number
of interrelated issues, which are addressed in this book.

Stringency of the Standards

Among the firms that have borne the brunt of environmental control
outlays, there is a strong consensus that environmental standards are
too stringent and that the incremental costs of abatement often greatly

2. See Steven Kelman, *What Price Incentives? Economists and the Environment*
(Auburn House, 1981).

exceed the incremental benefits of the environmental improvement they generate. The latter observation does not permit a conclusion that too much is being controlled; it may simply reflect the inefficiencies of current control policies.

Inefficiency of the Standards

The prevailing method for regulating environmental discharges is the setting of standards for individual point sources of pollution. In the case of air pollution these standards may be set by the states, the federal government, or a combination of the two. Such standards are numerous, complicated, and guided by statutory language that does not require and often shuns economic efficiency. It is not surprising that these standards do not generate pollution reduction at the lowest possible cost. The inefficiency of the standards that result from the current maze of regulation is the principal source of concern to economists who argue for pollution taxes or transferable pollution rights. The EPA itself has begun to produce evidence that its standard-setting process is inefficient; this evidence is reviewed and expanded in chapter 3.

Barriers to Growth

The 1970s were launched by Earth Day and the Club of Rome's *Limits to Growth*.[3] They ended with the developed world growing much more slowly, though not because of the exhaustion of raw materials or the oppressive forces of overcrowding and pollution. The attempt to combat inflation, in part generated by sharp rises in oil prices by the Organization of Petroleum Exporting Countries, led to deliberately slow-growth macroeconomic policies in most developed economies by the 1980s.

During the 1970s the new environmental, health, and safety regulation was beginning to take form. New products or new production facilities were subjected to the greatest scrutiny and the tightest standards. Air pollution regulation was certainly no exception, as successive statutes required increasingly stringent new-source standards. Legislators and

3. Donella H. Meadows and others, *The Limits to Growth*, Report for the Club of Rome's Project on the Predicament of Mankind (Universe Books, 1972).

lobbyists might have considered this inadvertant policy or at least no more than some naive technology-forcing. But with the 1977 Clean Air Act Amendments, which required utilities to install expensive equipment on new boilers regardless of the extent of the pollution produced by these facilities, this explanation began to seem unconvincing. The alternative theory, advanced in chapter 7, is that the new-source bias is a deliberate attempt by Congress to slow the decline of the older industrial areas of the country.

Ineffectiveness of the Policy

Perhaps equally important in the gathering consensus for a change in air pollution policy is the feeling that the current policies may not be particularly effective in reducing air pollution. It is common for participants in the environmental policy process to talk of the great strides made in cleaning up the nation's air and water. It is less common for them to provide evidence of these salutary results. Data on air quality trends through the 1970s are at best spotty; even these data do not suggest an acceleration in the rate of improvement over the 1960s. This is not to say that there has been no improvement, but it does generate disquietude in those who would like to see the substantial resources that are devoted to pollution abatement wisely used.

Fortunately, the EPA has already begun to change course. It is integrating economic incentives into its administration of the Clean Air Act through a variety of small but meaningful reforms. While the Reagan administration's commitments to these reforms were slow to form, much has been done. Unfortunately, much damage has also been done by a number of misguided policy initiatives in the areas of enforcement, new-source standards, and air quality standards. In this book I review these initiatives, providing a critical analysis of how some of them might be used as the foundation of a more rational, effective, and efficient set of policies.

I

Federal Air Pollution Policy

Air pollution policy in the United States seems to be regarded as a qualified success. People generally believe that air pollution has been reduced by federal standards for automobiles, industrial plants, and utilities, although the cost of these reductions might have been lower.[1] Suggestions for changing air pollution laws are usually advanced with a warning that progress must not be reversed. But has this policy been successful by conventional criteria? Is the air cleaner? If it is, can the improvement be attributed to regulation?

There is some evidence that emissions from automobiles have been reduced by federal new-car standards,[2] but no conclusive studies demonstrate similar success for federal stationary-source policies. While most studies of the automotive policy demonstrate that emissions could have been controlled at a lower cost,[3] at least regulation seems to have reduced them.

The regulation of emissions from industrial and utility sources—stationary sources—has consumed much of the resources and energies of the Environmental Protection Agency (EPA). However, stationary-source regulation has not been studied as intensively as automotive emission regulation. More than a decade after the Clean Air Act Amendments of 1970,[4] which gave the federal government primary responsibility for directing air pollution policy, it is not known how well the policy of controlling stationary sources is working.

1. National Commission on Air Quality (NCAQ), *To Breathe Clean Air* (Government Printing Office, 1981), p. 1.

2. Lawrence J. White, *The Regulation of Air Pollutant Emissions from Motor Vehicles* (Washington, D.C.: American Enterprise Institute for Public Policy Research, 1982).

3. Edwin S. Mills and Lawrence J. White, "Government Policies toward Automotive Emissions Control," in Ann F. Friedlaender, ed., *Approaches to Controlling Air Pollution* (MIT Press, 1978), pp. 348–409; and White, *Regulation of Air Pollutant Emissions.*

4. These amendments have become known as the Clean Air Act; they in turn were amended in 1977. The entire statute may be found at 42 U.S.C. 7401.

Federal Air Pollution Legislation

Major federal activity in regulating the environment is rather recent. Before the 1960s air and water pollution were problems left to state and local governments. The federal government assumed a minor role in water pollution control in 1948 and a somewhat greater role in 1956.[5] Not until 1965 did Congress establish a strong federal policy for the design and enforcement of water quality standards. Federal involvement in air pollution policy followed a similar course. The 1963 Clean Air Act gave the Department of Health, Education, and Welfare the power to convene hearings and conferences on state air pollution problems. HEW could pursue industrial polluters in federal courts if the states failed to act, but the department generally deferred to the states in the administration of the policies.

Between 1965 and 1972 Congress responded to public pressure for improvements in environmental quality with several statutes that expanded the federal role in both air and water pollution regulation. Surprisingly, federal environmental regulation grew most rapidly while a conservative Republican, Richard Nixon, occupied the White House. The turning point in air pollution policy came during this period, when Congress passed the Clean Air Act Amendments of 1970. By 1972 federal preeminence in both air and water pollution policy was firmly established.

In 1965 Congress began to focus on air pollution from the automobile. More than a decade earlier, scientists at the California Institute of Technology had established a probable link between hydrocarbon and nitrogen oxide emissions and the formation of smog in urban areas. By 1965 policymakers had generally accepted this scientific finding, and Congress was ready to pressure automobile producers into reducing the emissions from new cars. Senator Edmund Muskie drafted a bill to empower HEW to set federal standards for new-automobile emissions. Following this statutory mandate, HEW copied the 1967 California

5. For a brief review of the history of federal environmental policy, see J. Clarence Davies III and Barbara Davies, *The Politics of Pollution* (Bobbs-Merrill, 1975), chap. 2. For a critical review of air pollution policy, see Larry E. Ruff, "Federal Environmental Regulation," in *Study on Federal Regulation,* vol. 6: *Framework for Regulation,* Senate Committee on Government Operations, 96 Cong. 1 sess. (GPO, 1978), p. 251.

standards. These standards became the 1968 federal automobile emission standards.

The 1965 act provided little authority for federal intervention in air pollution from industrial sources. The federal government could convene conferences with state officials or regulate industrial sources that contaminated Mexico or Canada. Neither activity was pursued vigorously. The federal role in regulating air pollution from industrial sources would not begin in earnest until the 1970s.

The Air Quality Act of 1967 was a prelude to the legislation of the 1970s. The federal government was empowered by the 1967 act to designate air quality control regions (AQCRs) and to specify recommended control technologies, but the states retained the power to set individual standards and to enforce them. Unfortunately, there was little apparent progress.

In 1970 Congress, prodded by the new populism reflected in events such as Earth Day, passed a far-reaching set of amendments to the 1967 act, giving the federal government the power to set national air quality standards and to require states to develop implementation plans for attaining these standards. Standards for individual industrial sources were to remain the responsibility of the states, but the federal air quality standards were to be met by 1975 after allowing for expected economic growth. The Environmental Protection Agency was authorized to carry out federal air pollution policy and set uniform standards for *new* industrial sources of pollution.

The 1970 amendments specified standards for nitrogen oxides, carbon monoxide, and hydrocarbons emitted by new automobiles. These standards were to be tightened successively over a five-year period until emissions from new cars were reduced 90 percent from their 1970 or 1971 levels. The existing stock of cars on the road was not regulated. Thus for the first time the federal government assumed responsibility for regulating emissions from new industrial sources and new motor vehicles, and it began to supervise state plans for regulating older industrial sources of the major criteria pollutants.

Establishing a new agency, the EPA, to right in just five years problems that had been building up for decades was a phenomenon to be repeated many times in Washington in the 1970s. New agencies were formed to cope with problems of occupational safety and health and product safety or to assume expanded responsibilities for mine safety. In each case

Congress gave the agency little time to accomplish a difficult political task. Nevertheless Congress could take credit for having addressed some major problems.[6] But how well would its designs work? Who would be blamed if they failed? The succeeding years found the EPA embroiled in continuous controversy. In large part this controversy was inevitable—particularly in air pollution policy—because of the complex mandate that Congress had suddenly thrust on the EPA.

The Clean Air Act in Operation

The Clean Air Act Amendments of 1970 created a curious variety of federalism.[7] State governments set individual standards for existing polluters, but the federal government dictates the goals. New-source standards are issued by the EPA, but offsets of emissions from older sources against emissions from new sources are administered by the states. Most enforcement responsibilities reside with the states, but the federal government retains civil penalty powers for punishing violators. The EPA can declare an air quality control region in *nonattainment* for one or more pollutants, but it can force compliance only through indirect incentives such as the withholding of federal grant monies. Given these complexities, it is useful to begin with a summary of the various aspects of federal clean air policy.

Setting the Ambient Standards

The Clean Air Act Amendments of 1970 require the EPA to set primary and secondary ambient standards for all *criteria* pollutants, a category that now includes particulates, carbon monoxide, sulfur oxides, nitrogen dioxide, hydrocarbons, oxidants, and lead. The primary standards must protect the health of the most sensitive groups in the population with an adequate margin of safety. The secondary standards must protect the public "welfare," including private economic benefits such as crop yields and the prevention of property soiling. The 1977 amendments require that each of these standards be reexamined every

6. See Morris P. Fiorina, "Legislative Choice of Regulatory Forms: Legal Process or Administrative Process?" Social Science Working Paper 387 (California Institute of Technology, May 1981).
7. 42 U.S.C. 7401.

five years, but by the end of 1982 the EPA had revised only the oxidant standard. It has been unable to reach decisions on the revisions of standards for other criteria pollutants.

The 1970 amendments specified the criteria for the primary ambient standards. Congress apparently intended that these standards protect health absolutely, reflecting a belief that there is a "threshold" in the relationship between ambient concentrations and human health. That the evidence does not suggest such a threshold has never been recognized by Congress or the courts. With the existing scientific knowledge of the health effects of the criteria pollutants, the EPA cannot reject the theory that the dose-response relationship is linear.

Since there is only limited evidence of actual health effects from most of these pollutants at current pollution levels, the EPA administrator is forced to make a judgment from experimental and clinical evidence involving much higher concentrations. A linear extrapolation from this evidence toward a zero (or "background") concentration may lead to the prediction of *some* health effects at even the lowest concentrations.[8]

The absence of a cost-benefit test for setting mandatory air quality standards has been criticized widely.

On the face of it, carrying out such a policy literally would be madness; no reasonable person would spend a million dollars to eliminate a dime's worth of environmental damage. But since a rulemaking proceeding to determine a standard based on full analysis of the costs and benefits for many different locations throughout the country might prove unmanageable, it may be valuable to establish, as goals, what levels of contaminants are harmless—provided that the law also permits those goals to go unmet in the event their costs are excessive.[9]

Acknowledging that benefits and costs of air pollution control should be balanced against each other is difficult for a legislator. Thus the goal of absolute protection in the ambient air quality standards is likely to remain.

In addition to setting the ambient standards, the statute requires the EPA and the states to control emissions so that the primary air quality standards are met throughout each AQCR, not simply at an average site.

8. For an incisive critique of this process, see Lawrence J. White, *Reforming Regulation: Processes and Problems* (Prentice-Hall, 1981), chap. 4; and Lester B. Lave and Gilbert S. Omenn, *Clearing the Air: Reforming the Clean Air Act* (Brookings Institution, 1982), pp. 9–18. For further discussion, see chapter 8, below.

9. David P. Currie, "Federal Air Quality Standards and Their Implementation," *American Bar Foundation Research Journal* (1976), p. 368.

This can lead to substantial planning and control costs because of the necessity for assuring compliance in every location in the region.

The SIP Process

The responsibility for devising a plan for meeting the national ambient air quality standards for each pollutant rests with the states. The EPA has designated 247 AQCRs. Each state must submit to EPA a state implementation plan (SIP) describing its regulatory strategy for bringing each AQCR into compliance with the ambient standards set by the EPA under section 109 of the Clean Air Act. Plans for controlling the existing sources of each criteria pollutant must be detailed. The SIP must demonstrate that all AQCRs in the state will comply with the primary standards by 1982 or 1987, depending on the pollutant. The method for administering increments of additional pollution in prevention of significant deterioration (PSD) areas must also be specified. For nonattainment areas the method for administering the reasonably available control technology (RACT) requirements is to be specified. Reasonable progress toward attainment must be demonstrated in these areas, and comprehensive inventories of emissions must be calculated. If an area does not meet primary ambient standards for the automobile-related pollutants—oxidants (ozone) and carbon monoxide—a mandatory vehicle inspection and maintenance system must be implemented. This last requirement has been vigorously resisted by a few states, most notably the state with the greatest automobile pollution problem, California.

Critics of the SIP process contend that it is unduly cumbersome and burdened by procedural requirements.[10] Each SIP revision must pass through both a state and a federal administrative process. At the federal level the revision is subject to the Administrative Procedures Act. The EPA must publish the proposed revision for public comment; the agency must consider all such comments before reaching a final decision. Most states require a similar procedure, creating additional administrative burdens and delays.

Each time an ambient standard is changed or a new set of new-source standards is promulgated or any adjustment is made in the regulation of individual point sources, a SIP revision must pass the administrative procedures gauntlet. Moreover, trading pollution rights through offset

10. William F. Pedersen, Jr., "Why the Clean Air Act Works Badly," *University of Pennsylvania Law Review*, vol. 129 (May 1981), pp. 1059–1109.

transactions has historically been handled as a SIP revision. The bureaucratic tangle created by such a process in the name of public access is a potent force for maintaining the regulatory status quo.

The EPA has little real power to insist that SIPs be reasonable, although it can disapprove SIPs if they do not provide adequate control standards. If a state persists in not offering its own plan or is unable to propose one that the EPA approves, the federal agency can propose its own SIP for that state. This requires an even more formal notice and comment procedure than the regular SIP process.

More important, the EPA cannot compel a state to enforce a SIP. It can suspend federal grants to the state for sewage treatment or transportation facilities. It can even begin to press civil court proceedings against sources that are not complying with the EPA-formulated SIP. But in practice these procedures are ineffective because the EPA lacks the manpower, the budget, and the political wherewithal to enforce standards in states that do not want them enforced.

New-Source Performance Standards

While existing-source standards are largely the states' responsibility, the new-source standards are the EPA's.[11] All new sources must meet engineering-based standards set by the EPA for each source category in each industry. These standards are set on a uniform national basis. For PSD areas, however, the 1977 amendments require a case-by-case determination of the required controls. In these areas the standards are to be based largely on the best available control technology (BACT).

New-source performance standards must be set by the EPA for each generic source of pollution. The administrator is to choose the "best system of emission reduction which . . . has been adequately demonstrated,"[12] but he must also consider the social costs of achieving this reduction. These standards are supposed to be performance standards, specifying a result rather than a technique, but the choice of technique is generally rather explicit in the EPA's standards. In the case of "fossil-fuel-fired stationary sources" the EPA was required by the 1977 amendments to specify a minimum percentage reduction in emissions from the

11. For a discussion of EPA's role in setting new-source standards, see David P. Currie, "Direct Federal Regulation of Stationary Sources under the Clean Air Act," *University of Pennsylvania Law Review*, vol. 128 (June 1980), pp. 1389–1470.

12. 42 U.S.C. 7411.

best available technological system of continuous emission control. This provision was inserted into the law under pressure from eastern high-sulfur-coal producers. It has the effect of requiring the EPA to mandate flue-gas scrubbers for all new coal- or oil-fired sources of emissions, regardless of the sulfur content of the fuel.

In areas that have not met national primary air quality standards, new sources must employ the lowest achievable emission rate (LAER) demonstrated anywhere in the country. These new sources may have to purchase offsets from other polluters—guarantees from other polluters that they will reduce their emissions of the same pollutant. These offsets amount to a transfer of pollution rights from old sources to new sources in an area where ambient concentrations of the pollutant exceed the national primary standard, but the transfer does not represent an even exchange. For each pollutant, new sources must buy offsets that exceed their prospective pollution, and they also must meet the tight LAER new-source standards.

On a case-by-case basis BACT and LAER are not likely to differ. The EPA and the states cannot hope to make these distinctions for every type of new source; the practical solution is to use the new-source performance standards for most purposes. But these new-source standards impose much higher costs per unit of pollution removed than most SIP standards for existing sources.[13]

The definition of new source in the Clean Air Act has created considerable confusion.[14] If a new piece of equipment is constructed in an existing plant, should it be considered a new source? Should it be exempted from new-source designation as long as it does not increase total pollution from the plant? What happens if the plant's owners increase the size of a given piece of equipment (such as a boiler) but offset the resulting pollution increases by reducing emissions elsewhere? Is this new, larger equipment a new source? Is the entire plant subject to new-source standards? After successive court rulings in *ASARCO* v. *EPA*[15] and *Alabama Power* v. *Costle*,[16] the EPA redefined a new source so that modifications do not trigger the new-source requirement for the

13. See chapter 3 for evidence on this point.
14. See the discussion of "source" in *Anne M. Gorsuch et al.* v. *Natural Resources Defense Council, Inc., et al.* (D.C. Cir. 1982).
15. *ASARCO, Inc.* v. *EPA*, 578 F.2d 319 (D.C. Cir. 1978).
16. *Alabama Power Co.* v. *Costle*, 636 F.2d 323 (D.C. Cir. 1980).

entire plant.[17] Unfortunately, even this new definition for nonattainment areas has been nullified by the courts.[18]

Nondeterioration Policy

In 1977 Congress wrote a PSD policy into the Clean Air Act Amendments. All areas meeting national ambient standards are to be designated class I, class II, or class III. Pristine national parks and wildernesses are included in class I. The remaining areas are designated class II unless a state chooses to designate them class III after a detailed process involving the governor, the state legislature, and the public. In each of these areas, new pollution sources may not contribute more than a fixed amount of additional emissions even though these increments do not lead to a violation of national ambient standards. Class I increments are smaller than class II increments, which in turn are smaller than class III increments. Each proposed source must also meet BACT standards, and its owner must provide a detailed engineering and environmental analysis demonstrating that it will not exceed the allowed increment or degrade the ambient air quality beyond national standards. This case-by-case review has been much criticized by the private sector because of its effect on the timing and level of new investment.

In short, through PSD and new-source policies Congress has probably impeded the growth of new facilities in the cleaner sections of the country. In part the motive for this pursuit of nondegradation is to preserve the remaining clean areas, although there may be other political goals driving this policy.[19]

Visibility

Section 116 of the 1977 Clean Air Act Amendments requires the EPA to identify class I areas where visibility is an important consideration. This identification is to be done in consultation with the Department of the Interior. After this step the EPA is to require of all relevant SIPs the installation of the best available retrofit technology (BART) on twenty-eight classes of major stationary sources. This provision was adopted in

17. See chapter 5 for further discussion of this point.
18. *Anne M. Gorsuch et al.* v. *Natural Resources Defense Council, Inc., et al.*
19. See chapter 7 for evidence on the political determinants of environmental policy.

order to force the agency and the states to compel existing polluters to reduce emissions in class I areas where visibility has been impaired by air pollution.

Interstate Pollution

An obvious reason for a *federal* air pollution policy is that many pollutants are carried great distances by air currents in the atmosphere. Policies to improve air quality in a given area may simply transfer the problem to other areas. For example, the use of tall stacks to disperse sulfur oxides or particulates may succeed in improving air quality near the source while reducing air quality in distant downwind locations. Sulfates are now considered more dangerous than sulfur dioxide; the use of tall stacks may actually increase the probability that sulfur dioxide is transformed into dangerous sulfates rather than falling to the ground unchanged.

In the 1977 amendments Congress empowered the EPA administrator to require pollution abatement from one state if its pollution affects air quality in an adjacent state. The aggrieved state may petition the administrator for such action; he must respond within sixty days.[20] This provision has not been used successfully for combating the long-range transport of sulfur oxides and photochemical oxidants, perhaps because of the political problems that it creates for federal officials. Recent concern about the transport of sulfur oxides from the Midwest to the Northeast and Canada has focused attention on the inadequacy of federal policy in this area.[21] The "acid rain" that results from these sulfur oxides and nitrogen oxides appears to be adversely affecting water, vegetation, and wildlife, but current policies seem unable to cope with the emerging problem.

Other Provisions

While these procedures may seem complicated, the Clean Air Act requires even more of the EPA. The agency is responsible for testing new automobiles to determine their compliance with congressionally set emission standards for carbon monoxide, nitrogen oxides, and hydro-

20. Sec. 126 of the Clean Air Act.
21. NCAQ, *To Breathe Clean Air,* chap. 9.

carbons (as amended in 1977). It is responsible as well for setting emission standards for hazardous pollutants in a uniform national manner despite the local nature of the hazardous-pollutant problem. It must design and fund a monitoring network. It must devise a civil penalty program under two different sections of the act. The agency must regulate the lead content of gasoline. It is responsible for enforcing warranties on automotive emission-control equipment. It is also responsible for researching the effects of air pollution, abatement techniques, and the cost of achieving healthy air.

، Summary

The detailed statutory provisions of the Clean Air Act, including the supervision of state implementation plans, are enough to occupy a large federal agency. The Clean Air Act is only one of many statutes administered by the EPA. The agency must also implement federal policies for water pollution control, toxic substances regulation, pesticide regulation, hazardous-waste disposal, and noise abatement. As a result, it is not surprising that many SIPs remained less than fully approved two years after the statutory deadline, that the precise RACT guidelines for nonattainment areas have been slow in coming, or that the definition of "new source" is still unclear. The Clean Air Act is at best a baroque statute; at worst it may be unenforceable.

II

The Effectiveness
of Clean Air Policy

It is frequently asserted that the air is less polluted than in 1970 and that government environmental policies are responsible for the improvement. For instance, the National Commission on Air Quality (NCAQ) concluded:

Since [1970] . . . the absolute level of improvement for the most widespread air pollutants has been significant. . . .

More significant than the level of absolute reductions, however, is the difference between current pollution levels and those that would have occurred if major control efforts had not been required . . . it is clear that for a number of pollutants the level of emissions would now be several times as great in many areas.[1]

Similarly the Reagan administration has endorsed the continuation of progress in cleaning up the nation's air. The first of the "eleven principles" that guide the administration's approach toward legislation is that "the Nation should continue its *steady progress* toward cleaner air."[2]

What evidence does the NCAQ or the administration use to conclude that progress has been made? How accurate is this evidence? Can the hypothesis of no change in air quality be rejected?

Air Quality Trends

Two types of data can be used to measure the success of air pollution policies: air quality data and emission estimates. The former are measures of the average concentration of the important pollutants, drawn from monitoring sites maintained by the Environmental Protection Agency and the states. The latter are estimates of total emissions based

1. National Commission on Air Quality, *To Breathe Clean Air* (Government Printing Office, 1981), p. I-1.
2. Statement, Anne M. Gorsuch, administrator, U.S. Environmental Protection Agency, August 5, 1981; emphasis added.

on theoretical models of emission rates, the extent of compliance, and industrial activity.

Air quality data are the more useful measures of progress against air pollution because they reflect the pollution levels actually encountered by the public. Unfortunately these data were not collected in a thorough, systematic fashion in the 1960s and 1970s. As a result the effect of the national air pollution policy cannot be measured with any degree of certainty.

Virtually all data on air quality trends come from the EPA. Each year these data are submitted to the Council on Environmental Quality (CEQ), which in turn publishes them in its annual reports.[3] The CEQ's 1981 report was less detailed than previous reports, but in 1982 the Conservation Foundation published a similar document, from which these data are drawn.[4]

There are few observations on air quality before 1974. The Conservation Foundation tabulations (figure 2-1) for the important criteria pollutants begin in 1974 for oxidants, carbon dioxide, and sulfur dioxide. Carbon monoxide data go back to 1970, and data for total suspended particulates (TSP) are shown for 1960 through 1980. There appear to have been substantial improvements in sulfur dioxide and carbon monoxide concentrations since 1974, no improvement in particulate concentrations, a modest improvement in oxidant levels, and a worsening of nitrogen dioxide levels. Even these data must be considered tentative because of the quality of the monitoring on which they are based.

First, there are often few monitors producing reliable data. Sulfur dioxide and carbon monoxide data shown in figure 2-1 are based on fewer than 100 sites.[5] Ozone (oxidant) data are drawn from 122 sites and nitrogen dioxide data from 338 sites. Given the considerable variation in air quality within a single air quality control region (AQCR), there is considerable danger in characterizing average *national* air quality from as few as 84 sites drawn from the 247 regions.

Second, monitors are not located randomly across a control region, nor are they located to measure the air quality encountered by the average resident. Instead they are apt to be near the sources of the

3. Council on Environmental Quality, *Environmental Quality*, 1978 and 1979 annual reports, chap. 1.
4. Conservation Foundation, *State of the Environment, 1982* (Washington, D.C.: CF, 1982).
5. These details may be found in ibid., p. 54.

Figure 2-1. *Air Quality Trends, 1960–80*

Average concentration
(micrograms per cubic meter)

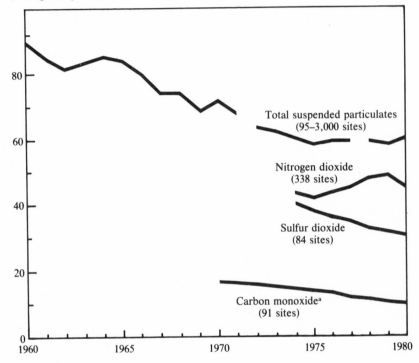

Total suspended particulates
(95–3,000 sites)

Nitrogen dioxide
(338 sites)

Sulfur dioxide
(84 sites)

Carbon monoxide[a]
(91 sites)

Average concentration
(parts per million)

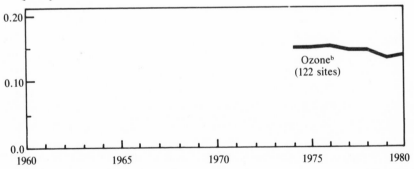

Ozone[b]
(122 sites)

Source: Conservation Foundation, *State of the Environment, 1982* (Washington, D.C.: CF, 1982).
a. Second highest eight-hour average.
b. Second highest daily maximum one-hour reading.

pollutant. This procedure is not conducive to capturing average air quality. Moreover, given changing demographics and industrial activity, the monitors can demonstrate improvement when pollution is redistributed but not abated. For instance, carbon monoxide monitors have been located primarily in the core of older cities. Since activity is declining in many of these cities, it is not surprising that measured concentrations of carbon monoxide have been falling. But has the average concentration of carbon monoxide throughout the country been declining? No definitive answer is possible from these ninety-one sites.

Third, observations are not available from each site in each year. As a result, the sample size in figure 2-1 is even smaller than indicated. When data points are missing, the EPA simply interpolates between the years for which data are available.

Finally, the data for total suspended particulates (TSP) are not quite as reliable as figure 2-1 might suggest. The improvement shown in particulate concentrations from 1960 through 1971 is based on just 95 monitoring sites. The 1972–77 data are drawn from over 3,000 sites, but the 1978–80 data are based on 1,925 sites. For this reason the TSP line in figure 2-1 is shown with discrete breaks to reflect the changing data base.

If the 1974–80 data seem unreliable, the earlier data are even less reliable. Nevertheless the fragmentary data available for sulfur dioxide and particulates show a rather interesting trend. The EPA has data from 32 sites for sulfur dioxide for 1964–71 and from 95 sites for particulates for 1960–71.[6] These data are plotted with alternative tabulations of the 1970s data drawn from various EPA and CEQ documents (figure 2-2). Every tabulation since 1972 shows less relative improvement than was achieved in the 1960s. Sulfur dioxide concentrations appear to have fallen 11.3 percent per year from 1964 through 1971 but no more than 4.6 percent per year in the 1970s. Similarly, the average concentration of TSP fell 2.3 percent per year in the 1960–71 period but only 0.6 percent per year from 1972 to 1980. Therefore, these data suggest that pollution reduction was more effective in the 1960s, before there was a serious federal policy dealing with stationary sources, than since the 1970 Clean Air Act Amendments.

In the 1970s two severe oil-price shocks clearly induced industrial

6. EPA, "Deputy Assistant Administrator's Report on Ambient Monitoring Activities—Air Portion" (EPA, 1980).

Figure 2-2. *Trends in the Ambient Concentrations of Particulates and Sulfur Oxides in the 1960s and 1970s*

A. TOTAL SUSPENDED PARTICULATES, 1961–71 AND 1972–80

Micrograms per cubic meter

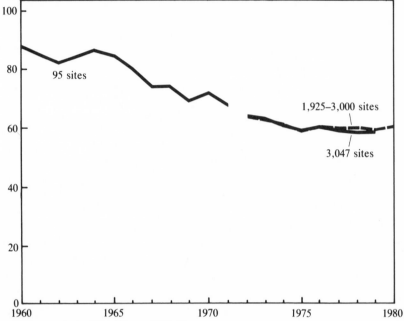

B. SULFUR DIOXIDE, 1964–71 AND 1972–80

Micrograms per cubic meter

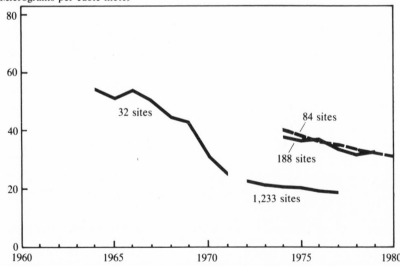

Sources: Environmental Protection Agency, ''Deputy Assistant Administrator's Report on Ambient Monitoring Activities—Air Portion'' (EPA, 1980), pp. 2-3, 2-5, and A-3–A-8; and Conservation Foundation, *State of the Environment, 1982.*

enterprises to reduce their consumption of fossil fuels. Since a large proportion of industrial and utility emissions of sulfur dioxide and TSP derives from fossil-fuel combustion, the 1970s should have witnessed an acceleration of progress against air pollution even without change in environmental policy. The deceleration of economic growth after 1973 also should have served to reduce air pollution. Despite these influences, the available data do not permit a conclusion that air quality improved more rapidly in the 1970s than in the 1960s. Given the quality of the data, no stronger statement can be made with confidence, but there certainly is no support for the NCAQ assertion that the Clean Air Act has reduced the absolute level of pollution. A system of state air pollution policies could have been equally or more effective.

Another index of air quality in major metropolitan areas is the pollutant standard index (PSI), which measures the degree to which the ambient air quality standards are being violated for any one of five pollutants. A value of 100 indicates that the area does not violate any of the five standards and just meets the standard for one or more pollutants. A value above 100 indicates that the ambient air quality standard for at least one pollutant has been violated. PSI values above 100 indicate an unhealthy situation; values above 200, a very unhealthy situation; and values above 300, a hazardous situation.

The Council on Environmental Quality has published a tabulation of the trends in PSI levels for twenty-three urban areas. These areas, generally the largest standard metropolitan statistical areas (SMSAs)—excluding New York—have reasonably satisfactory data for 1974 through 1978. Through 1978 eight of these areas evidenced a worsening trend in PSI levels, nine showed an improvement, and six were essentially unchanged. The total number of days with the PSI above 100 dropped from 1,985 to 1,637 in the 1974–78 period, a 17.5 percent decline. Virtually all of this decline is accounted for by reduced ozone concentrations in Los Angeles, San Bernardino, and Philadelphia.

Since 1978 the Conservation Foundation has found even greater reductions in the PSI levels in its twenty-three-city sample. Its data show a 39 percent decline in the number of unhealthy days between 1974 and 1980. This decline is almost entirely due to reduced concentrations of carbon monoxide and ozone. The decrease in the number of unhealthy days primarily due to carbon monoxide in six of the twenty-three cities accounts for three-fourths of this 39 percent decline.

Unfortunately, these PSI improvements may not be useful indicators of air quality. The PSI captures the ambient concentration for only one pollutant—the criteria pollutant with the greatest concentration relative to its primary ambient air quality standard. In twenty of the twenty-three cities cited by the CEQ this pollutant is either ozone or carbon monoxide. The level of particulates or sulfur oxides is rarely the determining criterion. If ozone or carbon monoxide concentrations decline just enough to reduce the number of days during which the PSI is above 100, the CEQ or the Conservation Foundation would call this progress a reduction in the number of days of unhealthy air. But if this decline is accompanied by rising levels of TSP or sulfur oxides, for which the area may be in attainment, the increase will not be captured in the PSI. Since fine particulates and sulfate compounds are likely to be more harmful than ozone or carbon monoxide, the PSI would give an inaccurate measure of the overall change in air quality.

The PSI measures have also been calculated for large cities during a period of declining city population and increasing gasoline prices. The twenty-three-city sample used by the CEQ experienced a 4 percent decline in population between 1970 and 1980. With declining population in the central cities and sharply higher gasoline prices, it is not surprising that indexes dominated by carbon monoxide or ozone showed an improvement in air quality for major urban areas. It is difficult to estimate the contribution of regulation to this improvement.

Emission Data

The data on total emissions (as opposed to air quality measures) are equally problematic. The EPA publishes estimates of total national emissions for each major air pollutant, based on a set of technical coefficients, estimated production levels, and assumed compliance rates. Actual emissions are likely to differ substantially from these estimates because of poor compliance data and errors in assumed technical coefficients. Hence these data are useful only for measuring trends— and then only if the relationship between assumed control or production techniques and actual emissions does not change over time. Without intensive EPA monitoring, the agency may be unduly optimistic about the degree to which controls are implemented and the efficiency of these control devices. On the other hand, the rising relative prices of fossil fuels in the 1970s may have made it more profitable to capture unburned hydrocarbons and other residuals, thereby reducing emissions from even

Table 2-1. *Estimates of National Air Pollutant Emissions, 1970–80*[a]
Millions of metric tons unless otherwise specified

Year	TSP	SO_x	NO_x	VOC	CO
1970	17.6	27.9	18.5	27.1	110.9
1971	16.4	26.5	19.0	26.4	110.5
1972	14.9	27.3	20.1	26.7	109.7
1973	13.9	28.4	20.4	26.2	107.4
1974	12.1	27.0	20.1	23.8	102.5
1975	10.1	25.6	19.6	22.8	98.1
1976	9.4	26.4	20.9	23.7	100.4
1977	8.5	26.4	21.3	23.8	97.8
1978	8.6	24.8	21.5	24.4	96.7
1979	8.5	25.3	21.5	23.4	92.6
1980	7.8	23.7	20.7	21.8	85.4
Change, 1970–80 (percent)	−55.7	−15.1	11.9	−19.6	−23.0

Source: EPA, *National Air Pollutant Emissions Estimates, 1940–1980* (1982).
a. TSP = total suspended particulates
   SO_x = sulfur oxides
   NO_x = nitrogen oxides
   VOC = volatile organic compounds
   CO = carbon monoxide.

noncomplying sectors. It is difficult to determine which factor is more important and whether both may not be swamped by random errors in the data.

The data on national emissions are as difficult to explain as the air quality trends (table 2-1).[7] Particulate emissions fell sharply in the 1970s, according to EPA data, declining 55.7 percent from 1970 to 1980. Both fuel combustion and industrial processes are estimated to have reduced particulate generation by about two-thirds between 1970 and 1980. Surprisingly, as table 2-2 shows, manufacturing industries reported a 9 percent *reduction* in particulates removed between 1973 and 1979 (the first year and the most recent year for which the Census Bureau data are available, respectively); however, the EPA showed a 49 percent decline in manufacturers' emissions in the same period.[8] These data can be consistent only if industrial output declined sharply between 1973 and 1979 (which it did not) or if new processes replaced older equipment requiring baghouses, precipitators, or other control equipment. Neither alternative is plausible.

7. EPA, *National Air Pollutant Estimates, 1940–1980* (EPA, 1982).
8. U.S. Bureau of the Census, *Pollution Abatement Costs and Expenditures,* Current Industrial Reports, annual edition; and EPA, *National Air Pollutant Estimates.*

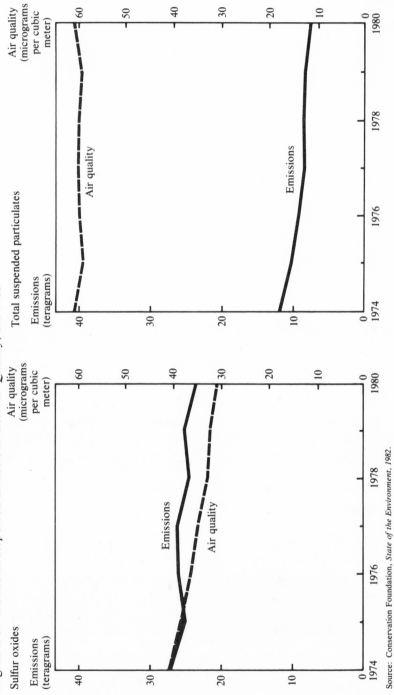

Figure 2-3. *Trends in Reported Emissions and Air Quality, 1974–80*

Source: Conservation Foundation, *State of the Environment, 1982.*

Table 2-2. *Pollutants Removed by Manufacturers, 1973–79*[a]
Millions of tons unless otherwise specified

Year	TSP	SO_x	NO_x, HC, and CO
1973	44.2	4.9	12.5
1974	40.1	5.4	11.0
1975	40.6	6.0	11.0
1976	42.7	6.7	11.8
1977	38.6	8.4	11.9
1978	40.1	8.7	12.9
1979	40.4	9.0	13.6
Change, 1973–79 (percent)	−8.6	83.7	8.8

Source: U.S. Bureau of the Census, *Pollution Abatement Costs and Expenditures,* Current Industrial Reports, annual editions.
a. HC = hydrocarbons. For explanation of the other symbols and abbreviations, see table 2-1.

As table 2-1 demonstrates, the emissions of the other pollutants did not decline as sharply in the 1970–80 period. Estimated sulfur dioxide emissions dropped 15.1 percent, but nitrogen oxides increased 11.9 percent. The volatile organic compounds (hydrocarbons) and carbon monoxide declined 20 and 23 percent, respectively. These modest trends compare with a 35 percent increase in industrial production during the eight-year period; hence some improvement in emissions per unit of output may have been occurring. How much of this was due to federal pollution control regulation is difficult to say. Census data show that sulfur dioxide removal, as reported by manufacturing firms, increased 84 percent between 1973 and 1979, particulate removal fell nearly 10 percent, and the amount of nitrogen oxides, carbon monoxide, and hydrocarbons removed increased 9 percent. Thus EPA policy probably contributed to reductions in sulfur dioxide, but regulation appears to have had less effect on the other major air pollutants from industrial sources.

Comparing Emissions and Air Quality Trends

The EPA's annual estimates of national emissions for sulfur oxides and particulates are not consistent with the reported improvements in air quality levels. Figure 2-3 juxtaposes the 1974–80 data from figure 2-1 and table 2-1 for these two stationary-source pollutants; clearly, measured ambient concentrations of particulates have not improved while estimated emissions have fallen more than 33 percent. Given the Census Bureau evidence that TSP *removal* has not increased since 1973, EPA data on emission reductions may be overstated.

Similarly, for sulfur oxides the timing and the degree of decline in ambient concentrations simply do not mirror the estimated decline in emissions. A number of explanations are possible. The ambient concentrations of sulfur oxides may have fallen much less than the 25 percent reflected in figure 2-3. Alternatively, sulfur oxide emissions may have been reduced more than table 2-1 suggests. Finally, the EPA's measurement of air quality may have improved near the EPA monitors because new power plants have been built away from urban areas. Such "progress" could obviously be a misleading indicator of air quality.

These divergent trends in emissions and air quality data reflect the difficulty of compiling accurate data on air pollution. The relationship between emissions and ambient air quality depends heavily on the spatial distribution of emissions and local meteorological conditions. This large stochastic component makes it necessary to take frequent measurements at numerous locations in order to obtain an indication of average air quality. Also, accurate emission data can only be produced by the EPA if it has a census of polluting facilities, good estimates of the emission profile of each type of facility, and precise data on compliance. Given the quality of the data with which the EPA has had to work, it is not surprising that there are doubts about the accuracy of its emission or air quality estimates.

Monitoring Air Pollution

The data on air quality trends are seriously deficient because EPA has not succeeded in establishing and maintaining a thorough monitoring network. Monitors are operated by state and local governments with federal guidance and funding. These monitors have not been operated consistently over time or across geographical jurisdictions, although improvements are being made. An interagency task force recently reported:

Over the decade of the 1970's the number of ambient air pollutant monitors increased dramatically from approximately 1800 in 1970 to approximately 8000 in 1979. The lack of uniform criteria for station locations, probe siting, sampling methodology, quality assurance practices, and data handling procedures resulted in data of unknown quality. In preparing "national" air quality trends data bases for the major pollutants, the number of monitoring sites changed constantly, reflecting the growth in state monitoring networks during this period. A conglomeration of different types of sites—rural, industrial, residential, commercial, etc.—evolved with no national plan. Some urban areas of the country had extensive monitoring while others did not.[9]

A high-quality national monitoring network is essential so that the EPA can chart its progress, determine how various policies are working, and launch needed research projects for new approaches.

In 1977 the EPA reported that of 4,008 monitors for particulates in the entire country only 2,699 generated valid annual data.[10] No estimated standard errors were reported, even for the valid data. Similarly, of 2,365 sulfur dioxide monitors, only 1,355 provided valid annual data. Both the TSP and the sulfur dioxide monitors have serious deficiencies. The sulfur dioxide monitors are primarily urban while the trend in sulfur dioxide source location has been away from urban centers. Moreover, concern seems to be shifting from sulfur dioxide toward sulfates, for which there are few monitors. The particulate monitors, while more numerous, generally fail to discriminate between coarse and fine particulates, complicating a shift toward controlling the potentially more dangerous fine particles.

The status of monitoring for pollutants primarily originating from mobile sources is much less satisfactory. As of 1977 the EPA reported only 524 ozone (oxidant) monitors, 456 carbon monoxide monitors, and 1,527 nitrogen oxide monitors (only 933 of the nitrogen dioxide monitors provided valid annual data). With 247 AQCRs there are not many sites for measuring ambient concentrations of these pollutants in each AQCR. While the number of monitors has increased since the early 1970s, data from these locations cannot be compared accurately over time because of the changing sample sizes. Thus information on pollution trends before 1973 is of little value. The CEQ and the EPA rarely report such estimates although the control of vehicle emissions began in the mid-1960s and state and local control of industrial sources began even earlier.

The poor quality of monitoring data has been recognized by the EPA for some time. In October 1975 the agency established the Standing Air

9. EPA, "Intra-Agency Task Force on Air Quality Indicators" (EPA, n.d.), p. 4-1.

10. These data and those that follow are drawn from EPA, *National Air Quality, Monitoring, and Emissions Trends Report, 1977* (GPO, 1979), pp. 4-4, 4-5. *Valid annual data* are defined as containing at least five 24-hour samples per quarter for intermittent sampling or 75 percent of all possible readings for continuous sampling.

Monitoring Work Group to review the air monitoring network and to suggest improvements.[11] In 1977 this group issued its report, finding serious shortcomings in the network. Sampling techniques, monitoring site locations, quality assurance, and data handling were criticized. Oxidant monitoring was found most unsatisfactory because of the lack of a monitor that responds uniformly to various nonmethane organic compounds.

In 1979 the General Accounting Office (GAO) released a report on the ambient air quality monitoring network.[12] It criticized the EPA's slow progress in improving the network and developing a standardized approach to monitoring. In reviewing the operation of 243 monitors the GAO found 197 of them with problems that would adversely affect the quality of the data. Of these 243 monitors, 174 were improperly sited and 142 used equipment that did not conform to EPA standards. Later the GAO noted that there had been no oversight hearings on this issue in the first twenty months after the release of its report.[13]

Because of the Clean Air Act's focus on *maximum* allowable concentrations of criteria pollutants, the Monitoring Work Group focused on monitoring the various pollutants at sites likely to reflect maximum pollution levels in an AQCR. Such data are not likely to be useful in determining the rate of improvement in the air breathed by the average citizen. Without demonstrated threshold effects for these criteria pollutants, averages of observations from sites designed to capture the worst pollution levels will not provide good indexes of the benefits of pollution control.

As a result of the 1977 report and of the 1977 Clean Air Act Amendments, the EPA promulgated new regulations for federal, state, and local monitoring systems in May 1979. These regulations provide separate monitoring criteria for the national air monitoring stations and the state and local air monitoring stations. Whether these regulations and the funding of monitoring facilities provide better air quality data remains to be seen, but early indications are far from favorable. In late 1982 the GAO once again reviewed the progress of the EPA in improving the

11. For a discussion of this effort, see SRI International, "Study of Air Monitoring Networks to Assess Utility and Consistency of Data," study prepared for the National Commission on Air Quality (NCAQ, 1980).

12. U.S. General Accounting Office, *Air Quality: Do We Know What It Is?* (GPO, 1979), pp. 5–12.

13. GAO, *Clean Air Act: Summary of GAO Reports (October 1977 through January 1981) and Ongoing Reviews* (GPO, 1981).

monitoring network.[14] It found that only 52 percent of the planned network was operating satisfactorily.

Monitoring and Enforcement

A major shortcoming of the EPA's enforcement policy is the absence of thorough monitoring of point sources or establishments to ascertain compliance. Except for electric utilities' emissions of sulfur dioxide (and even these sources are often monitored only on a spot basis), there is virtually no continuing, systematic monitoring of the actual output of pollution from various sources. Particulates may be tracked by periodic opacity tests, but most of the other pollutants are effectively unmonitored at the point of origin. How then does the EPA enforce existing standards?

According to EPA data, approximately 90 percent of the nearly 6,000 "major" stationary sources complied with applicable standards in 1979.[15] This estimate can be quite misleading given the differences in total emissions across sources. For instance, one steel mill may account for much more particulate matter than scores of other "major" sources. Only 13 percent of steel mills were in compliance. Even if the 90 percent compliance datum were an accurate measure of the proportion of *pollution* in "compliance," one cannot be sure that pollution is indeed controlled to the degree required by the standards.

The EPA certifies compliance by three methods: stack tests, on-site inspections of equipment, and voluntary certification by the polluter. The first method, stack monitoring, is used to certify compliance for only 5 percent of major sources; another 38 percent are found in compliance as the result of on-site inspections. The remaining 57 percent are simply voluntary certifications—unaudited reports from the polluter that it is complying with all relevant standards.[16] Given the problems in assuring performance to standards from only periodic on-site inspections (often with advance warning), it would be naive to think that this approach can assure compliance. Voluntary certification cannot be assumed to generate compliance unless followed by periodic verification through the use of stack monitors or other techniques. Apparently the EPA has

14. GAO, *Problems in Air Quality Monitoring System Affect Data Reliability* (GPO, 1982), pp. 8–9.
15. See EPA, *Compliance Status of Major Air Pollution Facilities* (EPA, 1980).
16. CEQ, *Environmental Quality*, 1980 annual report, p. 182.

not developed a method of stochastic or intermittent monitoring in which it has confidence and which is sufficiently inexpensive for widespread use.

In 1979 the GAO issued a report on a survey of major stationary air pollution sources reported in compliance by the EPA.[17] It found that 22 percent of the surveyed sources exceeded the maximum emissions allowed by the state implementation plan. In many regions compliance data are so poorly maintained that the GAO found it difficult to determine the effectiveness of the compliance classification process.[18]

A study made for the EPA in 1980 found that 70 percent of 180 sources reported in compliance had documented incidents of violations of their emission limitations.[19]

These data starkly illustrate the lack of enforcement of current standards that is largely the result of inadequate development of a system of source monitoring capable of detecting violations of existing regulations. Until a satisfactory monitoring system is developed in conjunction with a civil penalty policy for enforcing standards or marketable rights, it is difficult to see how any environmental regulatory system can work well.

Summary

This chapter has reviewed a variety of imprecise data on recent trends in air quality, emissions, pollution removal, and compliance. While there is some evidence that average pollution levels fell in the 1970s— particularly for carbon monoxide, sulfur dioxide, and TSP—the rate of reduction may well have been less than in the 1960s. Given the paucity and location of monitors, it would be difficult to conclude that the air quality experienced by the average citizen has actually improved.

The emission data are not much more helpful because they are not

17. GAO, *Improvements Needed in Controlling Major Air Pollution Sources* (GPO, 1979), p. ii.

18. Ibid.

19. These results are reported in Robert G. McInnes and Peter H. Anderson, "Characterization of Air Pollution Equipment Operation and Maintenance Problems" (EPA, 1981). The 180 sources had an average of thirteen breakdowns in emission control per year, each of which lasted an average of three days and generated emissions 25 percent above permitted levels.

drawn from actual monitoring of point sources. Using technical coefficients and assumptions concerning compliance, the EPA obtains national emission estimates that show substantial reduction in TSP but more modest improvement for other pollutants. Surprisingly, manufacturers do not report increased capture of particulates that mirrors the reduction in particulate emissions reported by the agency.

Finally, the EPA admits that most of its compliance information is drawn from unaudited reports from the polluters themselves. As a result, reports of compliance are likely to be exaggerated. The absence of continuous or intermittent monitoring at the pollution sources remains a major problem for any regime of pollution control.

In its first twelve years the EPA may have reduced stationary-source emissions, but the extent of this reduction and its impact on air quality cannot be assessed from current data. A top priority in any reform of air pollution policy must be a major infusion of resources into monitoring air quality and individual-source compliance.

III

The Efficiency
of the Current Standards

When Congress first established a major federal air pollution program in 1970, it could not have been expected to devote much attention to economic efficiency. Bringing air pollution under control in a few years would involve major expenditures and dislocations. The pain of adjusting to this new policy had to be distributed in a politically palatable manner, leading to policies that were likely to be quite inefficient. Imperfect information, tight timetables, and poor monitoring and enforcement systems could be expected to add inefficiencies to the program. In the 1980s, however, efficiency considerations may be expected to assume a more important role.

This chapter reviews the efficiency of stationary-source controls with particular emphasis on the difference in incremental control costs across sources in the same industry, across different industries, and between new and old point sources. This evidence is useful in projecting the potential for reducing the social burden of control costs through the reallocation of pollution control from the more costly to the less costly sources. It also sheds light on the effect of emission regulations on the construction of new facilities. Given the paucity of information on *actual* emissions, most evidence is derived from a priori studies of prospective control costs, not from the actual experience of polluters. The most compelling evidence of the new-source bias is, however, drawn from data on actual compliance costs.

The Cost of Stationary-Source Controls

The Department of Commerce has estimated that total outlays on pollution control by business, consumers, and government amounted to $55.7 billion in 1980.[1] Air pollution control accounted for $25.4 billion of

1. These data and those following may be found in Gary L. Rutledge and Susan L. Trevathan, "Pollution Abatement and Control Expenditures, 1972–80," *Survey of Current Business,* vol. 62 (February 1982), pp. 50–57.

this total; business expenditures for air pollution control alone cost $16.6 billion. Nearly two-thirds of the latter can be attributed to installing and operating stationary-source abatement facilities. Capital outlays for air pollution control by the nonfarm private-business sector alone accounted for $5.1 billion, or roughly 1.5 percent of all capital spending by this sector.

The cost of controlling air pollution is obviously substantial, but it appears to have been growing less rapidly in recent years than in the early 1970s. Between 1972 and 1975 total air pollution control outlays grew more than 25 percent per year.[2] In real terms they increased at a rate of 11.4 percent per year. From 1976 through 1978 the real rate of growth of outlays for air pollution control grew a much more modest 3.3 percent. Since 1978 there has been a renewed acceleration in these outlays, to an annual growth rate of 5.3 percent, caused almost entirely by increases in expenditures on motor vehicle emission control.

In real terms the spending on air pollution abatement equipment for stationary sources has declined almost continuously since 1975. In 1981 these capital outlays in constant dollars were 23 percent lower than in 1975. The 1977 Clean Air Act Amendments apparently have not led to a major surge in spending for stationary-source controls. Whether this is due to sluggish compliance rates or simply to a reduction in economic activity in the polluting industries is difficult to say. Industries such as copper, cement, steel, and electric utilities were not investing heavily in plant and equipment. Moreover, the copper and steel industries have received specific legislative extensions of deadlines of their pollution control requirements.[3]

Even if air pollution control expenditures are no longer growing rapidly, they remain sufficiently large to require careful scrutiny. Inefficiencies in a regulatory program that requires outlays of more than $15 billion per year can have severe impacts on the country's economic health. Alternatively, any saving in control costs can be used to purchase even greater improvements in the quality of life through other regulatory programs.

2. Most pollution control spending growth peaked in 1975. It is for this reason that Edward F. Denison has found that the impact of pollution control spending on productivity reached its peak in 1975. See Denison, "Pollution Abatement Programs: Estimates of Their Effects upon Output per Unit Input," *Survey of Current Business,* vol. 59 (August 1979), pt. 1, pp. 58–59.

3. The stretchout for copper is in section 117 of the 1977 Clean Air Act Amendments. The steel stretchout was legislated separately in 1981 (P.L. 97-23, 97 Cong. 1 sess.).

Evidence on Control Costs

Economic efficiency in air pollution abatement is related both to the degree of control and to the technique used to obtain this abatement. One often hears the complaint that environmental authorities have gone "too far" in mandating pollution control because the cost of obtaining the last few percentage points of reduction far exceeds the social value of this abatement. If true, this excessive control contributes to economic inefficiency because some resources that are employed in pollution control could be more productively utilized elsewhere.

The type of inefficiency addressed in this chapter concerns the strategies used to obtain a given level of emission abatement. If the cost of abatement is to be minimized, the cost of an incremental improvement in air quality in a given airshed should be equated across all sources of the offending pollutant. In practice this would require knowing with precision the contribution of a gram of pollutant from each source of air quality degradation. In the absence of such precision in air quality modeling, a proxy for the cost of air quality improvement is the incremental cost of emission reduction for each source of the pollutant in an airshed. Any set of policies that generates equal incremental costs across sources—new and old—is referred to as *cost-effective*.

In 1978 the Environmental Protection Agency commissioned a study by the Battelle Laboratories of the incremental cost-effectiveness of air and water pollution control strategies employed by the agency.[4] Subsequently EPA staff prepared its own estimates for internal policymaking purposes.[5] Neither report has been officially released, although both have been available to the public on an unofficial basis. These reports appear to contain the best information available to the EPA (or anyone else) on control costs across various sources of air pollution.

The EPA and Battelle studies estimate the incremental costs of various control options on major sources of eight different pollutants: particulates, hydrocarbons, carbon monoxide, sulfur dioxide, nitrogen oxides, vinyl chloride, mercury, and fluoride. These estimates are based on engineering analyses of model plants that are approximately equal to the median size in the industry. Since only a few, discrete standards are

4. D. M. Jenkins, J. E. Burch, and C. Buoni, "Draft Report on Incremental Cost Effectiveness for Airborne Pollution Abatement to U.S. Environmental Protection Agency" (Columbus, Ohio: Battelle Laboratories, June 5, 1979).

5. Environmental Protection Agency, "The Incremental Cost Effectiveness of Selected EPA Regulations" (EPA, January 23, 1981).

considered for each point source, the incremental cost estimate is actually the average cost per unit of emissions removed over the increment of control in question. If 10 grams of sulfur dioxide are released per kilogram of a product without controls and 8 grams are removed at a cost of $8 through the imposition of the weakest engineering standard, the incremental cost of this removal is an estimated $1 per gram. If a more stringent standard would remove another 1.9 grams at an additional cost of $19, the estimated incremental cost of removing these 1.9 grams would be $10 per gram.

In table 3-1 the range of incremental control costs for three major pollutants—particulates, hydrocarbons, and sulfur dioxide—is arrayed by industry. Wherever possible the control costs for existing sources and for new sources are listed separately. The existing-source estimates are based on state implementation plans (SIP) or reasonably available control technology (RACT) standards issued by the EPA. The new-source standards are either the best available control technology (BACT) or lowest achievable emissions rate (LAER) standards. The LAER standards are required for new sources in nonattainment areas. Since most new sources of particulates in the steel industry can be built only at existing plants in nonattainment areas, the LAER estimates are used for the steel industry wherever they are available.

The data in table 3-1 reveal a remarkable range of potential control costs even for existing sources. For instance, particulate control in the utility sector costs only $36 to $680 per additional ton removed while it can cost as much as $1,010 to $3,030 in a secondary aluminum plant or $30,880 in a coke oven. Were all these facilities' emissions of particulates equally dangerous and were all facilities located in the same airshed, increasing the stringency of controls on, say, eastern utilities and relaxing the standard for coke ovens would lower control costs while preserving air quality.

The Battelle and EPA cost estimates differ considerably, with the former often higher. In some cases the EPA estimates are higher than the Battelle data by only the rate of inflation between 1979 and 1980. In others EPA staff claim to have used more recent documents in developing the estimates.[6] In both cases there is an enormous range in the incre-

6. Telephone conversation with EPA, Office of Planning and Evaluation. Even these data are controversial within the EPA. The estimation of incremental control costs from background information documents is as much an art as a science. As this book goes to press, EPA staff continue their attempt to construct a comprehensive data base on control costs across industries.

Table 3-1. *Estimates of the Incremental Costs of Removing Pollutants from Existing Sources and New Sources*
Dollars per metric ton removed

	Existing sources		New sources	
Industry and pollutant	Battelle study (1979 dollars)	EPA memo (1980 dollars)	Battelle study (1979 dollars)	EPA memo (1980 dollars)
Particulates				
Electric utilities				
Eastern coal	36–680	252	. . .	2,577
Western coal	80	. . .	. . .	66
Coal cleaning	10	. . .	10	29
Petroleum refining	573	1	479	1
Chemicals				
Phosphate fertilizer	10–96	9–128	. . .	. . .
Phosphorus	22–45	. . .	. . .	. . .
Defluorinated phosphate rock	18–30	. . .	. . .	. . .
Dicalcium phosphate	1,200–2,600	. . .	. . .	. . .
Iron and steel				
Raw materials	823–7,359	982	194–126,243	1,759–2,872
Sintering	246–1,683	260–670	442–8,306	470–21,459
Coke ovens	16–17,759	179–6,285	1,360–38,734	1,356–27,387
Blast furnaces	990–7,542	308–10,429	1,170–297,570	2,130–16,600
Basic oxygen furnaces	87–3,735	353–3,110	1,380–101,000	2,461
Electric arc furnaces	254–8,165	1,291–2,448	4,020–160,654	15,589
Automatic scarfing	12,080–23,472	25,473	. . .	. . .
Continuous casting	. . .	. . .	6,300–23,646	. . .
Secondary aluminum	1,010–3,030	. . .	810	. . .
Secondary brass and bronze	100–28,900	24–569	. . .	. . .
Ferroalloys	400–760	. . .	. . .	602–1,259
Secondary lead	40–70	34–124	. . .	. . .
Asphalt and concrete	. . .	22	60–1,790	343–1,030
Lime	10–80	27–132	. . .	. . .
Feed mills	340–630	1,745	370	1,525
Grain handling	90–210	96–20,397	160	176
Pulp and paper	0–160	0[a]	120–2,440	92–7,206[a]
Hydrocarbons				
Petrochemicals	40–621	34–260	. . .	. . .
Structural clay products	1,001	4,143	. . .	. . .
Paint	1,250	998	. . .	. . .
Dry cleaning	163–2,070	. . .	. . .	105–6,905
Motor vehicles	186–2,720	20–154	. . .	. . .
Wood furniture	5,460	. . .	. . .	. . .
Coil coating	. . .	. . .	73–127	145
Sulfur dioxide				
Electric utilities				
Eastern coal	60–280	412	150–370	265–298
Western coal	. . .	. . .	1,090	1,167–1,414
Natural gas processing	118–372	340–824	. . .	. . .
Petroleum refining	217	409	164	0[b]
Iron and steel coking	295–473	513	560–700	184–579
Sulfuric acid	170–290	210	54	. . .
Primary copper	380–700	24–28	1,750	22

Table 3-1 (*continued*)

Industry and pollutant	Existing sources		New sources	
	Battelle study (1979 dollars)	EPA memo (1980 dollars)	Battelle study (1979 dollars)	EPA memo (1980 dollars)
Sulfur dioxide (continued)				
Primary lead	150	64–346	. . .	315
Primary zinc	780	38	. . .	222
Structural clay products	530–650	530–841	. . .	. . .
Paper (total reduced sulfur)	80	0–324[b]	. . .	92–12,437[b]

Sources: D. M. Jenkins, J. E. Burch, and C. Buoni, "Draft Report on Incremental Cost Effectiveness for Airborne Pollution Abatement to U.S. Environmental Protection Agency" (Columbus, Ohio: Battelle Laboratories, June 5, 1979); and Environmental Protection Agency, "The Incremental Cost Effectiveness of Selected EPA Regulations" (EPA, January 23, 1981).

a. Existing plants are said to have negative control costs; new plants remove particulates and sulfur as joint products.

b. Some estimates are negative; others are joint with particulate removal.

mental costs of control. The EPA has displayed the variance in these costs diagrammatically; figure 3-1 demonstrates the greater range in hydrocarbon and particulate control than in sulfur oxide control. Even in the latter case the range is approximately $4,000 per metric ton of sulfur dioxide removed. Given the large volume of sulfur dioxide emitted and abated, such a range could translate into a considerable misallocation of resources.

Unfortunately, it is difficult to use the data in table 3-1 to measure the excessive costs of existing control. These data, even if accurate, reveal nothing about compliance. The tighter standards are most likely to be violated, particularly where discharge rates are high. It is not surprising that the steel industry has been one of the slowest industries to comply with air pollution standards. The potential cost of one set of standards, the total suspended particulate (TSP) standards for coke ovens, could exceed the entire annual outlay by the industry on all environmental controls. Either the coke oven standards are regularly violated or the estimate of their cost is much too high.[7]

The data in table 3-1 are engineering costs, not economic costs. They do not capture the effects of substitution in production or consumption on pollution control costs. For instance, a tighter standard on primary-metal smelters might induce a substitution of a different process to produce the primary metal, a substitution of secondary metal for the primary metal, or even the substitution of a different metal altogether for this metal in various uses. The incremental cost of the standard would

7. The noncompliance problem is severe for steel plants, and the coke oven standards have been extremely controversial.

Figure 3-1. *Ranges in Incremental Control Costs for Existing and New-Source Standards in Various Industries*

Dollars per metric ton

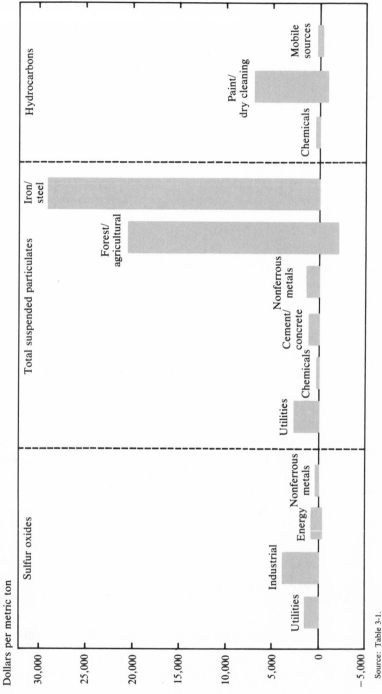

be the addition to total economic costs from controls and these various substitutions per additional unit of emissions abated.

Further, the geographical distribution of facilities determines the magnitude of prospective trade-offs between sources. For instance, most air quality control regions (AQCRs) are without major primary nonferrous smelters. Therefore, trade-offs between these smelters and older power plants cannot occur. In many AQCRs, the power plant may be the only major source of sulfur dioxide.

It is by no means obvious that the incremental cost of control should be the same across AQCRs. Some areas, such as Los Angeles, should have tighter point-source standards than others, such as Boise. In order to assess the efficiency of air pollution standards, one needs data on the density of emissions and transport conditions by AQCR.

Finally, the differences in table 3-1 may be misleading if the actual emission *rates* from most sources are extremely low while the emission rates from a few sources are large. For instance, the actual savings from reducing electric utility control costs for sulfur dioxide while increasing control costs on paper mills may be quite small. The incremental control costs might be equalized after only a few thousand pounds of sulfur dioxide emissions had been transferred from one to the other. This would save society little in control costs, and the bureaucratic costs of changing the standards might swamp the savings.

New-Source Bias

Perhaps more important is the difference between the new-source and existing-source standards for various industries. The most obvious example of this difference occurs with the electric-utility sulfur dioxide standards. At the instruction of Congress, the EPA has been forced to establish a continuous-emission-reduction standard requiring flue-gas desulfurization systems for all new coal-fired utility boilers regardless of the coal's sulfur content.[8] This was a deliberate attempt to increase the demand for high-sulfur eastern and midwestern coal.

---

8. See section III of the 1977 Clean Air Act Amendments. For a discussion of the EPA's options in setting this standard, see Bruce A. Ackerman and William T. Hassler, "Beyond the New Deal: Coal and the Clean Air Act," *Yale Law Journal*, vol. 89 (July 1980), pp. 1466–1571; and chapter 7, below.

The cost of sulfur abatement in new western-coal-fired plants is approximately four times the incremental cost in existing power plants (table 3-1). With a differential this large, the true cost of the new-source standard is actually greater. Utilities are induced to postpone replacement of older, obsolete units, thereby saddling consumers with higher power generation costs. The Battelle and EPA estimates cannot include these opportunity costs of forgone replacement investment. On this account alone, the estimate must be biased downward.

An equally glaring example of new-source bias is apparent in the steel industry's TSP control costs. In many cases incremental control costs for new sources exceed $2,000 per ton of TSP abated. For many installations the cost of these new-source controls is so high that replacement of older facilities is seriously discouraged. Even here the Battelle estimates are biased downward because of the enforcement powers granted the EPA by the 1977 amendments. Most steel mills have some facilities that fail to meet existing-source standards of the relevant SIP. Since new investment can occur only at existing sites, given the cruel economics of today's steel business,[9] obtaining a permit for a new source requires dealing with the same authorities that are responsible for enforcing standards on existing (noncomplying) sources. The steel-maker's cost of obtaining a permit, therefore, is the cost of meeting existing standards plus the incremental control costs on the new source. This combination of new-source standard setting and enforcement practice cannot contribute to capital formation in the steel industry.

Examining the data in table 3-1, one may reasonably conclude that new sources of particulates and sulfur oxides in the electric utility, metal, and paper industries regularly incur higher incremental control costs than existing sources. In other industries the pattern is less clear. (For hydrocarbons the two studies generally do not provide separate new- and existing-source cost estimates for the same industry.) Whether this new-source bias carries over into practice cannot be determined without data on actual compliance costs.

The Census Bureau collects compliance cost data for the entire manufacturing sector of the economy.[10] Compliance costs are broken

9. Robert W. Crandall, *The U.S. Steel Industry in Recurrent Crisis: Policy Options in a Competitive World* (Brookings Institution, 1981).

10. U.S. Bureau of the Census, *Pollution Abatement Costs,* Current Industrial Reports, annual edition.

down into capital outlays and current operating costs. The latter estimate includes depreciation of pollution abatement equipment but no estimate of the opportunity cost of capital invested in this equipment. Nevertheless these data are probably the best available for annual control costs by industry and by state.

If air pollution control policies are biased against new sources, control costs per unit of economic activity can be expected to be higher where facilities are newer. In states where industry is growing rapidly, the costs of air pollution control per dollar of economic output should be higher than in states where growth has been slower. If there is a bias against new sources, control costs per dollar of output should be higher in southern and western states than in northeastern and north central states.

The data in table 3-2 confirm this theory. Control costs (operating costs) per dollar of value added are aggregated by census region for the eight two-digit census industries with the greatest air pollution control problems. It would have been preferable to use three- or four-digit industries in order to avoid lumping steel and copper or automobiles and aircraft manufacture together, but data are not available at this level of disaggregation. Nevertheless this pattern strongly confirms the theory that air pollution standards are biased against new sources. In six of the eight industries the average cost of pollution control per dollar of value added in 1977 was much greater in the Sun Belt states than in the Frost Belt states, and in each of these six industries the average rate of growth was greater in the Sun Belt states. In two industries, food processing and transportation equipment, the older areas actually suffered the higher pollution control costs per dollar of value added. In transportation, this result may well reflect higher growth in the Frost Belt than in the Sun Belt. In food processing, air pollution control costs simply are not large.

The importance of the bias is perhaps best demonstrated by the results for the paper and chemicals industries. In both industries air pollution control costs are relatively high; in each industry a movement toward the Sun Belt is evident. The paper industry in the high-growth states encounters control costs roughly four times as high as its counterpart in the older regions ($10.81 versus $2.58 per $1,000 of value added). In chemicals the disparity is on the order of two to one. These differences occur even though it should be cheaper to constrain pollution in new facilities.

Table 3-2. Air Pollution Control Costs per Thousand Dollars of Value Added in Eight Industries, 1977[a]

Industry and standard industrial classification number	Frost Belt						Sun Belt						
	North-east	Middle Atlantic	East North Central	West North Central	Average	Growth in value added, 1972–77 (percent)	South Atlantic	East South Central	West South Central	Mountain	Pacific	Average	Growth in value added, 1972–77 (percent)
SIC 20 Food processing	0.42	0.90	1.27	1.80	1.25	53.0	0.72	0.93	0.70	0.84	0.69	0.74	63.4
SIC 26 Paper	3.32	1.89	2.81	2.63	2.58	10.3	13.60	11.99	8.67	1.95	7.85	10.81	78.3
SIC 28 Chemicals	1.80	3.85	4.07	4.60	3.90	58.2	5.59	10.30	8.73	6.72	3.96	7.44	94.0
SIC 29 Refining	. . .	36.70	23.80	12.70	26.97	200.3	22.50	. . .	37.10	16.10	57.80	42.52	238.0
SIC 32 Stone and clay products	4.05	7.49	5.76	8.92	6.95	47.6	7.27	8.97	8.76	8.71	10.30	8.78	60.5
SIC 33 Metals	2.93	19.36	15.70	13.90	16.20	54.6	21.10	18.80	21.40	136.00	19.40	24.52	72.6
SIC 34 Machinery	1.52	1.16	0.69	0.99	0.90	63.6	0.48	1.59	0.64	5.35	1.56	1.09	91.0
SIC 37 Transportation equipment	0.46	1.96	1.07	0.57	1.09	66.8	0.38	0.19	0.39	. . .	0.81	0.65	50.1

Source: Bureau of the Census.

a. The above data represent total outlays and value added in each industry in the states for which the Census Bureau reports the requisite information. Coverage ranges from 66 percent of value added in Frost Belt states in SIC 29 to 99 percent of value added in SIC 37. In all but three of the sixteen average entries, more than 90 percent of value added is included.

The results in table 3-2 should not be considered evidence that pollution controls are not important in the older industrial areas of the country. Capital expenditures for pollution control are often a larger share of new capital expenditures in these older industrial regions although the impact of these expenditures is greater in the growing Sun Belt. This apparent anomaly simply reflects the much lower overall investment in these industries in the older industrial states.

It is also possible that the results in table 3-2 are consistent with the imposition of equal incremental control costs across new and old sources. If, for instance, the incremental cost of control at new sources rises very slowly while the cost at older sources rises very rapidly over the feasible range of control, new sources could have tighter performance standards, higher *total* costs per unit of output, and incremental costs equal to those at older sources. That this is unlikely is suggested by the estimates in table 3-1 and the lax enforcement practices described in chapter 2. Knowingly or not, Congress, the EPA, and the states appear to have combined to make the construction of new sources much less attractive because of air pollution control policies.[11]

A recent study prepared for the EPA suggests that the costs of pollution control equipment do not have a major impact on investment decisions.[12] This study examines new-source and existing-source standards for three industries: steel, petroleum refining, and copper. The costs of the requisite environmental controls for a typical facility (for both air and water pollution abatement) are shown in table 3-3. The effect of these new-source standards is to reduce the return on investment in steel and refining plants 0.2 to 4.1 percentage points compared to the returns available when the looser existing-source standards are applied to these hypothetical investments. In the third industry, copper smelting, new-source controls are actually less onerous than existing standards,

11. For evidence that this is a deliberate choice by Congress, see chapter 7, below; and B. Peter Pashigian, "Environmental Regulation: Whose Self Interests Are Being Protected?" (University of Chicago, Graduate School of Business, 1982).

12. MathTech, "The Effect of New Source Pollution Control Requirements on Industrial Investment Decisions," report prepared for EPA (Arlington, Va.: MathTech, January 1979). A more recent paper, coauthored by an EPA economist, suggests that new-source performance standards may increase emissions for some time because of delay in replacing the capital stock. See Vincent H. Smith and Allen C. Basala, "The Economic and Environmental Impacts of New Source Performance Standards," paper presented at North Carolina State University Resource and Environmental Economics Workshop, September 1981.

Table 3-3. *Capital Requirements for Environmental Control in New Facilities in Three Industries*
Millions of current dollars

Industry and investment	Productive capacity investment	Environ- mental control investment	Investment share for environmental control (percent)
Iron and steel			
Expansion on site	1,567.0	106.9	6.4
New plant	8,181.0	276.3	3.3
Petroleum refining			
Replacement of catalytic reformer	15.7	1.9	10.8
New refining	449.2	49.6	9.9
Copper			
New smelter	197.3	41.4	17.3

Source: MathTech, "The Effect of New Source Pollution Control Requirements on Industrial Investment Decisions," report prepared for EPA (Arlington, Va.: MathTech, January 1979).

but the 1977 Clean Air Act Amendments specifically provided an even more lenient timetable for existing sources in the copper industry.

Even a 0.2 to 4.1 percentage point reduction can be significant in determining the rate of new-plant investment. However, this difference is understated because it fails to account for the likelihood of lax enforcement of existing-source standards. Since new-source standards are likely to be more rigidly enforced through the permit process, the new-source bias is undoubtedly greater than the EPA-sponsored study suggests.

The Social Cost of Inefficient Standards in the Steel Industry

While a thorough analysis of the social cost of the inefficient standards revealed in table 3-1 is difficult without knowing the distribution of all pollution sources and the extent to which standards are enforced, one example might help demonstrate the possible extent of this loss. The steel industry's struggle with particulate emissions is chosen for this analysis because a simple calculation can be made for a standard integrated plant. Assume that a plant has ore and coal yards, a sinter strand, coke ovens, blast furnaces, steel furnaces, a continuous caster, and an automatic scarfer.[13] If an average current facility were subject to RACT (because it is located in a nonattainment area), it would have to spend $28.41 (in 1979 dollars) per metric ton of slabs produced (table 3-4). A total industry output of approximately 100 million tons of semifinished products from integrated facilities in 1979 would mean that the industry would have to spend approximately $2.6 billion on TSP control alone, according to the Battelle study.

What would happen if the EPA selected the lowest-cost strategy for removing particulates in the steel industry? Battelle's estimate of the total cost of such a strategy (table 3-5) would be approximately $20.45 to remove 24.94 grams of the 27.53 grams of TSP emitted with every kilogram of steel produced (table 3-6). An efficient control strategy could lower control costs nearly 30 percent.

This example of particulate removal from steel processes is not necessarily typical. The differences in control costs across processes and the opportunity for substitution may be quite different in other industries. With so many particulate-emitting processes in the steel industry, such substitution is simple unless the type of particulate differs. The saving results primarily from substituting tighter sintering and coal yard standards for weaker blast furnace, open hearth, and scarfing standards as well as from a change in coke oven standards. Since the latter may be more dangerous than the former, the saving may not be nearly so great if standards are differentiated by *type* of particulate. Nevertheless considerable potential saving remains, as attested to by industry's support for the bubble concept.

Could the cost saving from allowing efficient particulate control offset the total taxes paid through an emission tax? Table 3-6 provides an answer. A tax of $5.93 per kilogram of particulates would generate the same amount of pollution removal as the "efficient" strategy, which in turn is somewhat greater than the RACT standards. The taxes paid on the 2.6 kilograms of pollution per metric ton of production would be $15.40. These taxes plus the efficient control cost of $20.45 per metric ton of production would be $7.00 per metric ton more than RACT.

Edward Burrows found a similar cost saving from the use of cost-

---

13. For a discussion of the technology, see Clifford S. Russell and William J. Vaughan, *Steel Production: Processes, Products and Residuals* (Johns Hopkins University Press for Resources for the Future, 1976).

Table 3-4. *Cost of Meeting RACT Standards for a One-Million-Metric-Ton Steel Plant*

1979 dollars

Process	Total suspended particulates		Cost	
	Produced (grams per kilogram of slabs)	Removed (grams per kilogram of slabs)	Marginal (dollars per kilogram removed)	Total (dollars per ton of slabs)
Ore yard	0.141	0.056	2.670	0.150
Coal yard				
Fugitives	0.029	0.012	7.359	0.088
Transfer	0.100	0.099	0.823	0.081
Sinter				
Windbox	0.473	0.416	1.683	0.700
Discharge	0.770	0.647	0.246	0.159
Fugitives	0.077	0.076	0.577	0.044
Coke ovens				
Charging	0.200	0.172	3.297	0.567
Pushing	0.998	0.978	2.114	2.067
Quenching	1.505	1.144	6.905	7.899
Discharge	0.124	0.099	17.759	1.758
Topside	0.086	0.078	7.784	0.607
Underfire	0.175	0.149	4.914	0.732
Handling	0.006	0.006	25.239[a]	0.151
Gas	1.239	1.065	0.473	0.508
Preheating	0.022	0.018	0.195	0.004
Blast furnace				
Cast house	0.207	0.186	7.542	1.403
Slag pouring	0.084	0.080	32.134[a]	2.571
Slag processing	0.072	0.036	0.992	0.036
Open hearth				
Hot metal transfer	0.0424	0.041	20.288	0.832
Refining	2.088	2.046	1.094	2.238
Slag processing	0.025	0.012	2.858	0.034
Basic oxygen furnace				
Hot metal transfer	0.102	0.099	3.735	0.370
Refining	14.79	13.874	0.135	1.873
Charging and tapping	0.29	0.174	2.764	0.490
Slag pouring	0.035	0.029	1.042	0.030
Slag processing	0.049	0.026	0.695	0.018
Electric arc furnace				
Refining	3.60	3.24	0.383	1.241
Slag pouring	0.008	0.004	8.165	0.033
Slag processing	0.012	0.001	5.715	0.006
Continuous casting	0.064	0.059	23.646[a]	1.395
Scarfing	0.120	0.014	23.472	0.329
Total	27.533	24.936	. . .	28.414

Sources: Jenkins, Burch, and Buoni, "Draft Report"; and EPA.
a. BACT.

Table 3-5. *Changes in Controls from RACT to Obtain Efficient Control for a One-Million-Metric-Ton Steel Plant*

Process	Incremental particulates removed (grams per kilogram)	Marginal cost (dollars per kilogram)	Savings (−) or cost (+)
Ore handling	+0.049	5.588	+0.276
Coal yard			
Transfer	+0.009	2.647	+0.024
Fugitives	−0.012	7.359	−0.088
Sinter			
Windbox	+0.024	4.116	+0.099
Discharge	+0.116	0.442	+0.051
Coke ovens			
Quenching	−0.438	6.905	−3.024
Discharge	−0.099	17.759	−1.758
Handling	−0.006	25.239	−0.151
Gas	+0.087	0.534	+0.046
Gas	+0.074	0.702	+0.052
Topside	−0.078	7.784	−0.607
Blast furnace			
Cast house	−0.186	7.542	−1.403
Slag processing	+0.029	5.930	+0.172
Slag pouring	−0.080	32.134	−2.571
Open hearth transfer	−0.041	20.288	−0.832
Basic oxygen furnace slag processing	+0.020	4.282	+0.086
Electric arc furnace			
Refining	+0.609	5.623	+3.424
Slag pouring	−0.004	8.165	−0.033
Continuous casting	−0.059	23.646	−1.395
Scarfing	−0.014	23.472	−0.329

Sources: Same as table 3-4.

effective standards.[14] He estimated the actual- and least-cost control strategies for three different standards regimes: RACT, BACT, and the Illinois SIP. In each case, the choice of efficient, least-cost standards lowers the control costs by roughly 30 percent (table 3-7).

These analyses are of *purported* EPA standards. If the model plant analysis is accurate, total particulate controls in an integrated steel works would be almost $30 per ton. Average production from integrated works of 100 million tons per year would require particulate control costs of

14. Edward M. Burrows, Jr., "Cost-Effectiveness of Alternative Air Pollution Abatement Strategies in the U.S. Iron and Steel Industry" (unpublished paper, November 1, 1980).

Table 3-6. *Summary of Estimated EPA Standards (RACT)*
and Efficient Control Costs for One Million Metric Tons
of Slabs in Typical Steel Plant

| | Total suspended particulates | | |
| | Produced (grams per kilogram) | Removed (grams per kilogram) | Total cost (1979 dollars per ton) |
Item			
EPA (RACT)	27.533	24.936	28.41
Efficient	27.533	24.936	20.45
Pollution tax ($5.93 per kilogram)	27.533	24.936	35.85[a]

Sources: Tables 3-4 and 3-5.
a. Control costs of $20.45 plus $15.40 in pollution taxes.

nearly $3 billion per year for the integrated sector alone. Even if these control costs are too high by a factor of two because of the relatively small model plant used in the analyses, TSP control costs would approximate $1.5 billion. Actual air pollution control costs in the entire steel industry are probably less than $400 million per year.[15] Hence the industry must be considerably out of compliance, or the projected costs are too high.

The EPA's own estimates of the total capital costs to the industry of complying with all air pollution standards is somewhat more than $700 million,[16] but there are no estimates of the annual operating costs associated with this outlay. The outlay could hardly bring the industry's total annual air pollution control costs to even $1 billion. The cost coefficients upon which the control cost estimates are based in the analysis are undoubtedly too large or the EPA has no intention of enforcing the letter of the standards. Nevertheless, the wide variance in incremental costs across the different processes should be a major cause for concern.

Other Studies

Virtually every other study of the cost-effectiveness of air pollution standards shows that existing air pollution policy is quite inefficient. In 1979, for example, MathTech studied alternative strategies for meeting

15. Bureau of the Census, *Pollution Abatement Costs,* Current Industrial Reports, 1977.
16. Memorandum from EPA administrator Douglas M. Costle to Senator Jennings Randolph, November 25, 1980.

Table 3-7. *Alternative Estimate of Control Costs for a 900,000-Ton Steel Plant*
Millions of dollars

Strategy	Actual cost	Lowest cost
RACT	30.45	18.91
BACT	43.42	31.36
Illinois SIP	39.31	32.79

Source: Edward M. Burrows, Jr., "Cost-Effectiveness of Alternative Air Pollution Abatement Strategies in the U.S. Iron and Steel Industry" (November 1, 1980).

a 250 micrograms per cubic meter, short-term nitrogen dioxide standard.[17] It found that the most efficient set of controls would cost $21 million per year for the Chicago AQCR alone (table 3-8). A sophisticated RACT strategy would cost $44 million annually, or nearly twice the efficient cost. A proportional rollback approach, the most common strategy used in controlling emissions, would cost $243 million to $254 million, or twelve times the efficient cost. MathTech concluded that a marketable permit system would save 50 to 90 percent of the costs that are likely to be incurred in a conventional regulatory approach.

A 1974 study by Atkinson and Lewis obtained similar results for TSP control in the St. Louis area.[18] They modeled the least-cost approach in two ways—one includes transport characteristics and one does not. The solution that minimizes the cost of achieving the primary ambient standard throughout the St. Louis area requires that incremental control costs vary according to the area in which the discharge occurs. This approach is only one-fourth as costly as a control strategy using the same emission tax or freely transferable rights throughout the entire AQCR. However, even the latter reduces control costs by two-thirds over those required under the SIP regulatory approach. Like the MathTech study, this study suggests that the current approach to regulatory policy may be as much as twelve times as expensive as necessary to achieve the environmental quality goal.

Other studies of the St. Louis, Washington, D.C., and Kansas City areas reach similar conclusions.[19] Particulates and sulfur dioxide can be

17. MathTech, "An Analysis of Alternative Policies for Attaining and Maintaining a Short-Term NO₂ Standard," report prepared for CEQ (Princeton, N.J.: MathTech, September 17, 1979).

18. Scott E. Atkinson and Donald H. Lewis, "A Cost Evaluation Analysis of Alternative Air Quality Control Strategies," *Journal of Environmental Economics and Management,* vol. 1 (November 1974), pp. 238 ff.

19. E. Burton and W. Sanjour, "Multiple Source Analysis of Air Pollution Abatement Strategies," *Federal Accountant,* vol. 18 (1969).

Table 3-8. *Cost of Nitrogen Oxide Control in Chicago*[a]

Control option	Pounds of nitrogen oxide emissions (10^3 pounds per hour)	Annual control costs (millions of 1978 dollars)
Proportional rollback		
90 percent	106	254
80 percent	104	243
RACT at least cost	40	44
Least cost	5	21
Maximum feasible control	106	254

Source: MathTech, "An Analysis of Alternative Policies for Attaining and Maintaining a Short-Term NO$_2$ Standard," report prepared for the Council on Environmental Quality (Princeton, N.J.: MathTech, September 17, 1979).

a. Standard is 250 micrograms per cubic meter for one-hour averaging period at all AQCR receptors.

controlled at a small fraction of the current costs if efficient control strategies are used. Each of these studies, however, proceeds from an assumption that control costs are known. Given the uncertainty in these estimates, the potential resource misallocation may be greater. A more recent study by Hahn and Noll estimates that a system of marketable permits for sulfur oxide emissions in the Los Angeles Basin would save only 8 percent of current control costs, but they admit that this estimate is probably biased downward.[20] It is also important to note that California has the most sophisticated air pollution program in the country; therefore, it is likely to have a rather efficient control strategy. In other jurisdictions the Hahn-Noll analysis would probably uncover much greater savings.

Studies of plantwide standards have been conducted for the iron and steel and the petrochemical industries. Each concluded that substantial cost savings would be available if the EPA moved from point-source to plantwide standards. Putnam, Hayes, and Bartlett concluded that a saving of 13 to 21 percent would be available in four model steel plants if coke oven emissions could be traded against other particulates.[21] If such trades were not allowed, the saving would fall to the range of 4 to 10 percent. Maloney and Yandle estimated even greater savings from plantwide standards in the petrochemical industry.[22] Using duPont data,

20. Robert W. Hahn and Roger G. Noll, "Tradable Air Pollution Permits in the Overall Regulatory System: Problems of Regulatory Interactions" (California Institute of Technology, 1982), p. 12.

21. Putnam, Hayes, and Bartlett, Inc., *Analysis of the Cost Impact of Plantwide Emissions Control on Four Domestic Steel Plants* (EPA, 1979).

22. M. T. Maloney and Bruce Yandle, "Bubbles and Efficiency: Cleaner Air at Lower Costs," *Regulation*, vol. 4 (May–June 1980), pp. 49–52.

Table 3-9. *Estimated Average Cost of Pollution Removal, 1975*
Dollars per ton

Industry	SIC[a] code	Total suspended particulates	Sulfur oxides	Hydrocarbons, carbon monoxide, and nitrogen oxides
Paper	26	12.03	69.44	. . .
Chemicals	28	13.42	245.19	25.97
Petroleum and coal products	29	6.10	87.21	. . .
Metals	33	46.53	26.66	. . .

Source: Robert W. Crandall, "Pollution Controls and Productivity Growth in Basic Industry," in Thomas Cowing and Rodney Stevenson, eds., *Productivity Measurement in Regulated Industries* (Academic Press, 1981).
a. Standard industrial classification.

they found that savings are 60 percent for a single plant and 86 percent for the entire company (if emissions can be traded among plants of the same company).

In an earlier study I attempted to measure differences in the *average* cost of air pollution controls for cross-sectional data reported by the Census Bureau for 1975.[23] The dependent variable was the cost of air pollution controls in a two-digit industry within a state. Four industries— paper, chemicals, petroleum and coal products, and metals—were used in the analysis. The estimated cost per ton of pollution removal varied from $6.10 to $46.53 for TSP and from $26.66 to $245.19 for sulfur dioxide (table 3-9). While these estimates reflect the average cost of controls across states and therefore do not adequately measure the differences in incremental costs in the same location, they are consistent with the hypothesis of substantial differences in control costs for the same pollutant across industries. In particular, the chemical industry is saddled with the highest average control costs for sulfur dioxide while metals escape with lower costs. On the other hand, metals incur the highest TSP control costs and petroleum and coal products the lowest.

Are the Benefits of Air Pollution Control Greater than the Costs?

The evidence discussed thus far leads inevitably to the conclusion that the effectiveness of the Clean Air Act in improving air quality is uncertain and that the costs are substantially greater than necessary for

23. Robert W. Crandall, "Pollution Controls and Productivity Growth in Basic Industry," in Thomas Cowing and Rodney Stevenson, eds., *Productivity Measurement in Regulated Industries* (Academic Press, 1981), pp. 347–68 (Brookings Reprint 375).

the improvement achieved. If the EPA knew the control costs across sources with precision, its regulations might be more cost-effective. If it could have devoted more attention to monitoring, perhaps it would have provided a better set of data from which to estimate benefits. But these deficiencies in knowledge make it difficult to know whether the benefits of air pollution control are sufficient to justify the costs imposed by the regulations.

Most studies of the benefits of air pollution control focus on the effects of reductions in ambient concentrations on human health, visibility, or crop yield.[24] It is difficult to estimate these effects because of poor data and the practical limitations on laboratory experimentation. With imprecise monitoring and limited information on the history of exposure experienced by individuals in the population, epidemiological studies of health effects are subject to criticism. Clinical health studies are limited by ethical considerations, and the results of laboratory experiments are not easily extrapolated to the general population. Moreover, most studies of the impact of air pollution on human health deal only with the relationship between pollution and premature death. Data on morbidity are generally unavailable; when available, they are subject to substantial potential bias in reporting.[25]

Nonhealth benefits are equally difficult to quantify because the aesthetic values of clean air are not traded in the marketplace. Increases in visibility may be valuable, but this value is not easily measured. For instance, even if photochemical smog is not a major health threat, it is generally unpleasant in high concentrations. The effect of smog on vegetation involves an additional aesthetic component in damage to residential shrubbery, local parks, and even national forests and parks. The impact on marketable crops is perhaps the only effect readily estimated by conventional techniques.[26]

Even if the relationship between air pollution and human health,

24. See A. Myrick Freeman III, "The Benefits of Air and Water Pollution Control: A Review and Synthesis of Recent Estimates," report prepared for CEQ, 1979, for a detailed review of these studies. An updated version has been published: A. Myrick Freeman III, *Air and Water Pollution Control: A Benefit-Cost Assessment* (Wiley, 1982).

25. For a recent study addressing morbidity, see Bart D. Ostro and Robert C. Anderson, "Morbidity, Air Pollution, and Health Statistics," paper presented at the joint statistical meetings of the American Statistical Association and the Biometric Society, August 12, 1981.

26. Freeman, "Benefits of Air and Water Pollution Control," reviews studies of vegetation loss.

visibility, and vegetation were well understood, it would be difficult to estimate the benefits from current policies. The calculation of the overall benefits requires several other steps. First, the effect of policy on emissions must be calculated. Second, any reduction in emissions must be translated into an effect on ambient air quality. Third, the population (or agricultural land) exposed to these pollution levels must be identified since it is unlikely that abatement policies have affected all areas of the country uniformly. Fourth, the impact of the reduction in ambient pollutant levels on health or other phenomena (visibility, crop damage) must be estimated. Fifth, the value of each incremental improvement in health, other amenities, or crop yields must be estimated. Finally, the total benefits must be calculated by multiplying the estimated improvements in health, amenities, or crop yields by the incremental value of these phenomena.

Uncertainty clouds every step of the process. Even if one knows how much pollution has been *removed,* one cannot be sure of the effect on ambient concentrations or the distribution of these concentrations. The major uncertainty in estimating the impact of such changes on mortality or the quality of life is compounded by the difficulty of placing a value on these changes at the margin. Estimates of the value of life are difficult to obtain, and they are even more difficult to justify in an emotion-laden public debate.[27] Given these problems, sharp disagreement about the value of the benefits from enforcing the Clean Air Act is hardly surprising.

Three recent studies of the value of emission reductions illustrate the range of disagreement over the benefits from air pollution control. Lave and Seskin attempted to estimate the impact of air pollution upon mortality from epidemiological data.[28] They concluded that a 1 percent reduction in particulates and sulfates would reduce mortality rates by 0.1 percent. From this they attempted to estimate the impact of abatement policies given assumptions about the degree of control and the value of life. Their estimate of the total value of these health benefits is $23.1 billion (1978 dollars).[29]

27. Martin J. Bailey, *Reducing Risks to Life* (American Enterprise Institute for Public Policy Research, 1980).

28. Lester B. Lave and Eugene P. Seskin, *Air Pollution and Human Health* (Johns Hopkins University Press for Resources for the Future, 1977).

29. This is Lave and Seskin's estimate stated in 1978 dollars. See National Economic Research Associates, *Cost-Effectiveness and Cost-Benefit Analysis of Air Quality Regulation,* report prepared for the Business Roundtable Air Quality Project (New York: Business Roundtable, 1980), pp. 6-29–6-43.

Freeman borrowed from Lave and Seskin and other studies to estimate the total benefits from air pollution control. He used a lower estimate of the potential health effects than Lave and Seskin, but he included nonhealth benefits and the benefits from automotive controls. His total estimate is $21.4 billion, of which $20.2 billion derives from stationary-source controls.

The National Economic Research Associates (NERA) attempted to synthesize the available evidence and to calculate total benefits in a study for the Business Roundtable.[30] By quarreling with Lave and Seskin's estimates of the impacts on mortality, using lower estimates of the improvements in air quality achieved through regulation, and using a different technique for extrapolation, the NERA estimated the benefits from air pollution abatement at only $8.5 billion per year, of which $4.5 billion represents health benefits, and the benefits from stationary-source controls at $7.7 billion, of which $4.4 billion is health benefits.

All these studies agree that most of the benefits from air pollution control come from reductions in the ambient concentration of particulates and sulfates. More recent evidence suggests that sulfates are probably the most serious problem, requiring far more attention than Congress gave them when it was debating the 1970 Clean Air Act Amendments.[31] The range of $8 billion to $23 billion in estimated benefits for controlling industrial sources is obviously wide. These estimates are often compared to the total estimated costs of control in order to assess the wisdom of current policy. Unfortunately, the cost data are also imprecise. More important, the simple comparison of *total* costs and benefits may generate misleading conclusions.

The estimated incremental costs of abating industrial and utility emissions rose from $7.8 billion in 1978 to $12.7 billion in 1979 in current dollars, according to the CEQ.[32] These costs are at best rough estimates because of the formidable problems in assembling the requisite data. For instance, investments in recycling industrial wastes may reduce

30. NERA, *Cost-Effectiveness*.

31. Mike Chappie and Lester Lave, "The Health Effects of Air Pollution: A Reanalysis," *Journal of Urban Economics*, vol. 12 (November 1982), pp. 346–76. Ostro and Anderson, "Morbidity, Air Pollution, and Health Statistics," on the other hand, find that particulates are more important than sulfates as contributors to morbidity.

32. CEQ, *Environmental Quality—1979*, p. 166, and *1980*, p. 394. These data differ from the Bureau of Economic Analysis data cited in footnote 1 in that they capture only the incremental costs of control arising from regulation. Expenditures that would have occurred without regulation are excluded.

Table 3-10. *Estimates of the Benefits and Costs of Stationary-Source Air Pollution Control*
Billions of 1978 dollars

| Study | Benefits | | | Costs | | |
	Health	Non-health	Total	Private	Public	Total
Lave-Seskin	23.1	. . .	. . .	. . .	. . .	. . .
Freeman	16.8	3.4	20.2	. . .	. . .	. . .
NERA	4.4	3.3	7.7	. . .	. . .	. . .
CEQ (1978)	. . .	. . .	. . .	7.8	0.8	8.6
CEQ (1979)[a]	. . .	. . .	. . .	11.7	0.9[b]	12.6

Sources: Lester B. Lave and Eugene P. Seskin, *Air Pollution and Human Health* (Johns Hopkins University Press for Resources for the Future, 1977); A. Myrick Freeman III, "The Benefits of Air and Water Pollution Control: A Review and and Synthesis of Recent Estimates," report prepared for CEQ, 1979; and National Economic Research Associates, *Cost-Effectiveness and Cost-Benefit Analysis of Air Quality Regulation*, report prepared for Business Roundtable Air Quality Project (New York: Business Roundtable, 1980).

a. 1979 costs are adjusted to 1978 dollars by deflating by the gross national product implicit price deflator for fixed investment.

b. Two-thirds of public costs are assigned to stationary-source controls—the remaining third is assumed to reflect the costs of controls on public-sector vehicles.

energy use and generate valuable by-products. Such investments may not have been undertaken without environmental laws, but their full cost should not be attributed to environmental policy.[33] The usual problems of separating joint costs, assigning overhead, estimating depreciation, and measuring the cost of capital cloud any estimates of the costs of pollution control. Nevertheless, the CEQ estimates appear to be as accurate as possible, given the existing data.

Can anything be said about the desirability of relaxing or tightening industrial (and utility) controls from these estimates of costs and benefits summarized in table 3-10? Unfortunately not, for two reasons. First, comparisons of total benefits and costs are meaningless for assessing optimality. Second, even if these estimates are accurate, the existing costs are not the minimum costs for the current degree of control. It is conceivable that even though benefits are greater than costs, a relaxation of environmental standards could increase economic welfare. Alternatively a more efficient strategy of control might allow an increase in economic welfare by making controls more stringent.

Figure 3-2 may help clarify these conclusions. Assume that the additional benefits from pollution reduction from each increment of control from 0 to 100 percent are measured by *MB*. The total benefits would be the area under the *MB* schedule between the vertical axis and

33. CEQ attempts to estimate the *incremental* costs caused by regulation.

Figure 3-2. *Comparison of Benefits and Costs of Air Pollution Control: A Hypothetical Example*

Dollars

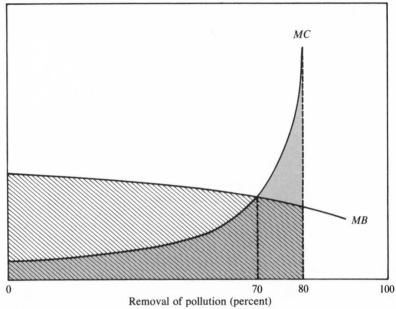

Removal of pollution (percent)

the indicated degree of control. Similarly assume that additional costs for each degree of control are given by *MC*. The total costs of control are the area under *MC* between the vertical axis and the chosen control level. For the sake of argument assume that 80 percent removal is mandated and that total benefits from this level of control greatly exceed total costs. (The shaded area under the cost curve is smaller than the crosshatched area under the benefits curve.) Despite this dominance of total benefits over total costs, a relaxation of control to 70 percent would increase economic welfare because the cost of adding controls to move from 70 percent to 80 percent removal exceeds the benefits from increasing controls. The additional (marginal) cost schedule is above the additional (marginal) benefit schedule everywhere to the right of 70 percent removal.

What happens if the *efficient* cost schedule is substantially below the *MC* schedule in figure 3-2? Obviously it would intersect the *MB* schedule to the right of the 70 percent abatement level. It could well intersect *MB* at abatement rates of more than 80 percent. Therefore, it cannot be concluded that controls are either too stringent or too loose from data on total current costs and total benefits. It is essential that the marginal costs of efficient controls be compared with marginal benefits. Such a comparison is extremely difficult.

Summary

There is overwhelming evidence that the current approach to setting environmental standards for air quality is extremely inefficient. Existing sources are controlled through state implementation plans, which are likely to use some variant of proportional rollback. Even the EPA's reasonably available control technology standards appear inefficient, presumably because *reasonably available* does not mean economically *efficient* to the engineers and lawyers setting the standards.

A further source of inefficiency is the stringent new-source standards—either BACT or LAER—which require far higher incremental control costs than existing sources. Such standards may be justified because new sources are more easily constrained than older ones, but the TSP and sulfur dioxide standards promulgated by the EPA for new sources are so stringent that the incremental costs of control seem to be higher than for retrofitted existing sources. This situation can only retard the development of new sources, increase the cost of pollution control, and slow the cleanup of the environment.

Nor can one conclude that the degree of current control is justified by estimates of the economic value of total benefits from current policy. Even if these benefits exceed estimated costs, controls may be too stringent. Alternatively, if regulation were efficient, it might be desirable to increase the degree of pollution control. Ignorance of the crucial data prevents any conclusion other than that air pollution policy could and should be much more efficient. A recent General Accounting Office report concludes that the data suggest a potential saving of 40 to 90 percent of current control costs from a more sensible policy.[34] This is sufficient justification for seeking alternative methods of control.

34. U.S. General Accounting Office, *A Market Approach to Air Pollution Control Could Reduce Compliance Costs without Jeopardizing Clean Air Goals* (Government Printing Office, 1982), p. ii.

IV

The Environmental
Control Problem

Economists, regulators, and environmentalists have long argued about the best method for regulating externalities, although the differences between them have narrowed.[1] Basically there are two options for controlling by-product discharges into the environment: economic incentives or legal compulsion (direct controls). Other indirect approaches are sometimes used. These include forbidding new product introductions, endlessly delaying permits, banning inputs to the production process that generate the discharges, and treating the discharges after they have been produced. Even these approaches are merely indirect quantitative controls.

In the public debate over economic incentives versus direct controls, there is a poor understanding of the basic economics involved. If the objective is to control the discharge to a precise, known level, direct quantitative controls are likely to be most effective in achieving the social goal. If they can be monitored and enforced, direct controls will "work" in the sense that they will reduce pollution to a known level.

It is far from obvious that policymakers should aim for a certain level of pollution. Knowing the "right" level of pollution requires information on costs and benefits that may be uncertain at best. Without this certain knowledge policymakers might choose a strategy that minimizes the social costs resulting from the wrong information on costs or benefits. This is likely to involve economic incentives rather than compulsory standards.

The Objective of Air Pollution Policy

While there are different opinions about the appropriate goal of environmental policy, this chapter presumes that environmental policymakers seek to maximize the economic welfare arising from their

1. See Jorge A. Calvo y Gonzales, "Markets in Air: Problems and Prospects of Controlled Trading," *Harvard Environmental Law Review,* vol. 5 (1981), pp. 377–430,

policy choices.[2] They are attempting to maximize an uncertain net-benefit stream, which is defined as the difference between the health, aesthetic, and material benefits of reducing air pollution and the costs of achieving this reduction. There are major problems of uncertainty in estimating the benefits or costs of control. The magnitude of prospective health effects, the relationship between point-source discharges and ambient air quality, the value of reduced morbidity or mortality, and the costs of control across myriad sources are the major contributors to this uncertainty. For each of these important relationships, objective or subjective estimates must be made by regulators if they are to pursue a systematic policy of welfare maximization.

Under current law the Environmental Protection Agency (EPA) is not always instructed to pursue this welfare-maximizing strategy. Indeed, the Clean Air Act Amendments of 1970 instruct the agency to set ambient air quality standards to protect the most sensitive groups in the population, apparently without regard to cost. Nevertheless, EPA administrators are guided by cost-benefit considerations. Since health-effect thresholds have not been found in most scientific studies, the administrator must make a determination within a wide range of potential ambient standards.[3] Congress has also instructed the EPA to use uniform national point-source standards for new sources of air pollution and for both new and old sources of water pollution. In either case there is no consistent strategy to maximize economic welfare. Inefficiencies arise in both air and water pollution policy because (1) the control of individual pollutants does not equate incremental benefits and incremental costs, and (2) incremental control costs are not equated across different point sources.

There is virtually no alternative to assessing benefits and costs in

---

for an exhaustive discussion of the trend toward market incentives in air pollution policy. The economics literature on the use of economic incentives in air pollution control is vast. See, for example, William J. Baumol and Wallace E. Oates, *Economics, Environmental Policy, and the Quality of Life* (Prentice-Hall, 1979); John H. Dales, *Pollution, Property and Prices* (University of Toronto Press, 1968); A. Michael Spence and Martin L. Weitzman, "Regulatory Strategies for Pollution Control," in Ann F. Friedlaender, ed., *Approaches to Controlling Air Pollution* (MIT Press, 1978), pp. 199–219; and Allen V. Kneese and Charles L. Schultze, *Pollution, Prices, and Public Policy* (Brookings Institution, 1975).

2. It is by no means clear that this was the goal of Congress in drafting the Clean Air Act. Nor is it clear that reducing air pollution is the only objective reflected in the act. See chapter 7.

3. See discussion in chapter 8 of the ambient standards.

designing a rational environmental policy. Resources spent on controlling one form of discharge cannot be spent on another. Minimizing some physical measure of pollution is meaningless because one cannot add tons of sulfur oxides to tons of heavy metals. If pollution is to be minimized, subject to some constraint, there must be a measure for calculating the value of total pollution reduction. If this is left to the policymaker, the rates of exchange among pollutants simply reflect his assessment of the relative social benefits of controlling each. Despite claims to the contrary, benefit calculations must be made in virtually any strategy.

It is often suggested that the objective of environmental regulation should be to protect human health. All pollution control would thus be pursued to the point where the community's health is maximized. This is the apparent legislative instruction in the Clean Air Act. Without threshold effects, such an objective may require elimination of all potentially harmful pollutants. This policy would not only be politically unpalatable but might be inconsistent with modern economic activity.

Another approach, used in both clean air and clean water policy, is to require that all polluters employ the best available technology (BAT). This engineering approach is often defended as a straightforward approach that obtains all reasonable or feasible protection. This strategy is neither simple nor reasonable. In the first place, there is no logical definition of the *best* technology. Technological choices depend on the relative prices of productive resources and the value of the output (pollution reduction in this case). Any technology that is deemed the best available for reducing pollution from a given source can be improved with the expenditure of additional resources. Second, choosing a different best available technology for hundreds or even thousands of different types of sources can be an administrative nightmare.[4] Third, using criteria such as best available or maximum degree feasible may lead policymakers to accept high rates of pollution from near-bankrupt sources even though the benefits from eliminating these firms' pollution might exceed the social loss of the output.

Thus the bureaucrat's search for the best available technology will not result in the most economic method for reducing pollution or the

4. For an insight into these difficulties, see the data compiled by Battelle Laboratories in a report to the Environmental Protection Agency: D. M. Jenkins, J. E. Burch, and C. Buoni, "Report on Incremental Cost Effectiveness for Airborne Pollution Abatement" (June 5, 1979).

most effective method. It would be better to let polluters choose their own best and most efficient technology, subject to some constraint.

In short, one cannot sensibly provide a simple engineering rule to guide environmental policy. Nor can the policy be guided by the instruction to maximize health subject to an unspecified expenditure constraint. Policymakers entrusted with protecting the population from the hazards of a myriad of substances must trade off degrees of control among these discharges and pay close attention to costs.

The Mechanics of Choosing the Optimal Control

Assuming that policymakers seek to maximize the net benefits from pollution reduction, the problem becomes one of choosing the policy instrument to achieve this goal.[5] In figure 4-1 the marginal benefits of controlling a given pollutant in a given area are depicted by negatively sloped curves. Total benefits are simply the area under the marginal benefits curve. In the top panel benefits rise at a declining rate as control gradually increases. Thus *incremental* benefits decline slowly with increasing pollution control. In the bottom panel benefits rise with pollution control but at a sharply declining rate. This is equivalent to assuming a rather sharp "threshold" effect that finds sizable benefits for controlling up to Q_1 but few additional benefits for controlling past Q_2. If, for instance, the pollutant is a toxic substance that generates major health effects above a particular concentration in water or air, the benefits of control are substantial until this concentration is reached. Thereafter they may be much lower.

In practice few pollutants fit the pattern of the lower panel in figure 4-1.[6] Hydrocarbons, nitrogen oxides, sulfur oxides, and photochemical oxidants appear to be pollutants for which the benefits function is fairly flat—reflecting no threshold effects upon human health, economic damage, or aesthetic values. Highly toxic substances, on the other hand, are more likely to fit the bottom panel's picture of the benefits relationship. However, since most air pollution policy is directed toward controlling

5. This discussion draws heavily on Martin L. Weitzman, "Prices *vs.* Quantities," *Review of Economic Studies,* vol. 41 (October 1974), pp. 477–91.

6. Bruce Ackerman and others contend that biochemical oxygen demand fits this description. See Bruce A. Ackerman, Susan Rose-Ackerman, and James W. Sawyer, Jr., *The Uncertain Search for Environmental Quality* (Collier-Macmillan, 1974), p. 265.

Figure 4-1. *The Economics of Alternative Pollution Control Techniques*

A. NO THRESHOLD

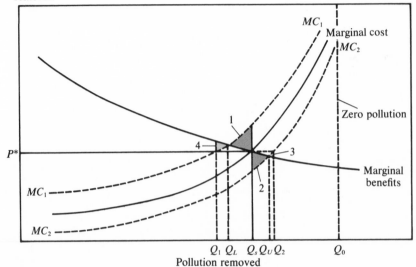

B. WITH THRESHOLD

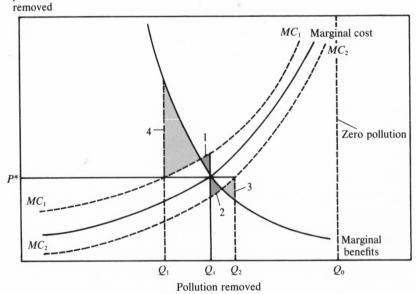

pollutants with no clear health effect thresholds, the top panel is likely to be more relevant for current discussions of regulatory policy.

The cost function in both panels is drawn in the same fashion, with sharply rising incremental costs of control as pollution removal approaches 100 percent. This is a reasonable assumption, given the engineering realities of control and declining marginal rates of substitution in production and consumption. As the attempt is made to control discharges more tightly, it may be assumed that in general the additional costs of control per unit of pollution will rise at an increasing rate. As pollution control forces substitution for products from polluting industries, the added costs to producers and consumers are likely to rise. Thus for any environmental policy that promises major reductions in pollution, it is reasonable to assume that costs rise rather steeply in the range of the desired or optimal degree of control.

Obviously policymakers cannot know precisely the shape and location of the benefits and cost functions such as those in figure 4-1. Benefits are difficult to measure,[7] but it can be shown that uncertainties in the measurement of benefits have little impact on the choice of control technique. Uncertainties about costs are more important.

The role of the cost function and the uncertainty surrounding it can be seen quite easily. The broken lines in figure 4-1 represent a hypothetical locus of points, for instance, one standard deviation from the expected marginal cost function, shown as a solid line. The greater this band of uncertainty is, the higher the social cost of errors in setting the control variable.

Regulators have a choice of control instruments: a pollution fee or quantitative standards. To maximize welfare, regulators equate expected marginal benefits with expected marginal cost. In figure 4-1 this equality occurs at Q_s. If regulators knew the location and shape of the cost and benefit functions, the choice of control instrument would be trivial. A pollution tax or fee set at P^* would lead businessmen to reduce pollution to Q_s as they equated the price of polluting with the marginal cost of curtailing it. Regulators could set the quantity standard at Q_s with the

7. The literature on cost-benefit analysis for social regulation is extensive. For a recent analysis of the problems in valuing environmental improvements, see A. Myrick Freeman III, *The Benefits of Environmental Improvement: Theory and Practice* (Johns Hopkins University Press for Resources for the Future, 1979). For a thorough review of alternative frameworks for analyzing regulatory issues, see Lester B. Lave, *The Strategy of Social Regulation: Decision Frameworks for Policy* (Brookings Institution, 1981). See also chapter 3, above.

same result except for the impact on income distribution. Under the standard-setting regime, pollution taxes would not be collected on the remaining emissions $(Q_0 - Q_s)$, but the pollution level would be the same. This may be the main reason that businessmen generally prefer standards to pollution fees.

Uncertainty in the assessment of costs and benefits means that regulators must worry about the choice of control instrument. Assume that actual marginal control costs exceed their expected levels. If the regulators set the quantity standard at Q_s, they will have misallocated resources since marginal control costs (shown by MC_1 in figure 4-1) will exceed marginal benefits. Society will have paid more for pollution reduction between Q_L and Q_s than it is worth, thus generating a loss in economic welfare. The loss in welfare is represented by the dark area labeled 1 in figure 4-1. Similarly if control costs are below their expected value, as shown by MC_2, the standard, Q_s, will generate too much pollution $(Q_U - Q_s)$ and a welfare loss, as measured by dark area 2.

What happens if the regulator uses the pollution fee as the control instrument? If control costs are precisely as expected, the result is to generate Q_s in pollution reduction, the welfare-maximizing level. But if control costs are MC_1, the fee will lead polluters to reduce their control efforts to Q_1 when optimally they should have been induced to control to Q_L. This generates a welfare loss shown as shaded area 4. Similarly if costs are lower than anticipated, polluters will reduce their pollution even further, to Q_2, an excessive level of abatement since the fee is above the point of equality of marginal control costs and marginal benefits. As a result economic welfare equal to shaded area 3 will be sacrificed.

Which control instrument leads to the lowest potential welfare losses in the face of uncertainty depends on the shape of the benefit and cost functions. In the top panel the gradual decline in the benefit function, combined with sharply rising control costs, argues strongly for the use of the pollution tax. Shaded areas 3 and 4 are obviously smaller than darker areas 1 and 2. As Spence and Weitzman emphasize, "Standards fix pollution levels but leave cleanup costs uncertain; in contrast, fees fix (incremental) cleanup costs but leave pollution levels uncertain."[8]

When there is little slope to the marginal benefit function, controlling costs and leaving the pollution level uncertain are preferable. If incremental control costs are rising sharply, setting the "wrong" standard

8. Spence and Weitzman, "Regulatory Strategies for Pollution Control," p. 209.

can be far more costly than setting the wrong pollution fee. Thus, where there are no threshold effects, pollution fees or taxes are better than quantity standards whenever control costs are uncertain.

When there are distinct thresholds in the benefits function, however, the optimal instrument is the quantity standard. Since substantial potential welfare losses can result from the wrong pollution level, it is better to control pollution directly than to control costs. The bottom panel in figure 4-1 demonstrates this result clearly. Areas 3 and 4, the losses from using a pollution fee, are much larger than areas 1 and 2, the potential welfare losses from using the quantity standard Q_s for the same range of uncertainty in control costs.

Uncertainty in the benefits estimation does not influence the choice of control instrument (pollution fees versus standards) although it increases the range of potential welfare loss. If there is a range of uncertainty around the marginal benefits schedule in figure 4-2 similar to the range with expected marginal control costs, the potential welfare loss from setting the wrong standard or fee is increased, but the choice between the two control instruments is not affected. If the benefits exceed their expected value, as in the top panel of figure 4-2, the maximum potential welfare loss from setting the standard at Q_s is ACD. On the other hand, the maximum loss from a pollution fee at P^* would be GBC or EDF. Similarly, if benefits are below their expected value, as in the bottom panel, the maximum loss from a standard is abc, but the maximum loss from setting the fee P^* is bde or gfh. Without a threshold in the benefit function and with steeply rising incremental costs, the fee remains superior to the standard, although the potential losses from setting the wrong fee or standard are much larger. The case for the fee is much stronger than in the certain-benefits case because the cost of being wrong is greater. If there were a threshold in the benefit function and gradually rising incremental costs, this conclusion would be reversed. As in the certain-benefits case, the regulator would be advised to set the pollution level directly and pay the penalty in uncertain control costs.

These considerations point to the general supremacy of pollution fees over quantity standards in every case except where strong threshold effects exist in the relationship between pollution and human health or other human values. Given the paucity of evidence demonstrating threshold effects for most pollutants, fees appear to be a generally superior instrument. Uncertainty in the benefits function does not affect the choice of control instrument because these benefits are not traded. Private decisionmakers do not respond to the shape of the benefit

Figure 4-2. *The Choice of Control Technique with Uncertain Benefits and Costs*

Dollars per
quantity of
pollution
removed

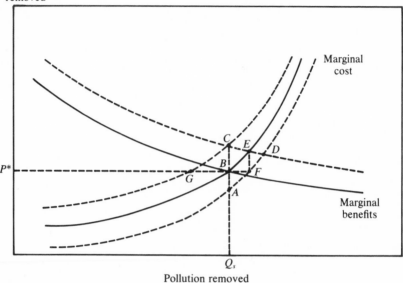

Pollution removed

Dollars per
quantity of
pollution
removed

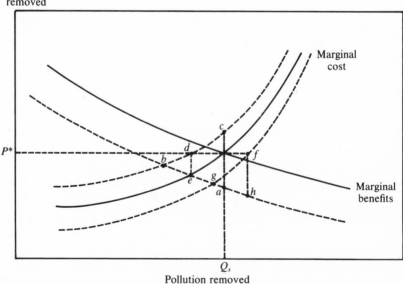

Pollution removed

function; they are influenced by the pollution standard, the fee, and the cost function. Regulators must agonize over the magnitude of the benefits, but their anguish is not likely to affect their choice of instruments.

Inefficiency from the Wrong Mix of Standards

Despite the preceding analysis, it is unlikely that the major source of inefficiency in the current standard-setting process derives from choosing the wrong aggregate goal, Q_s, as the basis for promulgating individual point-source standards. The marginal cost schedules in figures 4-1 and 4-2 are drawn under the assumption that emissions are reduced first by sources with the lowest costs of control, with additional reductions coming from slightly higher-cost sources or further reductions (at higher costs) from the first set of sources. As this process continues, marginal control costs rise with additional reductions. At any given control level the additional cost of abatement at all sources applying controls must be equal. If not, a transfer of control responsibility from the high-marginal-cost source to the low-cost source would reduce total costs to society.

Clearly the standard-setting process misallocates resources even more severely than the results in figure 4-1 or 4-2 suggest because regulators cannot have sufficient information to set individual standards efficiently. Indeed, because regulators cannot know the costs of abatement at every source, economists argue for a market-incentive approach (such as a fee) as a substitute for direct standard-setting regulation. Chapter 3 showed that control costs may well be two or three times as high as necessary for a given total emission target. The actual cost may be substantially above the marginal cost schedule in figures 4-1 and 4-2 for the standard-setting process. On the other hand, polluters presumably know their own marginal abatement costs much better and are therefore more likely to approximate the true marginal cost schedule in their abatement decisions. For this reason fees are likely to generate lower total control costs than a standard-setting regime that obtains the same degree of total pollution abatement.

The superiority of fees over standards is shown diagramatically in figure 4-3. The regulatory cost schedule is ragged, reflecting the unevenness of controlling pollution through a set of different standards for new and old sources in a number of different industries. Its shape and location

Figure 4-3. *The Social Costs of Inefficient Standards*

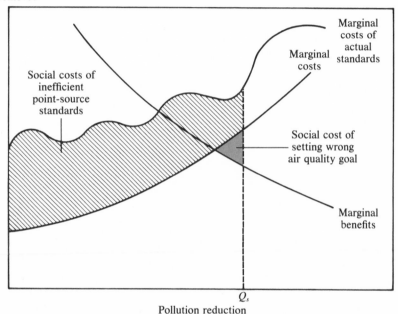

are arbitrary, drawn to represent the likely inefficiency in setting these standards. The total economic loss from inefficiency in the choice of control targets and technologies is shown by the crosshatched area, an area clearly larger than the social loss caused by choosing a quantity *target, Q_s,* instead of a fee. This suggests that the benefits of market incentives are likely to derive more from the proper selection of controls across sources than from the proper choice of an aggregate target under uncertainty.

The Opposition to Pollution Taxes

The relatively simple and compelling case for using pollution taxes or fees rather than direct quantity controls is recent, emanating from a classic article by Weitzman.[9] The economists' general predisposition for prices rather than quantities derives from concern that incremental

9. Weitzman, "Prices *vs*. Quantities."

control costs be equated across sources. This goal can be obtained by other means. Therefore, a system of pollution taxes is not required to generate this result. This is fortunate, given the strong opposition to pollution taxes.

The largely bureaucratic case against fees reflects a misunderstanding of the issues. A former EPA planning official referred to pollution tax proposals as an "effluent-fee chimera." He thinks that fees are unworkable because they must be based upon estimates of the damages (benefits) function:

This is the oldest, most classic, most unworkable (even theoretically), and longest-and-most-firmly-rejected version of the effluent fee. Even assuming that one could measure all the costs of a polluter's emissions (crop damage, dead birds, auto finish deterioration, aesthetic losses, and so on), society has never been able to agree on a measure of the most critical of costs—human disease, suffering, and death. (By contrast, the costs of compliance . . . are easily determined).[10]

He fails to recognize that the inability to measure damages from pollution (or benefits from pollution control) reveals nothing about the choice of instrument. It simply says that any form of control probably will fail to maximize welfare.

A more compelling objection, but one with little empirical support, is that fees require substantially more enforcement outlays than standards. The source of these purported economies in enforcement is apparently the ability to monitor "compliance" by simply determining that control equipment is in place. Standards are designed so that compliance can be assured by observation of the control equipment while fees must be enforced by monitoring emissions. This ignores the possibility of using the equipment-surveillance technique for enforcing fees. If a piece of control equipment is assumed to meet a quantity standard, that quantity can be used in computing the pollution tax. At the extreme a pollution fee system could require polluters to use one of a limited number of options of control or production techniques. With each option a presumed discharge level would provide the basis for estimating the tax liability. Although far from ideal, this would be an improvement over the regulation of the quantity of emissions when benefits increase at a gradual rate but costs do not. The imperfect monitoring of quantities of pollution, through verification of equipment, can be used for enforcing either a price or quantity mechanism of control. Since the total tax bill

10. William Drayton, Jr., "Comment," in Friedlaender, *Approaches to Controlling Air Pollution,* pp. 232–33.

under a pollution tax system is based on *quantities* of discharge, it would be difficult to argue that monitoring efficiencies make one system superior.

What has been generally overlooked in the debate over pollution taxes is how fees differ fundamentally from standards in their effect on the distribution of wealth. Quantity standards, such as the new-source performance standards (NSPS) for sulfur oxides or the best practicable technology (BPT) standards for various water pollutants, are in effect licenses to pollute at a zero price up to the standard and prohibitions on pollution above the standard. Polluters will favor such a system over one that imposes a tax equal to the marginal cost of control at the standard. If standards are uniformly set and enforced so that marginal control costs are equal everywhere, a shift to a tax will not affect production techniques, product prices, or pollution levels—if the tax is precisely equal to the marginal cost of control under the old standards. But polluters will suffer a loss of wealth because they must "lease" the air up to the standard by paying taxes rather than obtaining their standard ration at a zero price (figure 4-4).

The incremental control costs for an individual polluter are shown as *ABC* in figure 4-4, rising at an increasing rate as pollution is reduced. The standard is set at *FE* units of pollution per period, thus requiring a reduction of *GF* units from the "unconstrained" level. The firm's total *control* costs are equal to the shaded area *ABFG*—the area under the incremental control cost function between *G* and *F*. In a standard-setting regime these are the only costs of pollution borne by the firm. It pays nothing for the right to pollute *EF* units per period.

If a fee is imposed, inducing the firm to precisely the same rate of pollution control (and therefore pollution), the firm will continue to experience control costs of *ABFG* but will also pay pollution taxes equal to *BDEF* in figure 4-4. These tax payments are likely to be substantial as long as the fee is set so as to provide substantial cleanup but not zero pollution.[11]

The shift in the tax burden implied by a movement to pollution taxes from the current standard-setting process is unlikely to enjoy widespread support from the polluting industries. Given the concentration of pollution and pollution control in a few industries,[12] it would be difficult to offset this large increase in indirect taxes with compensating reductions

11. See chapter 10 for an estimate of these potential tax revenues.
12. For these data, see Robert W. Crandall, "Pollution Controls and Productivity Growth in Basic Industry," in Thomas Cowing and Rodney Stevenson, eds., *Productivity*

Figure 4-4. *Imposition of a Pollution Tax*

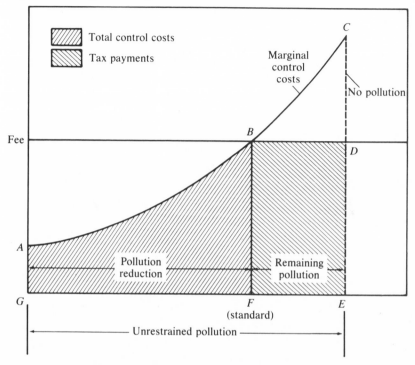

in taxes that affect only these industries. For instance, manufacturing industries accounting for less than 4 percent of the national income incur nearly half of all reported pollution control costs.[13] These industries— paper, steel, copper, chemicals, petroleum refining, cement, and grain milling—are unlikely to support a shift to pollution taxes even though substantial efficiency gains can be realized.

The guarantee of a property right—the pollution "standard"—at zero cost makes the current standard-setting process particularly attractive to businesses that pollute. Any proposal to reform the process of environmental control must grapple with this phenomenon. The whole-sale transfer of property rights from these businesses to the government will meet stiff opposition. While the current system may have transferred a large share of these rights, the share remaining with the industries responsible for the nation's pollution is substantial.

Measurement in Regulated Industries (Academic Press, 1981), pp. 347–68 (Brookings Reprint 375).
    13. See chapter 10 for a more complete discussion of this point.

The movement from a world in which pollution is largely unregulated and cleanup is not paid for by polluters to one in which increasingly strict regulation applies has not occurred without substantial political compromise. More stringent standards have been legislated for new sources than for older ones. Copper smelters have been given explicit dispensation in the form of more lenient timetables for achieving lower emission levels. Small firms and industries have been exempted altogether. Coal miners have been given protection even when they produce high-sulfur, polluting coal.

The use of a tax to ration pollution would make these exceptions somewhat more difficult to administer, but the tax code probably could accommodate even these political compromises. However, a standard-setting process gives the regulator additional discretion that Congress might be loath to give the Internal Revenue Service. Standards that have been set quite differently across industries can be concealed more readily than differences in tax rates. Whenever necessary, industries can be divided and subdivided for the purpose of defining best available technology.[14] Small firms can be given more lenient treatment without explicit exemptions. Some students of environmental policy suggest that regulators use their discretionary power to set standards that will tend to equalize control costs across sources in an industry in order to avoid altering the competitive positions of the firms.[15] This requires equalizing control costs per unit of output, not of pollution. Fees or taxes would equalize incremental costs per unit of pollution.

Practical Alternative Approaches to the Control Problem

The preceding discussion suggests that an efficient system for controlling pollution cannot be implemented without addressing the major problem of transferring property rights from producers to society. The present process distributes these rights in response to political pressures but then allows virtually no further transfer among claimants to assure economic efficiency.

Two potential approaches to the control problem would work much

14. See Robert A. Leone and John E. Jackson, "The Political Economy of Federal Regulatory Activity: The Case of Water Pollution Controls," in Gary Fromm, ed., *Studies in Public Regulation* (MIT Press, 1981), pp. 231–71.
    15. Ibid.

better: (1) transferable pollution rights and (2) pollution taxes with two-part tariffs. Each would allow the cleanup process to be undertaken far more efficiently. The latter would permit a better expected allocation of resources for pollutants without threshold effects.

Freely Transferable Rights

The idea of allowing polluters to transfer pollution rights granted to them by the standard-setting authorities has been entertained for at least a decade. Dales, Ackerman, Montgomery, Oates, and Hahn and Noll have suggested this approach.[16] In recent years the EPA has begun to move in this direction and even Congress has followed, in the Clean Air Act Amendments of 1977. This change has occurred through the offset and bubble policies (discussed in chapter 5).

A system of marketable rights would simply give a firm the right to emit pollution up to a specified regulatory standard or to sell this right. The firm would be able to offer the right to another potential source of the same pollutant in the same area. It could reduce its pollution by more stringent controls or by a reduction in its output; it could choose to abandon production altogether and to sell its pollution rights as it closed operations in that location.

A pollution rights market would require delineation by the government of the permissible range of transfers. One type of pollutant could not be traded for another. Presumably the initial endowment of pollution rights would specify the total allowable pollution level for each of a myriad of different discharges or emissions. Each category would be different because of the health and other welfare effects emanating from that pollutant and because of the associated transport characteristics of the pollutant. Thus, if authorities had set a level of 100 tons of sulfur dioxide and 1,000 tons of particulates for a given area, sulfur dioxide emissions could not be traded for particulates. Nor would trades be made across

16. See Dales, *Pollution, Property and Prices;* Susan Rose-Ackerman, "Market Models for Water Pollution Control," *Public Policy,* vol. 25 (Summer 1977), pp. 383–406; W. David Montgomery, "Markets in Licenses and Efficient Pollution Control Programs," *Journal of Economic Theory,* vol. 5 (December 1972), pp. 395–418; Wallace E. Oates, "Corrective Taxes and Auctions of Rights in the Control of Externalities," *Public Finance Quarterly,* vol. 9 (October 1981), pp. 471–78; Alan Krupnick, Wallace Oates, and Eric Van De Verg, "On Marketable Air Pollution Permits: The Case for a System of Pollution Offsets," Economics Working Paper (University of Maryland, 1982); and Robert W. Hahn and Roger G. Noll, "Designing a Market for Tradable Emissions Permits," in Wesley Magat, ed., *Reform of Environmental Regulations* (Ballinger, 1982).

geographical regions (although some attention to the possibilities for such trades might develop).

Benefits of a Marketable Rights System

There are a number of potential benefits to a marketable rights system, the most important being (1) efficiency gains, (2) accommodation of political problems in transferring rights, (3) elimination of new-source and old-source distinctions, and (4) signals to communities of the real costs of tighter controls.

First, a marketable rights system would lead those with generous initial allocations (generous standards) to think about sales to those less-favored in the standard-setting process. If a chemicals plant has a stringent hydrocarbon standard while asphalt or gasoline bulk depots have lenient hydrocarbon standards, the former could buy some rights from the latter. When the opportunity cost of rights is equated in all firms in the area—where incremental control costs are equalized—trades will cease. Society would be better served by lower-overall control costs without any degradation in environmental quality.

A marketable rights system also would encourage polluters to look for methods of improving pollution control techniques; such improvements would allow them to sell more of their endowments of pollution rights. One failing of a standard-setting approach is the absence of such incentives for improvement.[17] Of course, a pollution fee or tax is likely to be more efficient in its choice of pollution *level* than a quantity-setting regime. A marketable rights policy is clearly in the latter category because someone must choose the quantity of pollution to be distributed through the permits.

Second, the obvious advantage of this system over one of straightforward emissions fees is that the standard-setting process is used to generate the initial rights endowment. The political trades required to generate improvements in environmental quality can be accommodated without accepting the final allocation of resources implied by such deals.

Next, a major benefit of regulation by freely transferable rights is the elimination of the current distinction between existing and new sources. As demonstrated, standards for new sources are generally more stringent than those for existing sources on the basis of cost per ton of abatement.

17. Robert Hahn has reminded me that there is no empirical evidence supporting this assertion. "Best technology" standards may induce equipment suppliers to improve technology while a marketable rights system would provide the user of the equipment with the incentive.

It would be preferable to leave the relative distribution of emissions to a market test. If new plants are easier to control, businessmen will buy fewer rights for these facilities than for older plants of equivalent size. There is no reason to assume that this difference will be unchanging over time or across geographical regions. The danger in the present system is that it discourages new investment unnecessarily. Perhaps this is intended by Congress (see chapter 7). A marketable rights regime would correct this bias.

Finally, a much-needed reform in controlling pollution is a reduction of uncertainty for polluters so that they may plan their investment decisions. If a set of standards proves too lenient to attain the global environmental objective, a compensating mechanism is required. For instance, under current procedures state implementation plans (SIP) are drafted for achieving ambient air quality levels. These plans must be reassessed every four or five years. After this reassessment polluters may be asked to accede to more stringent (or more lenient) standards in order to allow the state to adjust for past errors in its plan. Standards are changed at considerable cost to the polluter and to society yet there is no assurance that these changes are carried out in the most cost-effective manner.

Were the state to issue marketable rights, a market would develop for each pollutant; this would generate a price for cleaning up each pollutant. If the citizens of the state wished even cleaner air or water, they could instruct state authorities to reduce the quantity of those rights through purchases from current owners. Voters would be directly informed of the cost of such a strategy by a simple calculation of market price multiplied by additional state purchases. They would thus be in a better position to know whether a reduction is worthwhile. Alternatively, if responsibility for the protection of human health remained with the federal government, it could calculate the price (and therefore the cost) of any further reduction in pollution necessary to protect human health.

Objections to Marketable Rights

The objections to a system of marketable rights can be anticipated from the literature on approaches to allocating rights to the electromagnetic spectrum.[18] It may be argued that these rights cannot be easily

18. See Arthur S. DeVany and others, "A Property System for Market Allocation of the Electromagnetic Spectrum: A Legal-Economic-Engineering Study," *Stanford Law Review*, vol. 21 (June 1969), pp. 1499–1561, for a discussion of these issues.

specified. Each plant is different; reducing emissions in one plant is therefore not equivalent to reducing them in another. Geographic location, coproducts, height of stacks, temporal distribution of output, and other variables affect the decision to control pollution.

The specification of the spatial distribution of optimal pollution levels is not easy, given different transport characteristics and synergistic effects among pollutants, but this hardly makes marketable rights unworkable. Under the standard-setting regime, trade-offs must be made among pollutants and across geographic areas. The marketability of rights can be constrained by the same algorithm used in setting standards under the current regulatory regime. The simplest approach would be to draw market boundaries, allowing trades within these boundaries but not across them. Alternatively, trades could be allowed at differing exchange rates across geographic boundaries.

A second objection might be that the marketability of rights would reduce the EPA's ability to monitor and enforce the actual levels of pollution.[19] Enforcement of a system of transferable rights requires some certification of the pollution discharged by both the buyer and the seller, before and after the trade, but this may be no more onerous than the current system. Low-cost, accurate monitoring approaches are a key to any efficient system of pollution control.

A third objection concerns the interaction of pollutants in creating damage. If several pollutants combine to form a social hazard, they should not be addressed separately (unless one pollutant is always redundant). This complicates administration, since rights might have to be defined as a set of maximum pollution constraints, no one of which may be exceeded by the polluter. This is not a reason to favor the current approach, since these interactions are not efficiently addressed in current EPA policy.

Finally, the marketable rights approach is unlikely to work if there are few buyers and sellers. To offer a marketable right to a lead smelter for lead emissions in a remote area may mean the right to sell the emission to nobody since there are no other actual or potential sources of lead discharges in the relevant market. Making the regulatory standard marketable harms no one; it simply confers no advantages. Where there is no market, the imposition of marketable rights will not shift from the current regulatory regime. One need not worry about such failures unless they are universal. Only if the rights markets are defined as the confines

19. Calvo y Gonzales, "Markets in Air."

of the current polluters' plants would a marketable rights system be valueless. There is no a priori reason to believe that all pollution markets should be so narrowly drawn.

Whether a pollution rights market can function efficiently has yet to be proved. Hahn and Noll have wrestled with this problem for sulfur dioxide control in Southern California; they have shown that market power can develop in a sulfur dioxide market because utilities would have a large share of the market.[20] For this reason they argue that the design and "initialization" of the market are crucial. The initial endowment must be distributed so as not to create monopoly or monopsony power.

A Two-Part Pollution Tax

There is no denying that pollution taxes are not now the popular route to reform of environmental policy. The income transfer and the uncertainty in settling upon the optimal fee are compelling reasons for opposing a movement toward pollution taxes. But perhaps even this type of economic incentive for pollution control should not be so quickly dismissed. There may be a mechanism for adapting such a price incentive to the harsh political and practical realities of environmental policy.

That a pollution fee would have to be adjusted to reflect new evidence (or new political pressures) is undeniable. But environmental standards are changed periodically without creating havoc. New categories, such as lowest achievable emission rate or best conventional technology, are introduced into environmental statutes. The view that a tax policy must be definite and unchanging while other policies may be changed to adjust to new information is difficult to justify. The Internal Revenue Code did not grow to its present proportions without frequent changes. This is not to say that changes in environmental tax rates would be welcomed but simply to suggest that pollution fees can be altered with changing perceptions of the underlying economic and health parameters. Moreover, these changes need not be frequent.

Spence and Weitzman have suggested that a pollution tax initially be set equal to the estimated marginal benefits from reducing emissions or discharges of a pollutant.[21] This is an upward-biased measure of the optimal rate, as figure 4-5 shows. If incremental benefits fall with each

20. Hahn and Noll, "Designing a Market for Tradable Emissions Permits."
21. Spence and Weitzman, "Regulatory Strategies for Pollution Control," pp. 204–06.

Figure 4-5. *Initial Selection of a Pollution Tax Rate*

Dollars

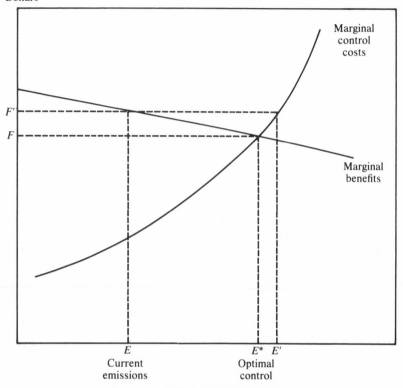

reduction of pollution levels, the equilibrium fee or optimal fee should be lower than the ex ante estimate of marginal benefits. Knowing control costs is an essential ingredient to setting the optimal fee; one can safely assume that these costs are not far from zero at pre–pollution control levels. When a fee equal to precontrol marginal benefits is set, firms will rush to exceed the optimal level of control, reducing pollution to E' rather than to the optimal level E^*. If the benefit function is gradually sloped or if control costs rise steeply, the Spence-Weitzman suggestion for a starting point will not misallocate resources greatly. Otherwise, it will lead to excessive control.

The practical political problem with fees is that they require payments for pollution rights now granted at a zero price. A way around this problem is to set two-part fees giving firms an allocation of zero-priced rights up to some finite limit and charging a fee for pollution beyond this initial level.[22] The rights could be traded, much as offsets are traded today, but without the constraints imposed by technology-based new-source standards under the current law.

The initial allocation of zero-priced rights would reflect a political decision, but the setting of the fee would represent regulators' (or Congress's) best judgment as to the appropriate degree of control. The fee and the resulting pollution would give citizens vital information on the cost of further cleanup or the benefits of relaxation. Given the appropriate levels of rights and fees, the collection of pollution taxes would provide much more information on control costs than is currently available.

If the resulting pollution levels were deemed too high, taxes could be raised. If necessary, lump-sum credits could be given to firms penalized by the need to change the tax rate, but credits based on the flow of tax payments would be counterproductive. The most important attribute of a pollution tax system is that it would induce efficient pollution reduction. Since all firms would be faced with the same incremental cost of pollution in each area for each pollutant, each firm would control pollution until its incremental control costs equaled this fee. In this sense pollution taxes are equivalent to marketable rights.[23]

The further advantage of fees lies in their effect on resource allocation in a world where benefits and costs are imprecisely known. When benefits are unknown but the benefit function is rising at a modestly declining rate, fees are likely to be the best choice of a control instrument (figure 4-1). If the optimal degree of control cannot be specified and if threshold effects of pollution do not exist, setting the wrong pollution tax is measurably better than setting the wrong standard (or the wrong total endowment of transferable rights).

Finally, the two-part pollution tax answers the unstated political objection to fees: that businesses will be forced to incur additional costs of scores of billions of dollars per year without being assured of corresponding reductions in other business taxes.

Summary

The simple economics of controlling an externality such as air pollution argues strongly for the use of fees or taxes rather than quantitative limits whenever the benefits of additional control decline

22. For a more detailed discussion of this proposal, see chapter 10.
23. It would be necessary to allow trading of the zero-priced rights to assure this efficiency condition. And the pollution fee would have to be binding.

slowly and the incremental costs of control rise rapidly. Fees or taxes minimize the costs of being wrong—and these costs can be substantial when there are uncertainties about the costs or benefits of control.

Most arguments against emission fees involve either the costs of monitoring or the income transfers inherent in the full reversal of property rights. The monitoring–enforcement costs argument applies similarly to fees or standards; any compromise that can be accepted for enforcing standards can be used in enforcing fees. The income-transfer problem is more serious. A two-part tariff with variable first parts across firms is probably the best solution to this problem.

V

The Movement toward Reform: Bubbles, Offsets, and Netting

The difficulties with the Clean Air Act's approach to stationary-source control have been recognized by the analytical staff at the Environmental Protection Agency for many years. Even before the 1977 amendments it was clear that the act's draconian approach to nonattainment policy could not be sustained politically. The Clean Air Act Amendments of 1970 required areas that did not meet ambient air quality standards to deny permission for the construction of new sources of these pollutants. Since a total ban on new sources would have substantial repercussions on local economies, the EPA was forced to devise a scheme that comported with the spirit of the Clean Air Act but allowed some new construction. This scheme was an offset policy requiring owners of new sources to buy pollution reductions—offsets—from other sources in the area. The unintended effect of this was to move the EPA toward market incentives in controlling air pollution.[1]

From this modest beginning in 1976 there has been a steady evolution toward a more comprehensive system of marketable permits. While most of these new tradable or "offsettable" pollution rights—or more properly, credits for emission *reduction*—are only now coming off the drawing boards and into practice, such markets are insinuating themselves into environmental policy to a degree that few environmentalists would have expected (or hoped) when the Clean Air Act was passed.

Statutory Complexity: PSD and Nonattainment Policy

In essence all areas of the country are classified as either a nonattainment area for a given criteria pollutant or a prevention of significant deterioration (PSD) area. That is, either an area exceeds the maximum allowable concentration of a pollutant or it is a nondegradation area. Its

1. *Federal Register,* vol. 41 (December 21, 1976), pp. 5525 ff.

classification into one of these two categories affects the regulatory approach that the EPA and the state must apply to new or existing sources of the pollutant.

Before the 1977 amendments new sources were apparently forbidden in nonattainment areas after a statutory deadline for attainment in 1975 or 1977. In 1976, however, the EPA proposed a method for allowing new sources in nonattainment areas after the statutory deadline in a way that would meet the requirements of the Clean Air Act.[2] Specifically, construction could take place if the new sources met a stringent new-source standard and if they purchased offsets from other pollution sources in the area. These offsets would be more-than-equivalent reductions in emissions of the same pollutant from other sources already in compliance. In short, pollution reductions by existing sources would exceed the prospective pollution from new sources, thus satisfying a statutory requirement that nonattainment areas demonstrate reasonable further progress toward attainment.

In 1977 the statutory deadlines for new sources were postponed to 1982 or 1987 (for automobile-related pollutants), and the EPA was instructed to require that states formulate plans to meet these deadlines.[3] The offset policy was codified in the 1977 amendments, but it expired at the 1979 deadline for submitting state implementation plans (SIPs). Thereafter, states could incorporate this approach into their SIPs as part of their new-source policy, at their own discretion. SIPs are to include provisions for requiring reasonably available control technology (RACT) for all sources in nonattainment areas and to require the imposition of vehicle-emission inspections in those areas not meeting ambient standards for oxidants or carbon monoxide by 1982.

For PSD areas the EPA is instructed to limit the growth of emissions of total suspended particulates (TSP) and sulfur dioxide to specific increments above a "baseline" level. It must require all new major sources of either pollutant to undergo a new-source review.[4] As part of this review the owners of the proposed new facility must provide state officials with the results of a detailed air quality modeling exercise demonstrating that the new facility will not violate ambient air quality

2. For a cogent review of the development of the offset policy, see Richard A. Liroff, *Air Pollution Offsets: Trading, Selling, and Banking* (Washington, D.C.: Conservation Foundation, 1980).
3. U.S.C. sections 7401–7642.
4. Ibid.

standards or the increments. Each such facility must be equipped with the best available control technology for that particular investment.

The use of offsets has been limited by other provisions of the Clean Air Act. New sources still must meet stringent new-source standards. Moreover these new-source standards are supposed to differ in PSD and nonattainment areas. Finally, the act limits the EPA's discretion in defining new pollution sources. Could any new facility in an old plant trigger a new-source requirement? Would the requirement cover the whole plant or one piece of equipment? Could offsets be made within the plant? If so, why should one bother with new-source requirements at all? These and many other questions were raised in a series of rule makings and lawsuits after the 1977 amendments. But before getting deeper into this, it is useful to introduce the EPA's next temporal step into the uncharted waters of pollution rights trading, the bubble policy.

Bubbles

The EPA bubble policy—a curious choice of nomenclature—allows existing plants to trade pollution at one source for emissions at another. This policy was first considered in 1977–78 in response to continual criticisms from Carter administration economists and various industrial groups that environmental policy is not cost-effective because firms are unable to make their own decisions concerning the mix of control strategies within a given plant.[5] There may be a number of different standards for the same pollutant for a single steel or paper plant, but the plant's managers could not adjust the emission rate at different points so as to equalize the marginal control costs across these different sources. Allowing a firm to do so would thereby lower total control costs without harming air quality.

By 1978 the EPA's Planning and Analysis Division was eagerly pressing for a bubble concept that would allow regulators and plant owners to manage emissions as if the entire plant were under an imaginary bubble.[6] This policy was advocated for both water and air pollution

5. See, for example, U.S. Council on Wage and Price Stability, *Report to the President on Prices and Costs in the United States Steel Industry* (COWPS, 1977).

6. For an example of this early attempt at reform, see U.S. Environmental Protection Agency, *Regulatory Reform Initiatives: Quarterly Progress Report, December 1978* (EPA, January 1979), pp. 6–7.

programs, but Senator Edmund Muskie's opposition after the promulgation of the air version left the water bubble on the administrator's desk for the remainder of the Carter administration.

The air pollution bubble policy was finally approved in December 1979,[7] but it was extremely limited in application. First, it could be used only in those areas that could demonstrate attainment with the ambient standards by the statutory deadline. Since the EPA and the states had not completed many of the new SIPs, this provision greatly reduced the use of such intraplant trades. Second, all bubble applications had to be treated as SIP changes and were therefore subject to the pertinent procedural requirements at both federal and state levels. Finally, the EPA added the requirement of air quality modeling (at the expense of the owner of the source) to demonstrate that the bubble would not lead to violations of ambient standards.

While these requirements severely limited the application of the bubble, at least the idea of trading pollution across existing sources was introduced. Bubbles and offsets became the jargon of the policymaker seeking to impose economic rationality upon a program that was constructed initially with little regard for economic considerations.

The bubble policy raised a number of troubling issues for the EPA. If bubbles could be used to lower costs in attainment (or prospective attainment) areas, why could they not be used in nonattainment areas? If a plant manager could adjust emissions levels across sources within his plant, why could he not offer to trade back and forth with the plant next door? If it made sense to reduce costs without increasing emissions by trading between existing sources, why should the plant manager not be able to do the same between new and old sources so as to reduce the onerous force of the new-source standards without increasing pollution? The EPA has been struggling with these questions since 1979.

New Sources, Facilities, and the Concept of Netting

If bubbles could allow firms to achieve an environmental goal at less expense, a similar approach could obviously allow a firm to escape the rigors of new-source requirements when only part of a plant was being

7. *Federal Register,* vol. 44 (December 11, 1979), p. 71779. See also Richard A. Liroff, "The Bubble Concept for Air Pollution Control: A Political and Administrative Perspective," paper delivered at the annual meeting of the Air Pollution Control Association, June 1981.

replaced or modernized. Assume that a steel plant was about to have its coke ovens replaced or modernized. Would this replacement require that the entire plant meet new-source performance standards? Is the coke oven itself deemed a new source? Alternatively, might it escape this designation altogether if the *plant's* emissions were not increased?

The EPA attempted to use a net concept for the new-source definition in 1975 by specifying that a modification of a facility in a plant did not qualify as a new source under section 111 of the act as long as the modification did not increase plantwide emissions, but a facility would be considered a source if it was entirely new. As long as the increased emissions from a modification were offset by reductions elsewhere in the plant, new-source requirements would not be triggered. This was referred to as the *netting* of pollution increments and decrements. This definition of source was rejected by the Circuit Court of the District of Columbia in *ASARCO* v. *EPA,* because it would allow firms to avoid installing the best pollution control technology on new installations in existing plants in nonattainment areas.[8] All major modifications of plants would have to install the specified technology and purchase offsets as part of an overall program to obtain reasonable further progress toward attainment.

In 1980 the EPA responded to the *ASARCO* decision by using a dual definition for new sources in nonattainment areas that included both the entire plant and an individual piece of equipment. In 1981, however, the agency attempted to return to a plantwide concept, arguing that this definition allows states greater flexibility in nonattainment policy and that it agrees with the definition in PSD areas.[9] Once again the court of appeals ruled that the plantwide definition is a violation of the nonattainment provisions of the 1977 Clean Air Act Amendments.[10] Nonattainment policy includes a requirement for new-source standards as a mechanism for generating *further progress* toward attainment. The plantwide definition allows firms to avoid triggering this new-source requirement and is therefore inconsistent with the statute. Such a requirement might reduce new investment in sources, facilities, or installations (or whatever the court chooses to call productive units) and therefore leave dirty, old facilities in place longer, but the court felt that

8. *ASARCO* v. *EPA,* 578 F.2d 319 (D.C. Cir. 1978).
9. *Federal Register,* vol. 46 (October 14, 1981), pp. 50766–71.
10. *Anne M. Gorsuch et al.* v. *Natural Resources Defense Council, Inc., et al.* (D.C. Cir. 1982).

such considerations were too speculative to negate the requirement for technology-based standards.

For nondeterioration areas the EPA attempted to solve the new-source definition problem differently. The agency issued regulations that allowed firms to offset any pollution increases from a major modification in a plant by reductions from other facilities within the plant.[11] As long as such a modification does not lead to increased emissions, the owner need not submit to the case-by-case best available control technology (BACT) requirement. Thus nondeterioration and nonattainment areas now have slightly different applications of new-source concepts. In the former case the netting of pollution of one source against another is allowed but not in the latter.

Banking

A final concept that further establishes the concept of a pollution right is *banking*. Firms that are in compliance with applicable standards may store the rights to the pollution that the plant was allowed under the SIP until they wish to use them for offsets against other sources or until they trade them in offset transactions. It is obviously bad environmental policy to induce firms to continue to operate old, polluting facilities in order to avoid sacrificing their valuable pollution rights. Firms might continue to operate dirty, old plants until they were ready to build new ones at the same locations or even longer if they had no plans to replace them at the same locations. It would be more efficient to allow them to store these rights for future use or sale to operators of economically viable facilities. And it would be sensible to reward them for reducing emissions below the standards for plants that continue to operate.

In January 1979 the EPA ruled that states may develop systems of banking emissions, thereby crediting firms for emission reductions below the applicable standards, including those obtained by closing facilities.[12] The details of the banking systems are left to the states, but the EPA must approve the banking schemes during the SIP approval process. As long as the emission rights reflect plants in compliance and the quantities can be verified, banking is generally permitted.

11. *Federal Register*, vol. 45 (August 7, 1980), pp. 52676–748.
12. *Federal Register*, vol. 44 (January 16, 1979), pp. 3274 ff.

A Fully Marketable Emission Reduction Credit

The EPA has evolved its view of emission trading from a cautious offset ruling in 1976 to a proposal for the full marketability of pollution rights. For political reasons these rights are being called *emission reduction credits* (ERCs), emphasizing the positive (emission *reductions*) rather than the negative (pollution *rights*). The opposition to such a system is slowly withering, although the attachment to technology-based new-source standards remains strong.

Changes in the Clean Air Act are required to make the ERCs fully marketable, but a number of obstacles must be removed before such legislation is likely. These obstacles concern (1) the abandonment of the concept of technology forcing in the pursuit of "further progress," (2) the solution of the monitoring and enforcement problems, (3) a consensus on the geographic limits of trading and the type of emissions that may be traded for each other, and (4) the problems of monopoly or monopsony power, which may emerge in ERC markets.

Forcing Technology for Further Progress

Nothing is more ingrained in pollution control policy than the idea that the government must always specify ambitious goals for new sources (automobiles, power plants, or polyvinylchloride plants) so that progress toward a safer, cleaner environment occurs as new plants or new products replace older ones. In part this approach derives from the observation that new facilities or products can be designed more readily to abate emissions or other discharges than older ones. Another argument in the defense of technology forcing is that the government must assure control equipment manufacturers a future market. Thus assured, these suppliers will respond with innovative products, and polluters will be unable to argue that suitable technology does not exist. Finally, the technology-forcing notion derives from a general feeling that proponents of more stringent controls will not be able to press continually for more and more progress against pollution if technology is not moving ahead with them. Thus new-source standards become inexorably tied to the drive for setting lower pollution targets.

The technology-forcing argument is usually made without acknowledging that strict standards for new sources or new products will inevitably slow the pace of adopting them. New plants are less likely to be built. Consumers are less likely to buy new products, such as automobiles, if the cost of the product is driven up relative to the cost of holding the older one. Gruenspecht has shown that weaker emission standards for new automobiles would have both increased new car sales and reduced pollution for several years.[13] Even the EPA's own studies of new sources show that new-source performance standards reduce the attractiveness of new investment.[14]

The resistance to offsets, bubbles, and banking has come largely from those who fear that technology forcing will be abandoned. If new sources or new facilities escape the lowest achievable emission rate (LAER) or BACT requirements in the Clean Air Act by simply reducing pollution elsewhere—perhaps even in the same plant—firms will escape the requirement to install the most advanced technology for controlling pollution. If a cheaper combination of strategies exists, why not let the firm choose it? The most advanced technology might never be the lowest-cost approach to reducing emissions. Suppose that wetting coal piles kept particulate emissions at zero tons per day but that a much more expensive system of enclosed sheds, conveyors, and bag houses could also eliminate emissions. Why should the latter strategy be required? Who gains from such a policy other than the sellers of the advanced technology?

Court reversals and the economic impracticality of imposing technology requirements on plant modernizations have frustrated the EPA's attempt to define "new source" as the entire plant for both attainment and nonattainment areas. The objective was to allow new pieces of equipment or new facilities to escape LAER or BACT requirements as long as they did not produce a *net* increase in emissions from the plant. The EPA had thus succeeded in disentangling the concept of *further progress* and the technology requirements for industrial plant modifications. For the present, however, the courts appear to have prevented this plantwide approach in nonattainment areas, and the EPA appears

13. Howard Gruenspecht, "Differentiated Regulation: The Case of Auto Emissions Standards," *American Economic Review*, vol. 72 (May 1982, *Papers and Proceedings, 1981*), pp. 328–31.

14. MathTech, *The Effect of New Source Pollution Control Requirements on Industrial Investment Decisions*, report prepared for EPA (Arlington, Va.: MathTech, January 1979). See also the discussion of new-source performance standards for electric utilities in chapter 7, below.

to be bound to the technology-based LAER or BACT standards for all completely new plants. It is perhaps no small coincidence that new-plant construction has been a declining share of private fixed investment in recent years.

Enforceability

Almost any proposal for the introduction of market incentives in air pollution policy encounters the objection that these instruments increase enforcement costs. With enforcement of the existing policy far from ideal, many observers are not eager to see the EPA or the states saddled with even more complex enforcement responsibilities. For this reason the agency stresses in discussions of offsets, bubbles, or other trades that all transactions must involve quantifiable and enforceable reductions in pollution. In view of the abilities of the states and the EPA to measure emissions from myriad point sources, it is not clear how a given polluter can assure the regulators that he is actually reducing pollution.

One suggestion in the literature is that emission reductions be marketable only if the buyers and sellers underwrite the cost of monitoring subsequent emission rates.[15] This approach is in the spirit of past policies involving bubbles and new-source permits and the continuing policy for PSD areas (requiring polluters to pay for air quality modeling). The problem with such a requirement is that the polluters must bear the costs of enforcement for only those exercises that increase economic efficiency. Existing standards are to be enforced at the expense of the state (or the EPA), but a better, more efficient set of standards can be introduced only if firms bear the costs of enforcement. This makes sense only if one assumes that the current system is in place and working, that any change from the current system will increase enforcement costs, and that the private costs of this enforcement are no greater than the EPA's costs of providing the additional monitoring or modeling. Therefore, any increase in economic welfare from more efficient abatement will be offset by the additional monitoring and enforcement costs. If the former does not exceed the latter, the change should not be allowed.

If one considers the benefits from reducing the costs of controlling a new facility, the presumption in favor of the traditional standard-setting

15. Jorge A. Calvo y Gonzales, "Markets in Air: Problems and Prospects of Controlled Trading," *Harvard Environmental Law Review,* vol. 5 (1981), pp. 377–430.

mode no longer exists. Why penalize only the pollution right bought in a market by requiring self-financing of monitoring costs while allowing the firm that follows the regulator's standard to escape without bearing the monitoring expense? To do so is to penalize the search for efficiency while excusing the inefficient choice.

Nor is it clear that a marketable system is much more difficult to enforce than one based on a distribution of licenses by government fiat. As long as the number of pollution sources is not greatly affected, the difficulty in constructing and maintaining a monitoring network should not vary between the two approaches. Calvo y Gonzales suggests that a regulatory system may be easier to enforce because regulators' standards are likely to admit fewer technological choices than firms' cost minimization strategies.[16] If true, this suggests that standards are inefficient. Why would firms choose a more diverse set of technologies unless cost savings were generated? Only if the choice offered savings lower than the costs of additional monitoring would this provide an argument for continuing only regulatory standards.

Geographical Limits on Trading

A critical decision in moving to a system of marketable rights is the delineation of the geographic market in which trades are to be allowed. The generic limits on the types of pollution that may be exchanged are also important. The issue of trading among different pollutants is not likely to be resolved soon. It is difficult enough to establish emission-level goals and offset transactions for single pollutants. It would be even more difficult to set the ratios for trading reductions in particulates for increases in hydrocarbons, for instance. Measuring the value of marginal reductions in each pollutant and establishing the appropriate trading ratios among them based on these values would only complicate the movement toward marketability. One would hope that independent markets for each pollutant could be shown to operate successfully before a more ambitious social calculus was attempted.

Perhaps the most serious problem in moving toward a system of tradable rights is the complex set of factors that influence ambient air quality. A given quantity of emissions may have quite different effects on various air quality monitoring locations; this depends on the atmospheric conditions, the height of the stack emitting the pollutant, the

16. Ibid.

terrain, and even the other pollutants. If the goal of air pollution policy is to ensure that a minimum air quality be maintained at all receptor points, a pound of emissions from one source may not be equivalent to a pound of the same pollutants from another source a few miles away.

The severity of the dispersion problem varies considerably for the major pollutants. For some, such as particulate matter, local plumes around the discharge point may degrade air quality at nearby receptors but not at more distant monitoring locations. Trades of these pollutants across considerable distances could therefore reduce air quality at some locations even if total emissions were not increased. For others, such as sulfates and photochemical smog, the mixing of pollutants in the atmosphere is more important than the local plume effects. The precursors to these pollutants, such as sulfur dioxide and hydrocarbons, affect air quality more or less in proportion to their total emissions into the airshed. Trades involving these pollutants are therefore likely to cause fewer problems, even if the trades are between discharge points several miles apart.

Many students of environmental policy have examined the problem of minimizing the cost of air pollution control with tradable rights.[17] The general conclusion is that a system of *emission* permits does not achieve a given air quality goal at minimum cost. A system of permits based on the effects of each receptor point is required. A given polluter would have to own a set of rights to affect each receptor, not a right to a given quantity of emissions. The environmental control agency would have to specify a set of coefficients relating emissions at each location to air quality at each receptor. This *ambient* permit system would obviously be much more complex than a system of emission permits.

An alternative approach is to limit emission trades to a narrow geographic area for pollutants causing local hot spots. Hydrocarbons or sulfur oxides might have fairly wide geographic markets for emission trading, but particulates and nitrous oxides would have narrower geographic markets under this approach if the goals were to maintain ambient air quality at all receptors. Or the system might resemble the marketable offset system suggested by Krupnick, Oates, and Van De Verg,[18] in which trades are allowed between sources as long as the owners of the

17. W. David Montgomery, "Markets in Licenses and Efficient Pollution Control Programs," *Journal of Economic Theory,* vol. 5 (December 1972), pp. 395–418.

18. Alan Krupnick, Wallace Oates, and Eric Van De Verg, "On Marketable Air Pollution Permits: The Case for a System of Pollution Offsets," Economics Working Paper (University of Maryland, 1982).

sources can demonstrate no adverse effect on any receptor. The latter approach would be similar to an ambient permit system, but it would only trigger scrutiny by the environmental agency of trades required to prevent ambient air quality from falling below desired levels at each receptor point.

The case for narrow geographic market limitations on individual pollutant trades is not necessarily compelling. While the effect of emissions on ambient air quality varies substantially with atmospheric and topographical conditions, as a practical matter it is difficult to control air quality throughout a region with specific point-source limitations. The modeling is always difficult and imprecise. It may not be necessary to be so precise, given existing knowledge of the benefits of pollution control and particularly the precision with which the current system is constructed and enforced.

Evidence on the damage from air pollution generally points to a linear relationship between exposure and damage.[19] A number of experiments suggest a threshold, but this may simply reflect the difficulty of obtaining statistically significant results in small samples for lower-level exposures. Should dose-response relationships for most air pollutants prove linear, it would be defensible to allow trades of pollution rights across fairly wide geographic areas of similar population density as long as the distributional consequences were accepted. Pollution control that generates equal ambient sulfur dioxide or particulate concentration across all portions of an air quality control region (AQCR) can never be achieved. The region immediately around an electric utility or steel plant will be somewhat more polluted than residential areas in the same AQCR. Some variations in ambient concentrations must be accepted. If twenty tons of sulfur dioxide emissions were taken annually from one side of the Pittsburgh standard metropolitan statistical area (SMSA) to allow a new source of sulfur dioxide generating fifteen tons of emissions to be built on the other side of the SMSA, would the trade be allowed? Would it be allowed if fewer people lived on the latter side of town? Since it is impossible to find trades that leave everyone in the community unaffected, where should the line be drawn?

A few jurisdictions have begun grappling with the problem of offsets across considerable distances.[20] The San Francisco Bay Area Air Quality

19. See Lester B. Lave and Eugene P. Seskin, *Air Pollution and Human Health* (Johns Hopkins University Press for Resources for the Future, 1977).
20. For a discussion of these early attempts, see Liroff, "The Bubble Concept."

Management District has established a rule that offsets be purchased at a ratio of 2:1 when trades are negotiated between sources five to ten miles apart if the pollutant involved is TSP, sulfur dioxide, or carbon monoxide. Within five miles the ratio falls to 1.2:1. For nitrogen oxides or volatile organic compounds, the larger ratio applies to trades between sources fifteen to thirty miles apart, and the lower ratio applies to trades within fifteen miles.

The Los Angeles Area's South Coast Air Quality Management District has proposed a continuous formula

$$R = a + b(x),$$

where R is the offset ratio, a is 1.2 for most trades, x is the distance between trading sources in kilometers, and b is 0.01 for distances of more than eight kilometers but zero otherwise.

These attempts to deal with the distance between trades reflect the general presumption that a SIP has been engineered to meet attainment in the entire air quality control region. Therefore, any trade across a considerable distance would interfere with this plan. If an overall reduction in pollution is obtainable through a trade, the environmental authorities are willing to upset their carefully crafted geographic plan depending on the amount of the reduction and the distance involved. If one had a linear net benefit function for all locations within an AQCR, a less restrictive approach might be justified. For most pollutants, offsets are only allowed within all or part of the AQCR. Why shouldn't trades be allowed across AQCRs? If the damage per individual is linearly related to the flow rate of emissions, would it not be desirable to allow any trade that shifted a given rate of emissions from a more populous to a less populous area? Under these conditions the gainers in the area from which pollution rights are sold would be more than able to compensate the "losers" in the less populous area that is suffering the increase in pollution. Moreover, given the other "neighborhood" effects in terms of employment, property values, and general multiplier effects surrounding the new pollution source, the "losers" may end up as net gainers.

Exceptions might be made for pollutants that are carried long distances by atmospheric currents, such as sulfur dioxide (which is transformed into sulfates). Otherwise trades among AQCRs would seem to merit strong consideration. Evidence of strong threshold effects in damage functions would change this conclusion, but such evidence does not exist for most pollutants.

Monopoly and Monopsony Power

There is no gain from trading emission reductions if there is only one source of pollution in a given area. A copper or lead smelter may be hard-pressed to find trades under a more stringent standard. Being the only source of sulfur dioxide or lead in the area, the smelter will be forced to control its emissions tightly enough to allow the area to achieve ambient air quality standards. Similarly, if there are only a few potential traders, the buyers or sellers may have monopsony or monopoly power and may exercise this power by buying or selling fewer rights than economic efficiency would require.

Hahn and Noll have investigated the market-structure problems for a sulfur oxide market in southern California.[21] They chose sulfur oxides as the first pollutant to investigate because the dispersion of sulfur oxides is easier to model than the formation and dispersion of photochemical oxidants. The sources of sulfur oxides are fewer and more easily identified than the myriad sources of hydrocarbons and nitrogen oxides, which include all motor vehicles.

Because there are only a few sources of sulfur oxides, monopoly-monopsony pose a serious problem for the design of an emission-trading system. If a large share of the initial endowment of sulfur oxide rights is in the hands of the two major utilities, these firms may recognize the impact of their own offer to sell emission rights on the price of these rights. They will offer fewer units for sale than a competitive market, and therefore economic efficiency, would require. But if these two utilities have been saddled with the highest control costs, they are more likely to be potential buyers, exerting monopsony power and purchasing fewer rights than under competitive conditions.

Hahn and Noll show that the monopsony problem for sulfur oxide trading in the Los Angeles area is real. The two largest utilities account for approximately 40 percent of all sulfur oxide emissions. The larger of the two utilities would increase its share to 48 percent under a competition for permits but only 44 percent under monopsony. Since this firm begins with 30 percent of emissions, it must buy rights to 14 percent of all sulfur oxide emissions in the area to reach the efficient, competitive result.

---

21. Robert W. Hahn and Roger G. Noll, "Designing a Market for Tradable Emissions Permits," in Wesley Magat, ed., *Reform of Environmental Regulations* (Ballinger, 1982).

This would represent virtually all rights actually traded; monopsony power is therefore a definite possibility.

Hahn and Noll suggest that the successful implementation of an emission-trading concept requires close attention to the initial distribution of these rights. Unfortunately, these rights have already been distributed. SIPs provide for emission limitations on all sources. Changing these plans to ensure that the distribution of emissions permits efficient trading may be politically difficult. For other pollutants the problems may not be as severe because emissions are distributed far more widely across myriad sources. This distribution, however, creates another problem: it increases the cost of enforcement.

The Impact of Offsets and Bubbles

Given the recent origins of both the offset and bubble policies, it is not surprising that little evidence is available on these policies' contribution to efficiency in emission abatement. EPA rulings on the definition of source have been evolving for a number of years. For instance, the EPA did not clarify the definition of source for nonattainment areas until October 1981, and this definition has already been overturned by the courts. Therefore, it is unlikely that the market for offsets could have developed rapidly. With the continuing evolution of the bubble concept, it is also unlikely that much data will be available on the actual effect of bubbles on efficiency.

In a recent study of these developing markets, the General Accounting Office (GAO) has undertaken to measure the potential for trading in southern California and the San Francisco area and to summarize the current obstacles to trading.[22] In both cases the investigators discovered that there were large potential gains from trading (in the form of reduced control costs) but that regulatory problems have greatly increased search and transactions costs. Defining the eligibility of emission reductions for offsets, the BACT requirements on new sources, and the magnitude of required offsets have all complicated trading.

A major obstacle to offset or bubble transactions has been the uncertainty created by the continuing SIP process. In nonattainment

22. General Accounting Office, *A Market Approach to Air Pollution Control Could Reduce Compliance Costs without Jeopardizing Clean Air Goals* (Government Printing Office, 1982).

areas where offsets are used, state officials have been required to propose new plans to meet primary air quality standards by 1982 or 1987. In this process they have been searching for additional progress in controlling emissions. Firms with potential offsets to sell may well find that they are identified as targets for stricter standards under the new SIP. Others that can reduce emissions with greater efficiency by altering their array of point-source controls are not likely to advertise this ability to the SIP planners. Thus it would not be surprising if the search for a supply of offsets in the market has been complicated even more than necessary. Pollution rights must be specified with some finality and permanence before sellers will willingly offer them on the market. If regulators are unwilling to specify these property rights with finality, trading will be difficult.

Despite these difficulties, offset transactions have occurred. In a study for the EPA, Vivian and Hall attempted to catalogue all offset transactions through 1980.[23] Their results show that most offset trans-actions through 1980 were internal, reflecting adjustments of emissions within a single firm or establishment. At most, there were thirty-two external transactions (table 5-1). The number of internal offsets was thirty to fifty times the estimated number of external trades. With SIPs being reissued, the EPA a year away from a "final" definition of new source, BACT and LAER requirements still uncertain, and many indus-trialists skeptical of trading, the scarcity of transactions is not surprising.

A further implication of the GAO study is that buyers of offsets appear unwilling to pay sellers for their pollution rights. In two cases cited for the San Francisco area, GAO investigators found that many firms were unwilling to part with their pollution reduction credits even though they could reduce their emissions through the application of additional controls.[24] Most firms cited their desire to keep these rights for their own future needs. In one instance the offerer's price for offsets appeared to be no more than the seller's additional control costs. Why should a seller part with these rights at effectively a zero price? In the other case the buyer purchased $70,000 worth of options on offsets that would have eventually cost $1.3 million to exercise. By comparison, retrofitting the buyer's facilities to achieve the same pollution reduction would have cost $19 million.

23. Wes Vivian and William Hall, "An Examination of U.S. Market Trading in Air Pollution Offsets" (University of Michigan, Institute of Public Policy Studies, 1981).
24. GAO, *Market Approach to Air Pollution Control.*

Table 5-1. *Offset Transactions through 1980*

	External offsets	
Pollutant	Approved	Pending, withdrawn, or uncertain
Hydrocarbons	20	8
Total suspended particulates	8	3
Sulfur dioxide	4	1
Carbon monoxide	0	1
Nitrogen oxides	2	0
Total[a]	32	12

Source: Wes Vivian and William Hall, "An Examination of U.S. Market Trading in Air Pollution Offsets" (University of Michigan, Institute of Public Policy Studies, 1981).
a. Numbers exceed total because several offsets were for multiple pollutants.

Why are buyers so unwilling to pay for pollution rights? The reason may be the exercise of monopsony power. Or it could simply reflect the reluctance of businessmen to transfer resources to other businessmen who appear to enjoy lenient pollution standards. One would expect the latter motive, if it is important, to wilt under the pressure for seeking cost-minimizing pollution control strategies.

The Continuing Evolution toward Tradable Rights

The EPA has not been able to waive technology-based standards required by the current law. However, it has recently proposed eliminating most of the other artificial barriers to emission trading that it imposed in earlier rule makings. In April 1982 it proposed to liberalize its rules on trading by the following measures:[25]
—Allowing states to develop their own generic trading rules as long as the emission reductions are permanent, quantifiable, and enforceable.
—Permitting areas that do not meet ambient air quality standards to use emission trading.
—Substituting trading for technology in meeting the RACT standards.
—Allowing trades for the purpose of coming into compliance.
—Eliminating burdensome requirements for air quality modeling, thus relieving the states of the need to submit revisions of SIPs.

25. *Federal Register*, vol. 47 (April 7, 1982), pp. 15076–86.

—Allowing some extensions of deadlines for volatile organic compounds or carbon monoxide sources involved in emission trading.

These rules, if finally approved, will permit the states to develop much more extensive trading systems without placing large burdens on the buyers and sellers of the emission reduction credits. The new-source standards remain; the EPA policy staff is trying to formulate a new-source bubble that might circumvent this impediment to trading. Whether such an effort can succeed and withstand court challenge remains to be seen.[26]

It would be an overstatement to say that the EPA has now begun to substitute marketable rights or emission reduction credits for the traditional administrative regulation of individual point sources. The federal-state air pollution program continues to be one of administratively imposed standards for individual point sources. Attainment of ambient air quality goals through enforcement of these standards is the principal goal of most air pollution control administrators in the states or at the EPA. Nevertheless, considerable groundwork has been laid for the movement toward tradable rights. Legislative hurdles, particularly in the area of new-source standards, remain. Considerable problems of relating emission trading to ambient air quality improvement must be overcome. Enforcement and monitoring must be improved if any system is to work satisfactorily. But we are surely closer to a system of economic incentives in air pollution control in 1983 than we were a decade ago, when a proposed sulfur tax disappeared without even serious legislative debate.

26. See Michael H. Levin, "Getting There: Implementing the 'Bubble' Policy," in Eugene Bardach and Robert A. Kagan, eds., *Social Regulation: Strategies for Reform* (San Francisco: Institute for Contemporary Studies, 1982), pp. 59–92, for a cogent review of the EPA's struggle to implement marketable rights. For a skeptical view, see Steven Kelman, *What Price Incentives: Economists and the Environment* (Auburn House, 1981).

VI

Civil Penalties

Debate over the movement by the Environmental Protection Agency (EPA) from a rigid standard-setting process to a flexible system of transferable pollution reduction credits may be irrelevant if the agency has neither the apparatus to monitor emissions nor the ability to impose penalties on owners of sources for failure to comply with their control responsibilities. A standard-setting process imposes a binding limit on emissions only if the polluter's expected costs from noncompliance exceed the costs of obeying the standard. That such a condition is satisfied by current policies is unlikely.

When the Carter administration assumed responsibility for the EPA, it immediately identified noncompliance with water and air pollution standards as a major problem. Since the agency lacked the ability to levy substantial civil penalties for noncompliance, polluters who faced major outlays for control had a strong incentive to delay compliance or even to postpone it indefinitely. The steel industry in particular was recognized as a major violator of state and EPA standards.

For environmental policy to work properly, the new EPA leadership reasoned, there must be a civil penalty policy with some teeth in it. As a result the agency successfully persuaded Congress to include a noncompliance penalty provision in the 1977 Clean Air Act Amendments.[1] This provision instructs the EPA to set penalties equal to the present value of failing to comply, thereby removing the incentive to flout EPA regulations. The agency failed, however, to get a similar provision written into the amendments to the Clean Water Act.

Delayed-Compliance Penalty Policy

The noncompliance penalty was originally developed in Connecticut as an economic incentive to gain compliance with environmental stan-

1. Testimony of Douglas Costle, in *Clean Air Act Amendments of 1977*, Hearings before the Subcommittee on Health and Environment of the House Committee on Interstate and Foreign Commerce, 95 Cong. 1 sess. (Government Printing Office, 1977), pp. 1680–81.

dards.[2] It was never seen as an instrument to achieve efficient pollution control, but only as a system of enforcing the existing technology-based standards system. A standards system without sanctions for noncompliance is no standards system at all. If firms can avoid compliance with impunity, there is little likelihood that the standards will be universally obeyed. Although criminal penalties have been imposed in some circumstances, enforcement officials are unlikely to use criminal sanctions often. If civil penalties are unavailable or too limited to be an inducement to expend thousands or millions of dollars on expensive control equipment, the standards system becomes a pollution tax system with extremely low taxes (penalties). In short, if a standards system is to work, the penalty for noncompliance, including nonmonetary costs, must be at least as great as the marginal cost of compliance. With less than perfect enforcement, the penalty must be greater than the marginal cost of compliance.

What is the appropriate penalty policy when the costs of compliance vary greatly across firms? If the regulatory authority could measure the discharge of pollutants from each source (a difficult problem for EPA), the obvious solution would be a penalty scaled to the rate of discharge. This would be no more than a pollution tax, or emission fee in the case of air pollution. Another alternative would simply be a prohibitive penalty rendering noncompliance an expensive option for any transgressor.

The problem with prohibitive penalties is obvious: a politically sensitive government agency cannot be expected to use the penalty because of its disastrous consequences. A small firm or even a large one in grave financial difficulty, such as the Chrysler Corporation, could not be expected to pay such a penalty because it was behind schedule in complying with a changing clean air policy. Just as important is the fact that almost any point-source standard is somewhat arbitrary since it results from a bureaucratic determination based on incomplete information. Even if the "best available" or "reasonably available" technology could be defined, the definition would be subject to all the problems of limited staff, budget, information, and time that bedevil any regulatory effort. It would be difficult to justify a prohibitive fine for failure to comply with a standard whose selection was based in part on hunch or imperfect information.

    2. See U.S. Environmental Protection Agency, *Economic Law Enforcement,* vol. 1: *Overview* (EPA, 1975).

If nominal fines make a mockery of a standards program and prohibitive fines are impractical, two alternatives remain: a pollution tax that reflects the anticipated marginal costs of control or a tax that equals the cost of complying with the technological standard. The delayed-compliance penalty reflects the latter strategy; Congress chose this approach over the pollution tax. However, the two approaches may converge in application simply because the delayed-compliance fee cannot work as designed.

The Application of Delayed-Compliance Fees

The rhetoric of regulatory reform embraces economic incentives wherever possible. Since command-control regulation is viewed as inefficient and perhaps ineffective, economic incentives are sought as a mechanism to guide the private sector to the efficient result. Delayed-compliance penalties, however, are designed only to induce firms to comply with existing regulatory standards, regardless of the efficiency of these standards. Therefore, the delayed-compliance penalties are not a substitution of economic incentives for command-control regulation.

It is not sufficient to point out that the penalty program is not a substitute of economic incentives for direct regulation. The delayed-compliance fees are a step backward in the effort to simplify and streamline regulation in order to make it more effective. The diversity of the standards faced by firms in different industries and at different locations and the variance in the costs of adapting control strategies to plants of different design and vintages make the administration of the penalty program a nightmare. Polluters must make complex calculations on virtually a case-by-case basis and present these calculations in an administrative proceeding. Because of inevitable differences over the precise calculations, the EPA will find itself enmeshed in hundreds of court suits. Since the required cost calculations involve a variety of assumptions concerning individual plant costs, discount rates, capital-equipment prices, and variable input prices, the EPA is volunteering to become the biggest traditional public-utility commission in the country.[3] A brief description of the calculations required illustrates the nature of

3. The full details of the requirements may be found at 40 C.F.R., pts. 66 and 67, reprinted in the *Federal Register,* vol. 45 (July 28, 1980), pp. 50086–258. The appendixes explaining the necessary calculations, variables, data sources, computer programs, and so on, require 136 pages in the *Federal Register.*

the task that the EPA is assuming. (A summary of the entire model is presented in appendix A.)

For each noncomplying facility a firm must obtain estimates of the cost of the equipment required for compliance. Then its problems begin. The assessment of the penalty requires that the firm work through a fifty-six-equation system to obtain the precise value of the penalty. Along the way it must manipulate more than seventy variables, which are carefully defined in an attachment to the final EPA rule.

The first nineteen equations in the EPA manual for calculating these noncompliance penalties are related to the cash flows required to amortize debt and pay off common and preferred stock required to support the asset used in reducing pollution. Two additional equations are needed for the flow of operating and maintenance costs. Another four equations address the flows required for additional "cycles" of equipment. The total return on equity is assumed to be the dividends paid; no appreciation of equity capital is allowed. Thus the cost of equity for some high-growth companies or for those in such difficulty that they cannot pay dividends may be zero.

Nine more equations are required to calculate the present value of equipment that has been fully depreciated on the firm's books. For some reason the instructions say that the discount rate—which is sometimes described as the firm's cost of equity capital—cannot exceed the inflation rate. Other instructions stipulate that the discount rate cannot be lower than the inflation rate, leaving as the only alternative a discount rate *equal to* the inflation rate.[4]

The present value of delay is calculated in another six equations, using data on actual cash flows of control expenditures and those required for timely compliance. The final sixteen equations deal with such topics as the effect of precompliance expenditure, the conversion into monthly equivalents, and the calculation of quarterly payments.

The framework is not only complex and burdensome; it invites legal challenges. The calculation of the discount rate provides perhaps the best example of an arbitrary and theoretically incorrect requirement. The discount rate used for calculating present values is to be the last five

4. At one point in this *Federal Register* notice (p. 50134), there is a careful explanation of why the EPA will not accept a discount rate lower than the inflation rate. Later (p. 50146) the reader is told that "the discount rate cannot exceed the inflation rate." The authors of the notice appear to be saying that the inflation rate must equal the discount rate so that the real discount rate is zero and there is therefore no value to delay.

years' average return on equity. If a firm were participating in a tight cartel, it would have an artificially high realized return on equity and therefore a lower present value of control costs, ceteris paribus. A "sick" industry, perhaps the steel industry, would face a much higher present value of compliance costs for the same assumed profile of cash flows. This is one example of the likely grounds for challenging the fee.

While the EPA plans to use industrywide averages for many of the necessary parameters, each calculation will be complicated and subject to considerable controversy. One cannot be sanguine about the operation of such a system, even if the agency is able to attract the considerable resources required for implementation. Moreover the cost to the firm of estimating the penalty will be substantial. The *Federal Register* notice that announced the final regulations contains a technical appendix explaining how the firm is to calculate the penalty. This appendix contains seventy-five pages of detailed instructions for implementing the fifty-six-equation system. No estimate of the costs of carrying out these computations is provided. For a considerable period, the delayed-compliance penalty will generate more legal fees than penalty payments.

Implementation

At this juncture it is not clear whether the delayed-compliance fee will actually be vigorously implemented, even if it withstands legal challenges. The EPA argues that it has exercised considerable discretion in granting exemptions for firms that have entered into consent agreements for delayed compliance or have difficulty attracting capital to finance the pollution control investment. If firms encounter financial difficulty, they may invoke both conditions for exemption—first, by obtaining extended compliance schedules, and second, by claiming that their current financial difficulties complicate raising the needed capital.

The steel industry, for example, has been beset with continuing financial difficulties since 1976.[5] It has negotiated a variety of agreements and has even obtained legislation to extend compliance deadlines. It will therefore escape most of the delayed-compliance fees. According to EPA data on major sources, only 13 percent of integrated steel mills were in compliance with their emission standards in 1980 and only

5. See Robert W. Crandall, *The U.S. Steel Industry in Recurrent Crisis: Policy Options in a Competitive World* (Brookings Institution, 1981).

another 32 percent were on a compliance schedule.[6] In 1979 the steel industry reported that it spent $450 million on air pollution control equipment.[7] The earlier analysis suggested that annual control costs for particulates alone could exceed $30 per ton of raw steel produced in integrated facilities. This would translate into as much as $3 billion a year in compliance costs. According to the EPA's calculations for the Steel Tripartite Committee, the steel industry must spend at least $700 million on pollution control equipment to meet existing air pollution standards.[8] This seems to suggest that the industry faces substantial delayed-compliance penalties, since it has been in arrears on compliance for many years.

Surprisingly, the EPA's estimate of the annual penalties owed by the steel industry is only about 10 percent of a recent year's expenditure by the industry on air pollution equipment. The 1978 estimates of the ensuing five years' penalties are shown in table 6-1.[9] Two situations are shown: one in which the industry begins to launch compliance expenditures immediately and another in which compliance is postponed one year. Both cases are unduly optimistic in view of recent EPA decisions, but the size of the penalties is remarkably small in either case, given the apparent noncompliance problem in this industry. With only 45 percent of its facilities in compliance, the industry will be saddled with penalties of no more than 9 percent of a recent year's (1979) outlays for air pollution control equipment. The reason for this apparent discrepancy appears to be the agency's determination not to apply the penalties to firms that are on a compliance schedule required by a consent order. As long as firms agree to abide by these schedules, they may be able to avoid the penalties.

The industry with the largest potential penalties is the electric utility industry. In the one-year-delay case, investor-owned electric utilities face estimated potential penalties of nearly $600 million over a five-year period even though only 13 percent of major utility sources are listed as not in compliance or not on a compliance schedule in March 1980. The potential penalties facing other major industries are minimal, reflecting

6. EPA, *Compliance Status of Major Air Pollution Facilities* (EPA, 1980).

7. American Iron and Steel Institute, *Annual Statistical Report* (AISI, 1979).

8. EPA, *Compliance Status of Major Air Pollution Facilities*, chap. 3.

9. Temple, Barker, and Sloane, Inc., *The Economic Effects of Noncompliance Penalties under Section 120 of the Clean Air Act on the Iron and Steel, Electric Utility, Pulp and Paper, and Petroleum Refining Industries*, report prepared for EPA (March 1979). Since these estimates were prepared, legislation has given the steel industry a longer period to comply with applicable federal requirements.

Table 6-1. *Projected Noncompliance (Section 120) Penalties, 1979–83*
Millions of 1978 dollars

Year	Steel No delay	Steel One-year delay	Electric utilities No delay	Electric utilities One-year delay	Pulp and paper No delay	Pulp and paper One-year delay	Petroleum refining No delay	Petroleum refining One-year delay
1979	56.1	59.9	95.2	124.9	3.0	3.5	11.8	13.8
1980	69.4	114.8	118.1	228.6	4.6	7.1	1.1	6.5
1981	13.2	69.4	58.6	145.6	0.0	5.5	0.0	1.5
1982	4.0	13.2	21.4	35.2	0.0	0.0	0.0	0.0
1983	0.0	4.0	0.0	23.1	0.0	0.0	0.0	0.0
Five-year average	28.5	52.3	59.7	111.5	1.5	3.2	4.0	4.4
Pollution control investment[a]	9.3	1.7	. . .	. . .	1.2	2.6	1.4	1.5
Major sources not in compliance, 1980 (percent)	55		13		9		14	

Sources: Temple, Barker, and Sloane, Inc., *The Economic Effects of Noncompliance Penalties under Section 120 of the Clean Air Act on the Iron and Steel, Electric Utility, Pulp and Paper, and Petroleum Refining Industries,* report prepared for EPA (March 1979); EPA, *Compliance Status of Major Air Pollution Facilities* (EPA, 1980); and U.S. Bureau of the Census, *Pollution Abatement Costs and Expenditures, 1978.*
a. As a percentage of 1978 air pollution capital expenditures, Census Bureau data.

the EPA's belief that compliance problems exist mostly in steel and electric utilities. Neither the pulp and paper industry nor petroleum refineries face any major penalties, according to EPA estimates (table 6-1).

Since the EPA needed more than three years to promulgate the section 120 noncompliance penalties, there are no data yet on actual collections. In the past the agency has not been successful in collecting major penalties from firms violating its standards. While this failure might have resulted from not having appropriate civil penalties powers, it also reflects the difficulties of prosecuting cases of noncompliance with complicated and perhaps even arbitrary standards. Without a clear set of standards and a defensible rationale for them, the EPA finds it difficult to convince judges of the equity of assessing major penalties.

With air pollution policy becoming more complicated since the 1977 Clean Air Act Amendments, similar problems are likely to arise as the agency attempts to collect section 120 penalties. The penalties program will probably provide the EPA with a slight increase in bargaining power when negotiating with firms with major compliance problems. This additional leverage might lead to slightly more accelerated compliance schedules, but it seems unlikely that the penalty program will have much effect. The program is so complicated that it merely adds to the backlog of legal challenges with which future administrators must deal. Adding complexities to an already complex framework is not likely to assist in moving toward a more efficient policy, but it will add to public and private costs of litigation.

Other Civil Penalties

While the EPA was slowly moving to implement its new delayed-compliance penalty, its Office of Enforcement published a general proposed civil penalty policy for violators of both air and water pollution standards. The statutory bases for such penalties are section 113 of the Clean Air Act and section 309 of the Federal Water Pollution Control Act, providing for civil penalties of up to $25,000 and $10,000 per day, respectively. Although neither section stipulates that the civil penalties be calculated in the manner of the delayed-compliance penalty, EPA enforcement officials took their lead from the noncompliance penalty and added a few twists of their own. The Office of Enforcement proposed that the penalties should be the sum of (1) the harm or risk of harm to public health or the environment; (2) the benefits realized by the polluting firm from failure to comply with pollution standards; (3) a sum sufficient to penalize the violator for recalcitrance or defiance of the standard; and (4) the cost to the public of the additional EPA and state enforcement costs required to assure compliance.[10]

The EPA was proposing to sum the benefits from noncompliance and the costs to the public of the environmental degradation that resulted from noncompliance, with additional penalties to penalize the willful violator. In short the agency was double-counting costs and benefits and then adding arbitrary penalties for good measure.

This double-counting was retained in the revised policy that was finally announced in 1979. Why the agency, so taken with "economic" law enforcement, should have proposed such an illogical policy in the middle of its struggle with the delayed-compliance penalty remains unclear. Nor is it clear how section 113 civil penalties and section 120 delayed-compliance penalties are to be used to enforce air pollution standards. Apparently the general penalties (section 113) will be used

10. EPA, Office of Enforcement, "Civil Penalty Policy," July 8, 1980.

Table 6-2. *Civil, Criminal, and Administrative Civil Penalties Resulting from EPA Enforcement Actions, by Statute, Fiscal Years 1977–80*

Dollars

Statute	Civil cases (federal) (court)	Criminal cases (federal) (court)	Adminis- trative civil cases (EPA assessed)	Total
Clean Air Act	27,065,970	20,000	14,814,701	41,900,671
Stationary sources				
MSEE cases[a]	26,783,600	. . .	. . .	26,783,600
Non-MSEE cases[a]	24,000	20,000	. . .	44,000
Mobile source tampering	168,370	. . .	. . .	168,370
Mobile source, other	90,000	. . .	14,814,701[b]	14,904,701
Clean Water Act	16,663,851	9,554,500	. . .	26,218,351
MSEE cases[a]	15,014,970	. . .	. . .	15,014,970
Non-MSEE cases[a]	1,649,490	9,554,500	. . .	11,203,990
Safe Drinking Water Act	26,400	. . .	. . .	26,400
Federal Insecticide, Fungicide, and Rodenticide Act	. . .	. . .	994,707[c]	994,707
Toxic Substance Control Act	. . .	. . .	253,930	253,930
Total	43,756,221	9,574,500	16,063,338	69,394,059
MSEE only	41,797,961	. . .	. . .	41,797,961

Source: Environmental Protection Agency, Office of Enforcement, 1981.
a. MSEE = major source enforcement effort; these are major facilities that failed to bring themselves into initial compliance with the major deadlines of the Clean Air and Water Acts.
b. Represents proposed administrative penalties.
c. Represents final civil penalties assessed.

infrequently, even though it appears at this writing that the delayed-compliance penalties will be much weaker than might have been supposed.

Civil Penalty Collection

The irrelevance of civil penalties can be gauged by examining data on the EPA's success in collecting them. In fiscal years 1977–80 the agency collected $69 million in penalties from all sources under all its programs (table 6-2).[11] Stationary sources of air pollution contributed a paltry $27 million in these four years, or roughly $7 million a year.[12] This is less than 0.1 percent of the estimated compliance costs for privately owned

11. EPA, Office of Enforcement.
12. Ibid.

stationary sources in 1978. In some cases penalties are reduced by the amount spent by the source to achieve compliance, but even these cases account for only a small share of total compliance costs.[13] Since the EPA has identified at least 10 percent of 5,378 major sources as not in compliance (and the actual number is probably much greater),[14] it is inconceivable that civil penalties have acted as much of a threat to those firms considering whether to achieve timely compliance with air pollution standards. The complexity of the delayed-compliance penalty and the logical absurdity of the general civil penalty policy do not augur well for an improvement in these incentives.

A Stumble or a Step in the Right Direction?

While the "economic" enforcement strategy has many problems from the standpoint of economic efficiency, the movement toward some systematic civil penalty policy is absolutely essential if air pollution policy for existing sources is to work at all. The delayed-compliance penalty as currently structured will either be ensnarled in judicial appeals or collapse of its own weight. However, a penalty policy could be constructed from this foundation.

If the delayed-compliance penalty is to work, it must be changed. The computational complexity of the penalty is a convenient reason for altering the entire concept. If all standards were set by an omniscient authority that had been instructed to equate the incremental cost of control across sources of the same pollutant in the same area, the delayed-compliance penalty could be calculated by simply measuring excess emissions from each source and multiplying by the incremental cost of control. This does not happen, not only because of a lack of perfect information, but also because environmental standards are set in an economically inefficient manner by statutory design. Differences in control costs across industries and between new and old sources within an industry would generate different compliance penalties per unit of emissions even if the compliance penalties could be calculated

13. The EPA has estimated that $5 million in judicial penalties was assessed in 1981 and $102.5 million in "money spent by the facility for environmental work" was credited to noncomplying facilities. Presumably some of this $102.5 million was induced by the threat of fines.
14. EPA, *Compliance Status of Major Air Pollution Facilities.*

efficiently. A simplification of the method of calculation, therefore, should not be thought of simply as a means of perfecting the penalty as originally conceived. If, however, the practical difficulties justify redirecting the penalty toward an emissions tax, the opportunity should be seized.

It could be argued that it is impractical to calculate the penalty on a source-by-source basis. Moreover, since there are many sources of each pollutant in each area, it does not make sense to penalize noncompliance so as to induce anything less than the maximum abatement per dollar imposed. To impose low penalties on one polluter because he has relatively low prospective compliance costs reduces his incentive to incur even these costs. Were he saddled with a penalty per excess ton of emissions more nearly equal to that of other firms in the area, he would rush to comply. The maximum abatement per dollar of control costs could be obtained by moving toward an equal rate of tax per unit of excess emissions in each area. Finally, publicizing the tax in terms of an estimated incremental cost of control for the entire area would give the tax a greater appearance of equity.

The civil penalty should vary across regions since the severity of the pollution problem varies from area to area. How the agency could move toward a regionally uniform penalty is unclear. Without changes in the law, it might be difficult to argue for equalizing the penalty rate per excess unit of emissions across sources. The best method might be a formula that served as a general guideline for setting standards in state implementation plans across the country. The EPA has a program similar to this in the preparation of control technology guidelines for reasonably available control technology. These guidelines could be used to calculate delayed compliance penalties for all excess emissions; the number of categories could be reduced with time, or an attempt could be made to set the guidelines at levels of roughly similar incremental control costs.

The grounds for simplifying both the guidelines and the regulations could be administrative simplicity. This simplification could then carry over into the setting of delayed compliance fees. Since the EPA could justifiably assert that a smaller set of different penalties generates more efficient and (if they are high enough) more rapid cleanup, the purpose of the delayed-compliance fee could be served without enmeshing the agency in a bureaucratic nightmare that could only induce inefficient compliance if it worked at all.

VII

The Struggle between the Regions

The first six chapters of this book examined the effectiveness and economic efficiency of the current policy toward stationary sources of air pollution. It is quite clear that despite its inefficiency the Clean Air Act is harsher on some sections of the country than others. The high-growth (Sun Belt) areas, not the northern industrial areas, bear the highest ratio of measured pollution control costs to output. This is not an accident but a reflection of the policies legislated by Congress and carried out by the states. Some industrial interests in the North may thus view the Clean Air Act as a blessing despite the direct control costs it imposes.

In this chapter I review the voting records of congressmen on key environmental issues to determine if there is a voting pattern that is consistent with the outcome of clean air policy—namely, a bias against the growing regions of the country. I also examine two of the more blatant examples of air pollution policy directed against the Sun Belt: the new-source performance standards for electric utilities and the prevention of significant deterioration (PSD) policy. Each case is concerned with the political motivations behind the policy as well as the resulting economic distortions.

Congressional Voting

The usual political argument for a national environmental policy is based on the need to prevent states from using environmental concessions to attract industry. Without uniform federal policies, it is argued, states would be forced to the lowest common denominator in environmental standards. This argument ignores the opportunity for states to offer prospective businesses other incentives if the citizens value environmental quality. Why should a state offer a business the right to discharge effluents or emissions rather than the rebate of property or other business taxes? If citizens would willingly pay for lower pollution in the form of higher taxes on themselves or fewer state government services, why should the political process lead to a socially less desired incentive?

Even if one believed that Congress in the late 1960s and early 1970s sought to reduce the states' use of environmental degradation as a competitive device for attracting or retaining business, one would expect most pressure to come from citizens of the states that are hotly engaged in the competition; these are the southern and western states to which industrial production is migrating. The residents of these states might support federal regulation as a means of constraining interstate rivalry that reduces their economic welfare. If, on the other hand, environmental policy was used as a mechanism for impeding growth in the Sun Belt, one would expect the congressional votes for environmental policy to come from the declining northern areas.

There is a considerable bias against new sources in clean air policy. New sources appear to pay more per ton of emission reduction and a larger share of the value of their output to control emissions, according to available data. Were federal environmental policy intended to prevent areas or states from using environmental degradation as a competitive tool for attracting business, forcing new sources to pay a larger share of the value of output than existing sources would be unnecessary. Moreover, one might have expected Congress to insist on enforcement of existing standards so that one state could not retain business that might have economically shifted to another state by failing to enforce standards on older plants. But in reality Congress has not provided this impetus, and as a result monitoring of and enforcement against older sources have not been strong features of the Environmental Protection Agency's air pollution program.

Since areas with the lowest air pollution levels are in the Sun Belt and these are the most rapidly growing states, any set of pollution policies that requires higher air quality goals for areas already in attainment and tighter standards for new sources benefits the older industrial regions to the detriment of the Sun Belt. The 1977 amendments to the Clean Air Act demonstrate a remarkable concern for both policy instruments. PSD policy was made explicit in the act, and the new-source performance standards were made even more onerous.

One might ask why Congress waited until 1970 and then 1977 to structure environmental policy so as to reduce the incentives for industrial growth in the Sun Belt. The answer may lie in the temporal pattern of industrial growth since World War II. Between 1947 and 1958 the

Table 7-1. *Share of Manufacturing Value Added, by Census Region, Selected Years, 1947–77*

Percent

Census region	1947	1954	1958	1963	1967	1972	1977
Frost Belt							
New England	9.2	7.8	7.4	7.1	7.2	6.4	6.0
Middle Atlantic	28.0	26.0	24.6	22.7	21.9	19.9	17.4
East North Central	31.6	31.2	28.9	29.3	28.6	28.2	27.0
West North Central	5.5	6.1	6.3	6.2	6.4	6.7	6.8
Total	74.3	71.1	67.2	65.3	64.1	61.2	57.2
Sun Belt							
South Atlantic	9.3	9.1	10.1	11.0	11.2	12.5	12.2
East South Central	3.9	4.0	4.5	4.8	5.2	6.0	6.1
West South Central	4.1	4.9	5.5	5.7	6.3	6.9	8.8
Mountain	1.1	1.2	1.6	1.8	1.7	2.1	2.3
Pacific	7.5	9.7	11.1	11.4	11.3	11.3	13.4
Total	25.9	28.9	32.8	34.7	35.7	38.8	42.8

Source: Bureau of the Census, *Census of Manufactures*, various years. Figures are rounded.

industrial regions of the country (the New England, Middle Atlantic, and North Central census regions) lost about 10 percent of their share of manufacturing to the South and West (table 7-1).[1] Their share of manufacturing declined from 74.3 percent to 67.2 percent in this period. The proportional shift of manufacturing slowed from 1958 to 1967 as the Frost Belt lost only 3.1 percentage points, or less than 5 percent of its share. In 1967, however, the shift accelerated sharply; in the next ten years the proportional loss was greater than that of the early postwar era. From 1967 to 1977 the Frost Belt's share of manufacturing fell from 64.1 percent to 57.2 percent of the national total, a decline of 11 percent. The real annual growth rate in manufacturing in 1967–77 (deflated by the producer price index for finished goods) was only 1.1 percent in the northern areas, but 2.2 percent in the Sun Belt. The loss of manufacturing to the South and West was accelerating; the full impact of the 1973–74 oil shock had not been felt. Moreover, the 1979–80 oil price increases were still to come. With the national economy growing slowly and manufacturing activity moving to the Sun Belt, northern congressmen should have felt more threatened by trends in the industrial economy than at any time since World War II.

The design of clean air policy and the regional trends in manufacturing

1. U.S. Bureau of the Census, *Census of Manufactures*, quinquennial editions.

point to the possibility that northern congressmen were voting to prevent the cleaner, dynamic areas of the country from attracting industry from the North. To test this theory I analyzed the environmental voting records of congressmen from 1975 to 1980, using tabulations prepared by a leading environmental lobbying group, the League of Conservation Voters (LCV).[2] Its selection of the important environmental and energy issues is useful since it is often difficult to separate the procedural and unimportant votes from those representing significant policy choices.

The votes for each congressman are recorded by the LCV each year for the environmental, water resources, mass transit, and energy roll-call votes that it deems major. These votes were aggregated over each of the fifty states to form the observations for the dependent variable in the following analysis. The state was chosen as the unit because many data are not available for individual congressional districts. In the Senate the voting record of each senator provides the observations for the dependent variable.

If congressional votes reflect concern about the quality of the environment and the recognition of a trade-off between jobs and a clean environment, one should expect congressional votes to be directly related to local pollution and to local economic conditions. Under this conventional theory, if the local economy is experiencing slow growth or if it is heavily industrial, the legislator may be expected to be less eager to vote for key environmental bills. On the other hand, if environmental policy is a mechanism to ward off new competition from the growing sections of the country, one might expect congressmen from the northern industrial states to vote for environmental measures, ceteris paribus. This latter theory predicts that congressmen from high-income, low-growth states would be likely to vote for strong environmental policy while those from low-income, rapid-growth states would be less likely to support strong antipollution policies.

To test these alternative theories a logit model was estimated for data for the 1975–80 period:[3]

2. League of Conservation Voters, *How Congress Voted on Critical Environmental Issues* (LCV, annual editions).

3. The logit specification constrains *VOTE* to values between 0 and 1. A simple linear model is less desirable theoretically but produces the same results. See Robert W. Crandall, "The Use of Environmental Policy to Reduce Economic Growth in the Sun Belt: The Role of Electric Utility Rates," in Michael A. Crew, ed., *Regulatory Reform and Public Utilities* (Lexington Books, 1982), pp. 125–40.

$$\log_e \left(\frac{VOTE_i}{1 - VOTE_i} \right) = a_0 + a_1 AIRPOLLUTION_i$$
$$+ a_2 WATERQUALITY_i + a_3 PARTY_i$$
$$+ a_4 NATLANDS_i + a_5 INCOME_i$$
$$+ a_6 INCOMEGROWTH_i + a_7 FROSTBELT_i$$
$$+ u_i,$$

where i is $1, \ldots,$ 50 states; $VOTE_i$ is the share of the state's congressional votes or the vote of each senator in the "right" direction on environmental and energy issues, according to the LCV; $AIRPOLLUTION_i$ is the share of a state's population living in counties exceeding the primary ambient air quality standard for one of three criteria pollutants: ozone, sulfur dioxide, or total suspended particulates [EPA]; $WATERQUALITY_i$ is the weighted average of fishable waters in state i in 1981 [Resources for the Future]; $PARTY_i$ is the share of Republicans in the state's congressional delegation (or in the Senate, for a Republican senator $PARTY$ is equal to unity; for a non-Republican senator $PARTY$ is equal to zero); $NATLANDS_i$ is the proportion of the state's land devoted to national parks, forests, and monuments in 1978 [Department of the Interior]; $INCOME_i$ is personal income per capita (less transfer payments) in the state in 1979 [Bureau of Economic Analysis]; $INCOMEGROWTH_i$ is the ratio of $INCOME$ in 1979 to $INCOME$ in 1959 [BEA]; and $FROSTBELT_i$ is a dummy variable equal to unity if the congressman is from a northern (North Central, New England, or Middle Atlantic) state and zero otherwise. (Data sources are given in brackets.)

The $NATLANDS$ variable was included to see if the presence of major parks or national forests increases the demand for environmental protection. The $PARTY$ variable captures the effect of philosophical differences between the parties that might affect environmental voting records. Finally, the three measures of economic activity are included to test for the effects of local economic conditions. The share of manufacturing activity was included in preliminary analysis, but this variable is inversely correlated with per capita income growth. Since $INCOMEGROWTH$ dominated the manufacturing variable in the analysis, the results with the manufacturing variable are not reported. The theory that environmental votes reflect protectionist sentiment in the states with older, declining industrial bases is consistent with a negative coefficient for $INCOMEGROWTH$ and a positive coefficient for $INCOME$. Exactly the opposite signs are consistent with the theory that politicians vote against environmental policy when their districts have a large share of industrial activity and therefore high per capita income. Finally, a dummy variable for the Frost Belt is included to determine if congressional votes can be explained by a simple geographic dichotomy rather than economic differences across states.

The results of estimating the equation are presented in table 7-2.[4] There are estimates for each of six years for the House of Representatives and for three Congresses for the Senate. In every case but one, air and water quality variables are not significant in explaining the environmental voting records of congressmen. (The negative coefficient for total suspended particulates in the 1975–76 Senate results suggests that senators from states with particulate pollution problems are less likely to support strong environmental policies than senators from cleaner states.) In later years the coefficients of the air quality variables are generally negative but not statistically significant. On the other hand, *NATLANDS* is inversely related to the environmental vote, suggesting that congressmen may be induced by such resources to vote against a strong environmental policy. Democrats are consistently more likely to support environmental measures than Republicans.

The results for the economic variables are clear. In every case the growth of per capita income is inversely related to the proportion of pro-environment votes, and in eight of nine cases the relationship is statistically significant. The Frost Belt dummy assumes a positive coefficient in three of the nine regressions and the level of per capita income has a positive but not significant coefficient in all but one equation. Per capita income is correlated with the Frost Belt dummy; collinearity therefore clouds the results. When the equations are estimated without the Frost Belt dummy, per capita income has a significant positive coefficient. Thus it may be concluded that states with high but slowly growing per capita income are most likely to generate political support for environmental measures before Congress. These states are primarily located in the Frost Belt, not the Sun Belt. Even after correcting for this difference,

4. The results are estimated for forty-eight states. Alaska and Hawaii are excluded because they are not as likely to attract industry from the Frost Belt states. All negative and zero values in the LCV tallies are set equal to 0.1 and all values of 1.00 are set equal to 0.99 for the purposes of the logit estimation. These adjustments affect none of the House votes in table 7-2; 3 of 288 observations for the House votes in table 7-3; 5 of 288 observations for the Senate votes in table 7-2; and 22 of 288 observations for the Senate votes in table 7-3. (See appendix B for a listing of all data series used in these analyses.)

Table 7-2. *Logit Analysis of the Determinants of Key Congressional Environmental Policy Votes, 1975–80*[a]

Year	AIRPOLLUTION Sulfur dioxide	Total suspended particulates	Ozone	WATER-QUALITY	PARTY	INCOME	INCOME-GROWTH	NATLANDS	FROST-BELT	$\bar{R}_2$
House										
1975	0.33	-1.01	-0.56	3.22	-0.63	0.21	-1.24*	-0.90	0.59	0.36
	(0.27)	(1.06)	(1.20)	(1.00)	(1.63)	(1.46)	(3.00)	(0.83)	(1.80)	
1976	0.69	0.42	-0.41	5.05	-1.58*	0.27	-0.83	-3.07*	0.53	0.41
	(0.50)	(0.39)	(0.79)	(1.40)	(3.62)	(1.66)	(1.79)	(2.49)	(1.43)	
1977	0.44	-0.36	-0.71	4.90	-1.22*	0.23	-1.43*	-2.52*	0.39	0.43
	(0.38)	(0.39)	(1.58)	(1.58)	(2.88)	(1.67)	(3.54)	(2.39)	(1.24)	
1978	-0.73	-0.37	-0.54	4.35	-0.89*	0.15	-0.86*	-2.21*	0.66*	0.37
	(0.63)	(0.41)	(1.22)	(1.42)	(2.13)	(1.12)	(2.16)	(2.11)	(2.13)	
1979	-0.82	0.35	-0.25	2.94	-0.51	0.16	-0.94*	-2.02	0.46	0.35
	(0.68)	(0.37)	(0.53)	(0.90)	(1.12)	(1.14)	(2.30)	(1.87)	(1.52)	
1980	-0.61	0.45	-0.62	4.39	-0.73	0.05	-1.34*	-2.34*	0.45	0.42
	(0.57)	(0.54)	(1.48)	(1.51)	(1.80)	(0.43)	(3.71)	(2.44)	(1.67)	
Senate										
1975–76	1.01	-2.14*	0.60	5.79	-1.91*	0.37*	-1.13*	-2.00	0.33	0.53
	(0.79)	(2.15)	(1.25)	(1.74)	(7.67)	(2.45)	(2.65)	(1.76)	(0.99)	
1977–78	-0.83	-0.53	-0.24	3.88	-2.02*	0.14	-1.24*	-0.66	1.06*	0.50
	(0.63)	(0.52)	(0.49)	(1.13)	(7.78)	(0.91)	(2.83)	(0.57)	(3.16)	
1979–80	0.72	-0.17	0.24	6.49	-0.69*	0.25	-1.03*	-1.57	0.90*	0.41
	(0.56)	(0.17)	(0.51)	(1.90)	(2.71)	(1.66)	(2.43)	(1.38)	(2.75)	

Source: League of Conservation Voters, *How Congress Voted on Critical Environmental Issues* (Washington, D.C.: LCV), annual editions. See also appendix B, below. Figures in parentheses are *t*-statistics.

* Statistically significant at the 5 percent confidence level.

a. Dependent variables:

Senate = share of each senator's votes for strong environmental policy (excluding Alaska and Hawaii) [LCV].
House = share of each state delegation's votes for strong environmental policy (excluding Alaska and Hawaii) [LCV].

Independent variables:

AIRPOLLUTION = percentage of population in the state living in areas not in compliance with the sulfur dioxide, total suspended particulates, or ozone primary standards [Environmental Protection Agency, 1982].
WATERQUALITY = the percentage of the state's waters that were fishable in 1981 [Resources for the Future].
INCOME = per capita income less transfer payments in the state, 1979 [Bureau of Economic Analysis].
INCOMEGROWTH = the ratio of INCOME for 1979 to INCOME for 1959 [Bureau of Economic Analysis].
PARTY = share of representatives in state from the Republican party.
NATLANDS = proportion of the state's land in national parks, forests, and monuments in 1978.
FROSTBELT = dummy variable equal to unity if the state is in the North Central, New England, or Middle Atlantic census regions and zero otherwise.

the growth of income is inversely related to a pro-environment voting record. This is evidence that voters in the declining states welcome stronger environmental measures; it is consistent with the theory that these measures, such as new-source performance standards (NSPS) and PSD, often thwart the migration of economic activity to the growing areas of the country.

The congressional votes analyzed thus far are for key environmental, water resource, mass transit, and energy issues because the LCV views energy conservation and water use as important to environmental quality. Combining votes on these types of issues may lead to some problems in interpretation, given the role of certain Sun Belt states as suppliers of energy. It is useful to delete these votes from the LCV tallies to determine if the results hold for purely environmental votes. The results for the 1977–78 period (reported in table 7-3) clearly are not affected much by the deletion of the votes on mass transit, water resources, and energy. The conclusions concerning the predominant influence of slow per capita income growth and Frost Belt location are unchanged, as is the conclusion that measures of air and water quality are unrelated to the environmental voting record of the congressman.

To conclude this analysis the voting equations for each year may be reestimated, omitting the variables that do not contribute to explaining the congressional votes. Table 7-4 displays these results for equations with five variables: *INCOME, INCOMEGROWTH, PARTY, NAT-LANDS,* and *FROSTBELT.* It is clear from these results that political party affiliation declined in importance for the environmental issues in the late 1970s. The share of land owned by the federal government continued to be inversely associated with strong environmental voting records. The coefficients of *INCOME* remained positive and were statistically significant in two of nine cases. Notable is the remarkable stability in the size and significance of the coefficient of *INCOME-GROWTH* throughout. Rapidly growing states with large amounts of federal lands send representatives to Washington who vote against major environmental measures.

New-Source Performance Standards

One might quibble with the preceding results, arguing that a more complete specification of the determinants of congressional votes would

Table 7-3. *Determinants of Key Congressional Votes on Purely Environmental Issues, with Energy, Mass Transit, and Water Resource Issues Excluded, 1975–80*[a]

Year	AIRPOLLUTION Sulfur dioxide	AIRPOLLUTION Total suspended particulates	AIRPOLLUTION Ozone	WATER-QUALITY	PARTY	INCOME	INCOME-GROWTH	NATLANDS	FROST-BELT	$\bar{R}_2$
House										
1975	0.85	−0.92	−0.57	4.18	−0.48	0.26	−1.32*	−0.88	0.50	0.40
	(0.69)	(0.97)	(1.23)	(1.31)	(1.25)	(1.78)	(3.24)	(0.81)	(1.53)	
1976	0.71	−0.61	−0.54	2.51	−1.04*	0.19	−0.96*	−1.16	0.76*	0.30
	(0.53)	(0.59)	(1.07)	(0.72)	(2.46)	(1.17)	(2.12)	(0.97)	(2.13)	
1977	0.33	−0.12	−1.24*	4.32	−1.62*	0.34*	−1.75*	−3.32*	0.15	0.50
	(0.28)	(0.14)	(2.78)	(1.40)	(3.87)	(2.46)	(4.36)	(3.17)	(0.47)	
1978	0.06	−0.58	−0.55	4.90	−1.82*	0.23	−1.14*	−3.21*	0.53	0.48
	(0.05)	(0.59)	(1.13)	(1.46)	(3.97)	(1.49)	(2.61)	(2.81)	(1.57)	
1979	−2.17	0.56	−0.78	5.81	0.19	0.17	−1.46*	−3.24*	0.40	0.26
	(1.26)	(0.42)	(1.16)	(1.24)	(0.24)	(0.85)	(2.51)	(2.10)	(0.91)	
1980	−1.97	1.77	−0.96	4.39	−1.97*	−0.23	−1.93*	−3.74*	0.81	0.40
	(1.13)	(1.31)	(1.41)	(0.92)	(2.98)	(1.14)	(3.25)	(2.38)	(1.83)	
Senate										
1975–76	0.79	−2.47*	0.65	4.72	−1.81*	0.35*	−1.35*	−1.79	0.43	0.48
	(0.55)	(2.19)	(1.20)	(1.25)	(6.42)	(2.03)	(2.80)	(1.38)	(1.16)	
1977–78	1.09	−1.75	0.16	4.18	−2.55*	0.22	−1.26*	−0.49	0.95*	0.49
	(0.68)	(1.40)	(0.27)	(0.99)	(7.99)	(1.15)	(2.35)	(0.33)	(2.30)	
1979–80	1.13	−0.75	−0.49	9.26	−1.88*	0.55*	−1.54*	−4.61*	0.85	0.39
	(0.54)	(0.46)	(0.62)	(1.65)	(4.51)	(2.23)	(2.20)	(2.47)	(1.58)	

Source: Same as table 7-2. Figures in parentheses are *t*-statistics.
* Statistically significant at the 5 percent confidence level.
a. For explanation of variables, see table 7-2.

Table 7-4. *Determinants of Congressional Votes
on Purely Environmental Issues, with Environmental Quality
Variables Excluded, 1975–80*[a]

Year	PARTY	INCOME	INCOME-GROWTH	NATLANDS	FROST-BELT	$\bar{R}^2$
House						
1975	−0.37	0.17	−1.05*	0.17	0.61	0.38
	(0.98)	(1.28)	(3.10)	(0.23)	(1.96)	
1976	−0.95*	0.11	−0.69	−0.37	0.84*	0.33
	(2.38)	(0.81)	(1.91)	(0.48)	(2.55)	
1977	−1.32*	0.28*	−1.11*	−1.70*	0.20	0.45
	(3.08)	(2.05)	(3.23)	(2.32)	(0.63)	
1978	−1.59*	0.19	−0.85*	−2.12*	0.58	0.47
	(3.59)	(1.32)	(2.40)	(2.79)	(1.79)	
1979	0.50	0.21	−1.07*	−1.94	0.33	0.26
	(0.87)	(1.14)	(2.27)	(1.91)	(0.78)	
1980	−1.77*	−0.16	−1.47*	−2.21*	0.75	0.40
	(3.00)	(0.87)	(3.08)	(2.15)	(1.77)	
Senate						
1975–76	−1.74*	0.26	−1.66*	−1.88*	0.56	0.44
	(5.98)	(1.61)	(4.01)	(2.11)	(1.52)	
1977–78	−2.45*	0.12	−1.34*	−0.15	1.09*	0.48
	(7.80)	(0.71)	(3.03)	(0.16)	(2.80)	
1979–80	−1.68*	0.45*	−1.38*	−2.75*	1.07*	0.39
	(4.19)	(2.04)	(2.38)	(2.16)	(2.09)	

Source: Same as table 7-2. Figures in parentheses are *t*-statistics.
* Statistically significant at the 5 percent confidence level.
a. For explanation of variables, see table 7-2.

result in a less significant impact of high income and declining growth on
the willingness of congressmen to support environmental policy.[5] Some
congressmen may *not* view the typical environmental policy issue as a
reflection of regional interests. The strong Frost Belt votes for environmental legislation and much weaker support from the Sun Belt may
reflect the relative health of the population, the differences in constituents' awareness of environmental issues, the differences in political

5. A lively literature is developing on the determinants of legislative voting. Joseph
Kalt and Mark Zupan, in "Amending the Economic Theory of Regulation: Ideology
and Capture in Legislative Politics," Discussion Paper 907 (Harvard Institute of
Economic Research, July 1982), argue that ideology accounts for a large share of
congressional votes on strip-mining issues. Sam Peltzman, in "Constituent Interest and
Congressional Voting" (manuscript, 1983), on the other hand, argues that ideology has
little influence on congressional views. The *PARTY* variable in the above analysis is
clearly an unsatisfactory proxy for ideology, but a more sophisticated approach to
modeling the ideological component does not affect the results reported in tables 7-2
through 7-4. Declining industrial growth, not local environmental quality, drives the
votes. Robert W. Crandall, "The Political Economy of Environmental Policy" (manuscript, 1983).

philosophy of the populace in each area, or any of a number of other influences that are difficult to measure.

It appears, however, that regional economic interests are reflected in the votes and in the consequent policy choices for enforcing environmental statutes. Certainly the political maneuvering over the new-source standards for sulfur dioxide emissions supports the view that politicians intended to use the Clean Air Act to redistribute economic activity across the regions of the country.

In 1975 a debate began in Congress concerning nondegradation policy and the regulation of new sources of sulfur dioxide. Ackerman and Hassler contended that the staff of the House subcommittee first proposed a major change in the language of section 111 of the Clean Air Act, specifying the requirements for new-source performance standards.[6] Apparently responding to the pressure from environmentalists to prevent the degradation of clean air areas, the staff drafted a proposal to require new sources of sulfur oxides to use the best technological system of continuous emission reduction. This proposal to require a "percentage reduction" in the concentration of sulfur dioxide in stack gases was designed to prevent western utilities from using low-sulfur coal without emission control equipment. In part this was in response to the pressure created by *Sierra Club* v. *Ruckelshaus,* in which the Supreme Court narrowly affirmed a lower court decision that required the EPA to prevent degradation of areas already meeting the ambient air quality standards.[7] Why the House staff wished to specify the technology rather than a result through a performance standard is unclear. Apparently this was another application of the technology-forcing theory of environmental control.

The search for supporters of the House staff proposal was not difficult. Eastern coal producers were becoming concerned about the prospective loss of markets to western coal. Western coal deposits are generally low in sulfur and easy to mine with strip-mining techniques. As clean air policy against sulfur oxide emissions became more stringent, utilities faced the choice of either using lower-sulfur fuel or burning high-sulfur coal and installing equipment to remove the resulting sulfur oxides from the stack gases. It became apparent that midwestern utilities would turn increasingly to western coal rather than install the expensive stack-gas

6. Bruce A. Ackerman and William T. Hassler, *Clean Coal/Dirty Air or How the Clean Air Act Became a Multi-Billion-Dollar Bail-Out for High-Sulfur Coal Producers and What Should Be Done about It* (Yale University Press, 1981), pp. 27–29.

7. *Sierra Club* v. *Ruckelshaus,* 344 F. Supp 253 (D.D.C).

scrubbers that constitute the best available continuous emission reduction technology. Western utilities with access to cheap low-sulfur coal would not need these scrubbers unless the performance standard for sulfur dioxide emissions became more onerous.

Environmentalists were eager to support a requirement for the installation of scrubbers since it fitted well with their general philosophy of forcing technology.[8] They reasoned that eventually all power plants would have this equipment, and the potential for emission reduction would be greatly enhanced. But how could they know that scrubbers would be the best technology for reducing sulfur dioxide emissions in fifteen or twenty years? Why should they wish to subsidize dirty coal? Would it not be more sensible simply to tighten the performance standard for existing and new sources of sulfur dioxide?

Apparently the environmentalists and the House staff felt that a coalition with eastern coal producers was required to attack the nondegradation and new-source issue. They could not simply press for a new-source standard of less than the prevailing 1.2 pounds of sulfur dioxide per million British thermal units (Btu) because there would be insufficient political support for it. Any attempt to tighten standards for existing plants would lead utilities to increase their use of low-sulfur coal dramatically. The political pressures in the eastern and midwestern coal regions where high-sulfur coal is mined would undoubtedly block this commonsense approach.

The impact of a proposal to require all new industrial and utility sources of sulfur dioxide to install scrubbers was thoroughly analyzed by the EPA staff in the months preceding the 1977 amendments and in the following year. These analyses demonstrated the following:[9]

1. Eastern and midwestern coal production would not decline between 1975 and 1995 even if the new-source standard of 1.2 pounds per million Btu were retained.

2. The imposition of a scrubbing requirement on all new sources would lead to a reduction in the rate at which new coal-fired utility boilers would replace older oil-, gas-, and coal-fired units.

3. The scrubbing requirement would scarcely reduce sulfur dioxide emissions in the Midwest, where much of the problem with acid rain

8. Ackerman and Hassler, *Clean Coal/Dirty Air*, pp. 35–37.

9. U.S. Environmental Protection Agency, "A Preliminary Analysis of the Economic Impact of Alternative Approaches to Significant Deterioration" (February 5, 1976), p. V-5; EPA, "Electric Utility Steam Generating Units," background information for proposed sulfur dioxide emission standards, supplement, August 1978.

originates, but it would have a substantial effect on the growing western and southern areas.

4. A strict scrubbing requirement would increase both costs and total emissions generated by 1990, when compared with a less strict, "partial" scrubbing option.

Without the scrubbing requirement, utilities would bid for low-sulfur western coal and pay to transport it eastward to the point where the cost of the low-sulfur coal plus transportation equaled the cost of high-sulfur coal plus the cost of scrubbing. Clearly the scrubbing requirement would lead to greater use of high-sulfur coal. The EPA's analysis of a full-scrubbing requirement in 1978 predicted that eastern and midwestern coal production would be 4 to 14 percent higher in 1990 with scrubbing than with the previous 1.2-pound standard. Western coal production, on the other hand, would be 6 to 15 percent lower.[10] Much of this added eastern production would be high-sulfur coal.

The EPA analyses of the effects of a full-scrubbing standard assumed that the scrubbers operate according to specifications. Unfortunately, these devices are extremely complex and require considerable care and maintenance for efficient operation. Unless regulators force utilities to monitor their stack gases carefully, the utilities may well allow these scrubbers to operate ineffectively for considerable periods. Since the utilities are often scrubbing high-sulfur coal, this may add substantially to pollution loadings. It is even possible that the scrubber requirement might not reduce emissions appreciably despite the approximately $3 billion to $4 billion (1978) a year added to utility costs in 1990. Even if the scrubbers work perfectly, the incremental cost of sulfur dioxide reductions from this regulation far exceeds the cost of sulfur dioxide abatement at existing utility plants or in many other industries.

During the rule-making period the EPA considered various options including partial scrubbing—the requirement that only a fraction of new sources meet a standard of 90 percent reduction of sulfur dioxide through stack-gas scrubbing. Lower-sulfur coals might be allowed lower post-combustion sulfur removal rates. Near the end of the rule-making period, the EPA began to consider seriously a proposal that new plants burning high-sulfur coal be required to remove 90 percent through the standard

10. EPA, "Electric Utility Steam Generating Units," table 2-4. A recent study by the Congressional Budget Office shows an even smaller effect on the distribution of coal production. The current standards increase eastern coal production only 1 percent and midwestern production 8 percent. Western coal is virtually unaffected. See *The Clean Air Act, the Electric Utilities, and the Coal Market* (CBO, 1982), p. 70.

Table 7-5. *Impact of Alternative Scrubber Requirements on Emissions, Coal Capacity, Oil Use, and Control Costs of Electric Utilities, 1995*

Description	1977 standards[a]	Full scrubbing (90 percent removal)	Final standard: dry scrubbing option (70 percent minimum removal)
National emissions (millions of tons)	23.8	20.7	20.5
Regional emissions (millions of tons)			
East and Southeast	11.2	10.1	9.7
Midwest	8.3	7.9	8.0
West South Central	2.6	1.7	1.7
West	1.7	1.0	1.1
Coal capacity (gigawatts)	554	520	537
Oil consumption in utilities (millions of barrels per day)	1.2	1.6	1.4
Incremental annualized costs of new standards (billions of 1978 dollars)	. . .	4.4	3.3

Source: EPA, "New Stationary Sources Performance Standards: Electric Utility Steam Generating Units," *Federal Register,* vol. 44 (June 11, 1979), pp. 33608–09.
a. Ceiling of 1.2 pounds per million Btu.

wet scrubber but that plants burning low-sulfur coal be permitted to remove only 70 percent of the sulfur dioxide through "dry" scrubbing, a less expensive form of flue-gas desulfurization. The agency appeared ready to advocate a maximum ceiling for sulfur dioxide emissions in the vicinity of 0.55 pound per million Btu, but aggressive lobbying by the eastern coal producers in April 1979, two months before the final decision, returned the EPA to a ceiling of 1.2 pounds per million Btu.[11] While the EPA finally relented and allowed the dry scrubbing alternative instead of full scrubbing for low-sulfur coal, its choice of ceiling left the agency in much the same position as before the 1977 amendments. Scrubbing might reduce sulfur dioxide emissions below this ceiling, but if the scrubbers failed periodically they might not reduce sulfur dioxide at all.

To see how the new-source performance standard for utilities affects emissions, compliance costs, and electricity prices, the EPA analyses, summarized in tables 7-5 and 7-6, may be consulted. Table 7-5 shows that the final standards promulgated by the EPA are projected to reduce total sulfur dioxide emissions 3.3 million tons a year, or 13.9 percent, by

11. Ackerman and Hassler, *Clean Coal/Dirty Air,* pp. 100–01.

1995. It may seem surprising that this option reduces emissions *more* than the full-scrubbing alternative. Clearly, much of the difference comes from the decision to postpone new plants. Under the full-scrubbing option coal-fired electric-utility capacity is 520 gigawatts in 1995 while with dry scrubbing it is 537 gigawatts. The smaller coal capacity reflects slower growth and a reduction in the rate of replacement of oil-fired capacity. Oil consumption at utilities would increase by 200,000 barrels per day in 1995 if full scrubbing were used instead of the dry-scrubbing option.

Emissions are reduced by the final dry-scrubbing rule 3.3 million tons a year in 1995; nearly half of this reduction comes from the western and southwestern areas of the country. These areas would have accounted for 4.3 million tons if the old standard (1.2 pounds per million Btu) had been maintained. Under the new standard they would be reduced 35 percent, to 2.8 million tons a year, in 1995. By the same year, eastern and midwestern emissions, which would have accounted for 82 percent of all emissions under the old standards, would be reduced only 9 percent. Thus the Sun Belt bears a disproportionate share of the burden of reducing sulfur dioxide, given its current contribution to the sulfur oxide problem. Midwestern emissions—thought to be a major source of the acid rain problem—are reduced only 4 percent under the new rule.

The EPA estimates that by 1995 the annualized costs of its final standard will be $3.3 billion (1978 dollars). Had full scrubbing been required, the cost would have risen to $4.4 billion, but emissions would have also risen from 20.5 million to 20.7 million tons a year in 1995. The choice of the full-scrubbing option would have increased 1995 emissions 200,000 tons a year and increased control costs $1.1 billion annually. This analysis assumes unrealistically that scrubbers work to theoretical capacity 100 percent of the time. Given the inevitable malfunctions with less than ardent enforcement, the perversity of full scrubbing is even more extreme.

There is more to the story. The impact of the new NSPS falls primarily on the western and southwestern states. As one might suspect, this is translated into higher electric utility rates for customers in these regions. Given the loss of industry by the Frost Belt to the Sun Belt, it would help the northeastern and midwestern areas slow the outmigration from their areas if their congressmen would vote for policies raising input prices in the Sun Belt relative to northeastern and midwestern costs. As table 7-6 demonstrates, the scrubber requirement accomplishes this. Full scrubbing, the only alternative analyzed for this purpose by the

Table 7-6. *Effects of Full Scrubbing of Sulfur Dioxide on Regional Electricity Rates, 1995*[a]

Cents per kilowatt-hour in 1975 prices

| | | Price in 1995 | | | |
| | | Moderate growth | | Rapid growth | |
Region	Price in 1976	Without mandatory scrubbing	With full scrubbing	Without mandatory scrubbing	With full scrubbing
New England	3.96	4.23	4.30 (1.7)	4.31	4.32 (0.2)
Middle Atlantic	3.75	3.58	3.65 (2.0)	3.83	3.91 (2.1)
East North Central	2.56	3.11	3.12 (0.3)	3.32	3.48 (4.8)
West North Central	2.57	2.73	2.78 (1.8)	2.95	3.11 (5.4)
South Atlantic	2.89	3.03	3.08 (1.7)	3.27	3.42 (4.6)
East South Central	1.68	1.32	1.35 (2.3)	1.42	1.46 (2.8)
West South Central	1.99	2.92	3.24 (11.0)	2.91	3.26 (12.0)
North Mountain	1.37	2.02	2.09 (3.5)	2.30	2.47 (7.4)
South Mountain	2.52	2.67	2.77 (3.7)	2.91	2.96 (1.7)
Pacific	2.11	2.75	2.80 (0.7)	2.90	2.93 (1.0)

Source: EPA, "Background Information for Proposed SO_2 Emission Standards, Electricity Steam Generating Units," July 1978, p. 7-44.

a. Numbers in parentheses are percentage increases resulting from full scrubbing.

EPA, raises 1995 electricity rates 0.3 to 2.0 percent under conditions of moderate growth in the Frost Belt while increasing rates as much as 11 to 12 percent in the booming southwestern area of the country. One could hardly imagine a better result for northern congressmen.

Nondeterioration Policy

The federal policy to promote nondegradation of air quality in regions where the air is cleaner than national standards has a long history.[12] It dates back to the 1967 Air Quality Act and was implicitly incorporated

12. For a discussion of this history of nondegradation policy, see Richard H. K. Vietor, *Environmental Politics and the Coal Coalition* (Texas A & M University Press, 1980).

into EPA policy by the 1970 Clean Air Act Amendments. While the agency initially balked at establishing nondegradation rules in 1971, a court challenge of this decision required it to reverse course.[13] In 1973 it proposed a set of nondegradation rules; in 1974 it offered a set of revised regulations that went into effect in December of that year. Subsequent controversy and numerous court challenges pressured Congress to clarify its intent. As a result Congress passed a complex set of amendments to Title I of the Clean Air Act detailing the obligations of the states and the EPA in establishing PSD areas, approving permits for new sources, and establishing increments of growth for emissions of criteria pollutants (initially sulfur oxides and total suspended particulates [TSP]).

The provisions of section 127 establishing this PSD policy can only be described as baroque. The requirements heaped upon a new source for obtaining a permit are numerous. Not surprisingly, Congress was virtually silent about requirements for existing sources in nondegradation areas.

Under the PSD policy all areas of the country are first designated as either attainment or nonattainment areas for the criteria pollutants. Those that satisfy the national ambient air quality standards (NAAQS) are attainment areas and therefore subject to PSD regulation. All such areas are classified class I, class II, or class III. Areas surrounding national parks or monuments must be designated class I. The remaining attainment areas are divided between class II and class III. Initially most areas are to be designated class II, but the states may designate some of these areas class III after a variety of procedural steps, including hearings.

The increments of additional criteria pollutants are set by statute. These increments represent a fraction of the difference between the ambient air quality standard and the current pollution level allowed. Class I areas have the smallest permissible increments; class III areas have the largest increments; class II areas are between the two extremes. These increments apply at first only to TSP and sulfur oxides. The EPA was instructed to prepare a PSD policy for the other criteria pollutants within two years, but it has not yet proposed such a policy.

One can question the underlying premise of PSD policy—namely, that it is unwise to allow cleaner areas of the country to increase their emissions rapidly, even to the levels deemed safe under the NAAQS. If the NAAQS are set to protect health and welfare, the less-polluted areas

13. *Sierra Club* v. *Ruckelshaus*.

should be allowed to reach this "safe" level. Some of the new-plant investment creating pollution in these areas substitutes for economic activity in the older, dirtier parts of the country. As a result, a strong PSD policy may slow the progress toward attainment in these older, dirtier areas. On the other hand, this policy relieves the northern areas of some of the competitive pressure from the Sun Belt, thus allowing them to tighten pollution standards.

The case for a national nondeterioration policy is based on the public goods aspect of natural vistas and parklands. The value of maintaining air quality in areas with these assets accrues to all citizens who may travel to enjoy them. Therefore, preserving clean air in these areas has a value quite distinct from the value of protecting the health of residents. It is difficult, however, to use this argument for the protection afforded by current PSD policy to vast class II and class III areas without such natural vistas. Regardless of the intention of Congress, PSD policy has the effect of protecting the older industrial areas from new growth in the cleaner Sun Belt and of keeping people in areas with presumably unhealthful air.

Pashigian recently analyzed congressional votes on PSD and found that its strongest supporters in Congress are from the densely populated urban areas in the northern and northeastern states.[14] He concluded that their votes represent an attempt to reduce the outmigration of industry from their districts. Northern congressmen in less urbanized areas and congressmen from Sun Belt states are much less likely to vote for PSD because they wish to attract industry to their districts. Pashigian also found that pollution expenditures per dollar of manufacturing value added are much greater in the growing southern and western states than in the older areas whose congressmen vote for nondegradation, a result confirmed by table 3-2. The strongest influence on pollution control expenditures per dollar of value added is industrial growth in the area, a result that confirms the new-source bias.

The barrier that PSD prospectively places in the way of economic growth in the areas most likely to attract new investment in many industries—namely, the Sun Belt—is heightened by the procedural requirements of the policy. Had Congress been interested only in reducing the rate of growth of pollution in these cleaner regions, it might have instructed the EPA to establish total emissions growth increments

14. B. Peter Pashigian, "Environmental Regulation: Whose Self-Interests Are Being Protected?" (University of Chicago, Graduate School of Business, 1982).

Figure 7-1. *The PSD Permit Process*

NEW-SOURCE REVIEW
PSD PROCESS

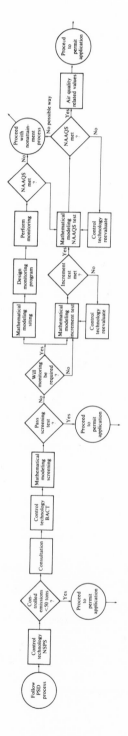

NEW-SOURCE REVIEW
PERMIT APPLICATION

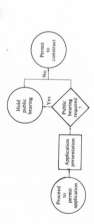

Source: Environmental Research and Technology, Inc., *ERT Handbook on Industrial Expansion and the 1977 Clean Air Act Amendments* (ERT, June 1979), pp. 6–10.
a. See the Glossary for definition of abbreviations.

for each air quality control region and to allow any new source (or modification of an existing source) to begin construction if it obtained a license for its additional pollution from the state or from existing polluters. Increments could have been auctioned off or given away according to some other plan. New sources would not have faced major bureaucratic hurdles to enter these nondegradation areas.

Instead, Congress and the EPA combined to establish potentially formidable barriers to growth. The full rigors of the PSD application process are best seen in a schematic diagram provided by a consulting firm advertising its abilities to usher firms through the process (figure 7-1). While this schematic may be designed to dissuade prospective clients from facing the process alone, it is a useful summary of the number of steps potentially required. As the figure demonstrates, these requirements apply only to "major" sources. At first this meant that sources emitting less than fifty tons of a pollutant per year were exempt from PSD. However, since being criticized by the Circuit Court of the District of Columbia for its definitions of major new and modified sources, the EPA has changed to a de minimis definition, which essentially reduces the criterion to forty tons per year for sulfur dioxide and twenty-five tons per year for TSP.[15]

Recent analyses of the PSD policy suggest that it has had little effect upon growth in the affected areas,[16] but it is far too soon to discern any such effect. The policy is quite consistent with the theory that environmental policy is increasingly being designed to impose much harsher requirements on new sources than on existing sources. Moreover, given the EPA's difficulty in designing simple methods for allocating or trading increments and existing pollution rights in nondegradation areas, the policy is even more hostile to economic growth than required to meet its ostensible policy objectives.

Concluding Assessment

The evidence from congressional voting records and the impact of recent developments in federal air pollution policy are clear. The burden of national air pollution policy is borne disproportionately by the growing

15. *Federal Register,* vol. 45 (August 7, 1980), p. 52707.

16. National Commission on Air Quality, *To Breathe Clean Air* (Government Printing Office, 1981), chap. 5. For a different view, see A. D. Little, "The Effects of Prevention of Significant Deterioration on Industrial Development," prepared for the Business Roundtable (November 1980).

southern and western regions of the country. This is not an accident but rather a deliberate choice of Congress, particularly its members from the northern industrial areas.

It is possible to construct a theory that rescues this regionally biased policy and makes it consistent with the view that residents of northern industrial states desire to improve environmental quality. Both northern and southern residents may value a clean environment equally, but those from southern and western areas have more to lose from a stringent environmental policy. Moreover, the western regions have greater environmental value than areas such as downtown Detroit.

The theory does not withstand the evidence. One need not apply strict new-source requirements to all utility plants in the West and South, for example, in order to preserve the wilderness areas, national parks, or other natural treasures of the country. If northern congressmen were voting to place tight restrictions on new plants in the South and West so that their constituents' desire for more environmental control in the North could be realized without inducing industrial flight, one might expect that northerners would be willing to tighten the controls on their industries, equating their control costs to those of the southern and western industries. Yet the high-income northerners accept a lower rate of pollution control spending than their poorer southern and western counterparts. Moreover, since the enactment of tighter new-source performance standards and the formalization of PSD policy in the Clean Air Act Amendments, air pollution control spending in the North has not accelerated in real terms. The southern and western areas were increasing their expenditures at the same rate in 1977–79 as in 1973–76, but northerners' spending on air pollution control was growing much less rapidly in the later period.[17] Apparently northerners had not yet resolved to increase their commitment to clean air in response to legislation designed to reduce migration to the Sun Belt.

Perhaps the new policies have not worked to slow this migration. On the other hand, why should one believe that residents of the northern industrial areas will reverse their policies of spending a lower share of income originating in basic industries on air pollution control than those in other areas? It is probably too soon to tell how the antigrowth policies will affect air quality management in the northern industrial region, but the early indications are not favorable.

17. Bureau of the Census, *Pollution Abatement Costs and Expenditures,* Current Industrial Reports, annual editions.

VIII

The Ambient Air
Quality Standards

Regulatory reform efforts in the Environmental Protection Agency's clean air program have been confined almost entirely to the setting and trading of point-source standards for new and existing plants. These reform efforts are devoted to reducing the cost of achieving satisfactory air quality. The controversial air quality goals—expressed in the national ambient air quality standards—have not been the targets of reform. The difficulties of setting these national ambient standards are considerable, given the quality of the evidence linking pollution to health. The task is further complicated by the statutory provisions of the Clean Air Act Amendments of 1970 that have proved difficult to change.

The Statutory Mandate

The Clean Air Amendments of 1970 required the EPA to set primary and secondary standards for the major criteria pollutants. The primary standards are to be set at levels that protect the public health with an adequate margin of safety.[1] These standards are to be uniform across the country, regardless of the topography, climate, or industrial base of individual air quality control regions (AQCR). While some observers believe that the agency is not precluded from considering costs in setting primary ambient standards, the general presumption is that these standards are to protect public health regardless of cost.[2] The current primary and secondary standards for each criteria pollutant are shown in table 8-1.

The secondary standards, far less important in the execution of state implementation plans, are "to protect the public welfare from any known

1. See the discussion in chapter 1, above, and in sections 108 and 109 of the Clean Air Act, 42 U.S.C. 7401.
2. Lester B. Lave and Gilbert S. Omenn, *Clearing the Air: Reforming the Clean Air Act* (Brookings Institution, 1981), pp. 13–14.

Table 8-1. *National Ambient Air Quality Standards*

Criteria pollutant	Averaging time	Primary standard levels	Secondary standard levels
Particulate matter	Annual (geometric mean)	75 micrograms per cubic meter	60 micrograms per cubic meter
	24 hours[a]	260 micrograms per cubic meter	150 micrograms per cubic meter
Sulfur oxides	Annual (arithmetic mean)	80 micrograms per cubic meter (0.03 part per million)	. . .
	24 hours[a]	365 micrograms per cubic meter (0.14 part per million)	. . .
	3 hours[a]	. . .	1,300 micrograms per cubic meter (0.5 part per million)
Carbon monoxide	8 hours[a]	10 milligrams per cubic meter (9 parts per million)	10 milligrams per cubic meter (9 parts per million)
	1 hour[a]	40 milligrams per cubic meter[b] (35 parts per million)	40 milligrams per cubic meter[b] (35 parts per million)
Nitrogen dioxide	Annual (arithmetic mean)	100 micrograms per cubic meter (0.05 part per million)	100 micrograms per cubic meter (0.05 part per million)
Ozone	1 hour[a]	240 micrograms per cubic meter (0.12 part per million)	240 micrograms per cubic meter (0.12 part per million)
Hydrocarbons (nonmethane)[c]	3 hours (6 to 9 a.m.)	160 micrograms per cubic meter (0.24 part per million)	160 micrograms per cubic meter (0.24 part per million)
Lead	3 months	1.5 micrograms per cubic meter	1.5 micrograms per cubic meter

Source: Council on Environmental Quality, *Environmental Quality—1980* (Government Printing Office, 1980), p. 172.

a. Not to be exceeded more than once a year.

b. The Environmental Protection Agency has proposed a reduction of the standard to 25 parts per million (29 milligrams per cubic meter).

c. A non-health-related standard used as a guide for ozone control.

or anticipated adverse effects" from the criteria pollutants. Some critics have contended that even these standards are not affected by prospective costs, but there appears to be fairly widespread consensus that the term *public welfare* connotes economic welfare.[3] In practice, secondary standards are usually identical to primary standards (table 8-1).

3. David P. Currie, "Federal Air Quality Standards and Their Implementation," *American Bar Federation Research Journal*, 1976, p. 368.

Finally, the EPA has the authority to set standards for hazardous emissions under section 112 of the act. These standards are not ambient quality standards but point-source standards. Once again, it appears that these standards are to be set without regard to cost and with an "ample margin of safety." This mandate has been difficult to implement because of its potential impact on individual polluters. As a result few hazardous pollutants have been actually regulated under section 112.

Choice of Criterion

Most of the discussion of the EPA standard-setting process has focused on procedural and scientific issues.[4] How is scientific information to be analyzed and evaluated by the EPA? What is the role of the Science Advisory Board or the Clean Air Scientific Advisory Committee in reviewing proposed standards or criteria documents? How is the diverse literature on the prospective health effects of individual pollutants to be synthesized by EPA so that an appropriate decision may be made? Are meetings of the advisory committees to be open to the public?

Much less attention has been focused on the criteria for setting primary health-related standards. In its review of the standard-setting process, the National Commission on Air Quality (NCAQ) gives rather cursory attention to the problem:

Like the language of Section 109, portions of Section 112 have raised questions of interpretation. The requirement of allowing an ample margin of safety in setting standards presumes a threshold concentration below which there is no adverse health effect. For pollutants that cause or are suspected of causing cancer, it is currently assumed that any level of exposure may be harmful.[5]

Does this mean that the NCAQ is advocating zero emission levels (under section 112) for all substances "that cause or are suspected of causing cancer"? Given the absence of thresholds in the health effects for the criteria pollutants, would the NCAQ be compelled to suggest ambient standards of zero parts per million for these pollutants?

---

4. The National Commission on Air Quality provides a thorough review of the procedures required to set the ambient standards in its report, *To Breathe Clean Air* (Government Printing Office, 1981), pt. 3, chap. 1. More detailed reviews of the basis for setting standards may be found in Lave and Omenn, *Clearing the Air;* and Benjamin G. Ferris and Frank E. Speizer, "Criteria for Establishing Standards for Air Pollutants," *The Business Roundtable Air Quality Project*, vol. 1 (New York: Business Roundtable, 1981).

5. NCAQ, *To Breathe Clean Air*, p. 3.1-3.

Figure 8-1. *Extrapolating Evidence on the Dose-Response Relationship for Criteria Pollutants*

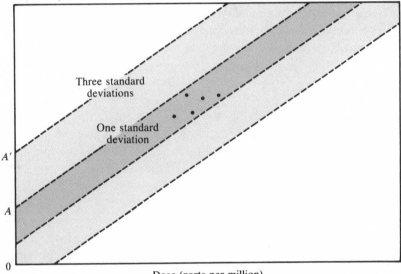

Dose (parts per million)

    The difficulty in setting an absolutely protective standard is demonstrated in figure 8-1. Excess mortality or morbidity is plotted on the vertical axis; concentration of a pollutant is plotted on the horizontal axis. Hypothetical scientific evidence on health effects is reflected by the dots, with each dot reflecting the dose-response relationship from one investigation. These investigations may reflect research on animals, clinical investigations with humans, or epidemiological studies. All results are subject to some uncertainty because researchers cannot identify perfectly all causes of the given health effects. Thus the array of dots is surrounded by a shaded area reflecting a given statistical confidence level.

    If excess morbidity or mortality is to be reduced to zero (with an adequate margin of safety), how should the EPA use results such as those in figure 8-1? Adverse health effects exist at the lowest concentration reflected in one of the dots. That the scientific evidence does not provide observations of health effects at lower concentrations does not allow one to conclude that none exists at lower concentrations. The limitations of sample size or equipment may complicate capturing these effects, but they may exist all the same. The most obvious example of this problem derives from carcinogen tests with rodents. Given the practical limitations on sample size, tests of suspected carcinogens must be carried out at high doses. The discovery of a positive result at these doses does not permit the researcher to say much about the carcinogenic effect of low doses. He usually must resort to theoretical extrapolations of the results to lower dosages in order to say anything pertinent about the doses encountered by humans in their daily lives.

Extrapolations of the results in figure 8-1 to lower dosages may generate a nonzero predicted excess morbidity or mortality at even the smallest possible doses. If linear extrapolation techniques are used (reflecting the absence of a threshold), the chances that this will occur are enhanced by a wide confidence interval around each of the observations. In figure 8-1 the upper range of two alternative confidence intervals, when projected toward the vertical axis linearly, generates the prediction of some excess mortality or morbidity ($0A$ or $0A'$) at even the lowest concentrations. In such a case the adequate margin of safety could only be obtained at a concentration of zero parts per million.

Assume that the extrapolated results generate a zero level of excess mortality or morbidity at a nonzero (or threshold) concentration (figure 8-2). What is an adequate margin of safety? Is it the extrapolation of a one-standard-deviation confidence level ($0B$) or should it be a three-standard-deviation level ($0B'$)? The Clean Air Act provides no definition of *adequate* to guide the EPA administrator.

Even greater difficulties arise with defining public health. If all primary standards are to protect the public health with an adequate margin of safety, should the risk of exposure to pollutants that add substantially to the risk of early death be treated the same as the risk of smarting eyes? Should public health authorities assign their priorities to the first class of pollutants and be more concerned about the adequacy of the margin of safety for these pollutants than for the latter group? The language of section 108 does not appear to permit such distinctions. Adverse health effects are not defined; all health risks appear to be treated equally under the law.[6]

Regional Uniformity of Standards

The public health criterion for ambient standards forces the EPA to neglect regional differences in setting the nation's air quality goals. Differences in climate, topography, or industrial structure might have a

6. See Ferris and Speizer, "Criteria for Establishing Standards."

Figure 8-2. *Extrapolating Evidence on the Dose-Response Relationship: A Threshold?*

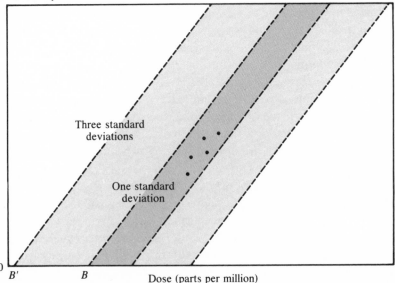

Excess mortality
   or morbidity

Three standard
   deviations

One standard
   deviation

0

B'   B   Dose (parts per million)

major effect on the cost of achieving a given air quality, but these differences are to be ignored in establishing public policy. If it should cost, say, $10,000 per capita to reduce the concentration of photochemical smog from 0.13 part per million to 0.12 part per million (the current standard) in Los Angeles, this expenditure must be made even though Boise or Cheyenne may stop at $100 per capita. The fact that Los Angeles residents might place a lower value on distant vistas and a higher value on large automobiles than their counterparts in Boise and Cheyenne makes no difference. Los Angeles is forced by national policy to pursue the same goal at a much higher cost than most other areas.

Apparently the NCAQ views this uniformity as a means of preventing other sections of the country from following the Los Angeles example of allowing relatively high ambient pollution levels.

In the Act, Congress recognized that while levels of air pollution at which public health is affected generally do not vary among different locations, the costs of meeting a specific standard can vary substantially from area to area, depending upon the severity of the pollution. Thus, if a national air quality standard were based in part on the costs of complying with it, the high cost of meeting the standard in a few heavily polluted areas could result in the standard's being set at a less protective level than is achievable in a reasonable, economic fashion in other areas.[7]

Why is a *uniform* national standard needed? Why should Los Angeles not have a looser oxidant standard than Boise or Cheyenne? Congress is willing to saddle PSD areas with tighter implicit standards, but it is unwilling to suggest that a similar rationale be used in setting the primary ambient standards.

It is difficult to comprehend how the EPA can set ambient air quality standards that are totally protective of health. The absence of thresholds in the dose-response relationships, the differing climatological and topographical conditions across the country, and the paucity of monitors make such standards impractical. As a result the absolutist tone of the Clean Air Act concerning the criteria for setting primary ambient standards cannot be fulfilled. It is inconceivable that an EPA administrator would choose a standard of zero parts per million. Nor is it likely that he would settle on a standard that protects a small minority of the population from a minuscule increase in expected mortality if the cost of this incremental reduction in the primary ambient standard were $100 billion per year. An implicit cost-benefit test must be used.

"Exceedances"

Even if there were a satisfactory health-based criterion for setting ambient air quality standards, how should this standard be defined for temporal variations in air quality? If there is evidence that ozone, for example, is harmful at concentrations above 0.15 part per million, how often should an area be permitted to exceed this level, and where should the compliance be measured? In any region there will be seconds, minutes, or even hours when the standard is exceeded at some location. Should the EPA attempt to limit these "exceedances" at every possible location? If so, how often may the standard be safely exceeded?

For most of the criteria pollutants, the agency sets a short-term standard, a long-term standard, or both. For sulfur dioxide, there are annual and twenty-four-hour standards. The twenty-four-hour standard may be exceeded no more than once a year at any monitoring location. Given the low density of monitors, there is no assurance that the standard

7. NCAQ, *To Breathe Clean Air*, p. 3.1-2.

will not be exceeded more than once at most locations where people breathe the air. The strictness of the standard is determined as much by the location of monitors as by the allowed number of exceedances.

Equally important is the possibility that the costs of limiting exceedances to one a year may be very high compared to the costs of allowing two or three exceedances. Will one additional day of "unhealthy" air add measurably to the health problems in an area? Would alleviating this additional burden on health be worth the cost? The absolutist nature of Congress's instruction to the EPA seems to make such questions irrelevant.

Primary Standard-Setting in Practice

Of the criteria pollutants, sulfates and particulates are by far the most dangerous, according to epidemiological research, and both are emitted largely by stationary sources. The other major stationary-source emissions, nitrogen oxides and hydrocarbons, are less important, but they combine to form photochemical oxidants with the aid of sunlight. Because the EPA chose to reexamine the oxidant standard first, this discussion begins with a review of the primary oxidant standard.

Ozone

The EPA's experience in setting the revised oxidant standard reveals the bankruptcy of the current approach to setting primary standards. In 1971 the agency had set the primary ambient standard for photochemical oxidants at 0.08 part per million. Oxidants are formed from unburned hydrocarbons and nitrogen oxides in the presence of sunlight. The oxidant standard is therefore important for both mobile and stationary-source emission policies. The decision to revise this standard in 1977–78, as part of the reexamination of all ambient standards required by the 1977 Clean Air Act Amendments,[8] had important implications for both the mobile- and stationary-source EPA programs.

The evidence on the health effects of breathing oxidants is sketchy. The major study cited to defend the 0.08-part-per-million standard in 1977 was the one used in establishing this standard in 1971: a 1956

---

8. 42 U.S.C. 7409, as revised by the Clean Air Act Amendments of 1977.

examination of 137 persons with asthma in the Los Angeles area.[9] This study found a weak relationship between the onset of asthma attacks and the existence of high levels of oxidants. Reexamining it twenty years later, the EPA discovered that the adverse effects probably did not begin until a concentration of 0.25 part per million was reached. Subsequent studies apparently did not reinforce this finding.

Since the 1956 study could hardly be used to justify the new standard, new evidence was sought. In its search through all past studies the EPA could find only five that detected some sort of "health" effect from concentrations of oxidants or ozone at less than 0.20 part per million, two and a half times the existing standard.[10] Most of these studies found that respiratory function was impaired slightly by these concentrations, so athletic activity was somewhat restricted during these periods and occasional headaches were reported. There is no mention of long-term effects at such concentrations.

Moreover, the statistical significance of most of these small-sample results is in considerable doubt. One study found some effects at 0.15 part per million, but with only six subjects, this finding is not statistically significant.[11] Constitutents of photochemical smog may have longer-term health effects, but most of the evidence on ozone and other oxidants does not suggest any effects below 0.20 or 0.25 part per million. More important, the EPA changed its standard from oxidants to ozone because it admitted that it could not measure the concentrations of all oxidants

9. Charles E. Schoettlin and Emanuel Landau, "Air Pollution and Asthma Attacks in the Los Angeles Area," *Public Health Reports,* vol. 76 (June 1961), pp. 545–49. (This study was conducted in the last three months of 1956.)

10. U.S. Environmental Protection Agency, Office of Research and Development, "Air Quality Criteria for Ozone and Other Photochemical Oxidants" (EPA, April 1978). Since 1978, a number of new studies of the effects of ozone have appeared, demonstrating some effect of oxidant concentrations on pulmonary function and reported asthma attacks. See Roger Detels and others, "The U.C.L.A. Population Studies of Chronic Respiratory Disease, IV: Respiratory Effect of Long-term Exposure to Photochemical Oxidants, Nitrogen Dioxide, and Sulfates on Current and Never Smokers," *American Review of Respiratory Disease,* vol. 124 (1981), pp. 673–80; and Alice S. Whittemore and Edward L. Korn, "Asthma and Air Pollution in the Los Angeles Area," *American Journal of Public Health,* vol. 70 (July 1980), pp. 687–96. On the other hand, there is evidence of an adaptation to the effects of ozone; see S. M. Horvath, J. A. Gilner, and L. J. Folinsbee, "Adaptation to Ozone: Duration of Effect," *American Review of Respiratory Disease,* vol. 123 (1981), pp. 496–99.

11. Anthony J. Delucia and William C. Adams, "Effects of Ozone Inhalation During Exercise on Pulmonary Function and Blood Biochemistry," *Journal of Applied Physiology,* vol. 43, no. 1 (1977), pp. 75–81.

well. Since it could measure ozone levels, the standard would be set for ozone. The limited evidence on the health effects of ozone per se put the administrator in a difficult position to justify a primary standard much below 0.20 part per million.[12]

The agency's reluctance to move much above its 0.08-part-per-million primary standard in 1977 reflected the dependence of much of the air pollution program on the continued determination that many standard metropolitan statistical areas were "nonattainment" for ozone. The EPA demonstrated that under the 0.08 standard, ninety AQCRs were nonattainment for ozone, but relaxing the standard to 0.10 part per million would reduce this number to only eighty-eight. Relaxing it to 0.20, which would be easily justified by the health evidence, would eliminate all but seventeen areas from the noncompliance status.[13] It would be difficult for the EPA to argue for strict *national* approaches to automobile emissions if the oxidant problem existed in only seventeen metropolitan areas.

A more embarrassing calculation was made by the Regulatory Analysis Review Group (RARG). It showed that keeping the standard at 0.08 part per million would cost $5,630 more per person-hour of "unhealthy" exposure than the 0.10-part-per-million standard.[14] The incremental cost of the standard proposed by the EPA, 0.10, was $2,180 per person-hour of unhealthy exposure. By contrast an 0.18-part-per-million standard would cost $90 per hour of additional exposure beyond the 0.20-part-per-million standard. Total costs of the 0.10 standard were estimated at $6.9 billion a year, and the costs of a 0.20 standard at $4.4 billion. The EPA might have conducted an experiment offering each potential "unhealthy" victim the choice between (1) a reduction in exposure from 0.12 to 0.10 part per million on the second-worst day or (2) a payment of $2,180 an hour for exposure to the concentrations of more than 0.10 part per million, which would occur under a 0.12-part-per-million standard. It is difficult to believe that, given the limited health evidence of any effect below 0.25 part per million, most would not have taken the money.

12. See report of the Regulatory Analysis Review Group (RARG) of the Council on Wage and Price Stability, "Environmental Protection Agency's Proposed Revisions to the National Ambient Air Quality Standard for Photochemical Oxidants," October 16, 1978, for a discussion of the health evidence. See also National Academy of Sciences, *Photochemical Oxidants* (NAS, 1977).

13. EPA, Office of Air Quality Planning and Standards, "Cost and Economic Impact Assessment for Alternative Levels of the National Ambient Air Quality Standard for Ozone," app. A, June 1978.

14. "Environmental Protection Agency's Proposed Revision," p. 24a.

The final decision was to relax the standard only to 0.12 part per million, thus preserving many of the accoutrements of the EPA nonattainment program.[15] Annual costs of this standard would be $5.9 billion, according to RARG, much of it in an increasingly unpopular inspection and maintenance program, which even California has been reluctant to implement. Why did the EPA keep such a strict standard? The political pressure from environmental groups that had supported President Carter had some effect. To relax to 0.16 or even 0.20 part per million would have antagonized these groups considerably. Yet the EPA could have said that a literal reading of its statute might require a zero standard since it could not reject the hypothesis of a linear dose-response curve with a positive intercept. Alternatively, it could have argued that, given the pressing environmental problems of the day, the agency would save the country $2.5 billion in pursuing this mild health problem in order to focus its efforts and the country's resources on sulfates, hazardous wastes, waterborne carcinogens, and toxic substances. Either approach would have been more defensible than the final decision. The EPA's compromise at 0.12 cannot be defended on any basis other than a desire to find a middle course between the inflation fighters at the White House and the ardent environmentalists.

Carbon Monoxide

The second ambient standard reviewed by the EPA after the 1977 amendments was the carbon monoxide standard. In August 1980 the agency proposed keeping the eight-hour standard at 9 parts per million but lowering the one-hour standard from 35 to 25 parts per million.[16] This proposal was based on studies of the health effects of carbon monoxide in persons suffering from cardiovascular and peripheral vascular disease. Most of the evidence of the effects of carbon monoxide on such people has been based on laboratory experiments with patients.[17] There is little epidemiological evidence linking carbon monoxide to heart disease. However, in attempting to set the standard to protect the most sensitive groups in the population, the EPA encountered the usual problem of justifying any standard above zero parts per million. There is every reason to believe that a small fraction of persons with cardio-

15. *Federal Register,* vol. 44 (February 8, 1979), p. 8220.
16. *Federal Register,* vol. 45 (August 18, 1980), pp. 55066–84.
17. National Academy of Sciences, Committee on Medical and Biological Effects of Environmental Pollutants, *Carbon Monoxide* (NAS, 1977).

vascular disease will suffer increased pain at slight concentrations of carbon monoxide; hence any nonzero standard will not be truly protective (with an adequate margin of safety) of their health.

As of mid-1982 the EPA had not promulgated the carbon monoxide standard. While this standard has little effect on air pollution policies affecting stationary sources, it exemplifies the problems that the agency encounters when setting ambient standards for pollutants with health effects that exhibit no thresholds. The Clean Air Act presumes a threshold, but the evidence for most criteria pollutants is to the contrary. The EPA can only exercise strained logic and hope to avoid an embarrassing showdown in the appellate courts.

Particulates and Sulfates

Recent research questions the validity of both the current particulates and the sulfur dioxide ambient standards.[18] Neither has been revised since the 1977 amendments, as the EPA has been unable to resolve a number of scientific controversies surrounding the two pollutants.

First, it is becoming increasingly clear that certain sulfate compounds, not sulfur dioxide, constitute the primary threat to human health from sulfur oxide emissions. The National Commission on Air Quality cites only preliminary evidence that sulfur dioxide causes significant reversible changes in the lung function of asthmatics, but it provides little further support for a sulfur dioxide standard.[19]

The recent research by Chappie and Lave[20] confirms earlier research by Lave and Seskin that sulfates, not sulfur dioxide, are associated with increases in mortality. Similar conclusions are reached by Rall and Wilson.[21] On the other hand Ostro and Anderson found that particulates, not sulfates, are important contributors to morbidity.[22]

The current particulates standard, expressed in concentrations of grams per cubic meter, does not distinguish among particles of various

18. Lave and Omenn, "Clearing the Air," pp. 16–17.

19. NCAQ, *To Breathe Clean Air*, pp. 3.1-11-12.

20. Mike Chappie and Lester B. Lave, "The Health Effects of Air Pollution: A Reanalysis," *Journal of Urban Economics*, vol. 12 (November 1982), pp. 346–76.

21. David P. Rall, "Review of the Health Effects of Sulfur Oxides," *Environmental Health Perspectives*, vol. 3 (August 1974), pp. 97–121; Richard Wilson and others, *Health Effects of Fossil Fuel Burning: Assessment and Mitigation* (Ballinger, 1980).

22. Bart D. Ostro and Robert C. Anderson, "Morbidity, Air Pollution, and Health Statistics," paper delivered at the joint statistical meetings of the American Statistical

sizes or between different chemical compounds. There is considerable evidence that fine, respirable particulates are more dangerous than the larger particles; hence the EPA has been attempting to recast the standard into a fine-particle standard. Moreover, certain particles such as sulfates are likely to be more dangerous than others. The merging of a sulfate and particulates standard thus seems appropriate, but the agency has not succeeded in doing this.

Hazardous Emissions

The EPA has moved slowly in setting hazardous emission standards, undoubtedly because these are point-source standards whose violation exposes individual polluters to possible criminal or civil penalties. Ambient standards, on the other hand, do not directly affect individual polluters. It has also been suggested that the EPA has found it difficult to resolve disputes about the appropriate trade-off between risk and economic costs, the exposed population, and the differences in the effect of a single emission standard across industries.[23]

Through 1982 the EPA had promulgated hazardous-emission standards for only four pollutants.[24] It has, however, enunciated a policy for airborne carcinogens, which does not require reducing these pollutants to a zero-risk level regardless of the cost of controls. Instead, it requires that individual sources use the best available control technology where *best* depends in part on the cost of compliance. This policy, assailed by environmentalists, is as yet largely unimplemented.

Summary

This chapter has not attempted a thorough review of the ambient air quality standards because such a review would plunge too deeply into the health sciences or epidemiology. Instead, the discussion has

Association and Biometric Society, August 1981. A more recent study by Philip E. Graves and Ronald J. Krumm, *Health and Air Quality: Evaluating the Effects of Policy* (American Enterprise Institute for Public Policy Research, 1981), argues that excess morbidity is caused by the *interaction* between sulfur dioxide and particulates (the coefficient of haze), but their results are generally plagued by low levels of statistical significance.

23. Conservation Foundation, *State of the Environment, 1982*, p. 69.
24. NCAQ, *To Breathe Clean Air*, pp. 3.1-15–22.

focused on the difficulty of defining a set of standards that are absolutely protective of health. This difficulty is demonstrated by the complex administrative process used by the EPA to revise the ambient air quality standards.

Five years after the Clean Air Act Amendments of 1977 the agency has been able to revise only the oxidant standard and then only in a way that has left many observers dissatisfied. The standard was changed from an oxidant to an ozone standard despite the limited evidence of health problems associated with ozone. While the standard was relaxed substantially, the goal remains expensive for many regions. Although economic considerations are not supposed to interfere with setting primary standards, they were very much part of the debate in revising the oxidant (ozone) standard.

The current procedure for setting ambient standards does not require the agency to use a cost-benefit test in setting its own priorities. Recent health evidence suggests that respirable particulates and sulfates are the most dangerous of the criteria pollutants. The EPA has moved more quickly to reexamine the standards for oxidants and carbon monoxide, two less dangerous pollutants, while wrestling unsuccessfully with the particulate and sulfur dioxide standards. Had the EPA been instructed to pursue the pollutants that most threaten health and welfare, it would have focused first on particulates and sulfates, not ozone and carbon monoxide. Ironically, the lack of instruction to regulate where the prospective net benefits to society are the greatest may have reduced public health.

IX

Modest Pressures
for Legislative Change

In 1981 there was a marked shift in political philosophy in Washington. The incoming Republicans established regulatory reform as a key issue on the first year's political agenda.[1] The president signed an executive order establishing a regulatory review office in the Office of Management and Budget to review all proposed regulations.[2] Senator Paul Laxalt drafted an omnibus regulatory reform bill requiring regulatory analyses of all major regulatory rules emanating from executive branch and independent agencies.[3] The administration launched a review of regulatory policies affecting the automobile industry.[4]

One might have thought that in this climate changes in environmental policy would be high on the list of priorities. If the concern of the new policymakers in Washington was the excessive cost of government regulation, environmental policy might be a good place to look for savings, particularly in the clean air or clean water areas. The Clean Air Act's authorization expired September 30, 1981, providing the administration with an ideal opportunity to launch a legislative program to streamline air pollution policy, to make it more cost-effective, and to reduce the burden of compliance costs on industry.

Surprisingly, there was little pressure for major legislative changes.[5] Had the automobile industry not been in its worst recession since the 1930s, there might have been even less interest in amending the act; the industry's plight generated mild support for some relaxation of emission

1. For a discussion of the Reagan program, see "Regulation: A Fast Start for the Reagan Strategy," *Business Week,* March 9, 1981, pp. 62–67; and Executive Office of the President, "Materials on President Reagan's Program on Regulatory Relief," June 13, 1981.

2. Executive Order 12291, February 17, 1981.

3. The Regulatory Reform Act, S. 1080.

4. Executive Office of the President, "Actions to Help the U.S. Auto Industry," April 6, 1981.

5. For an explanation of this inactivity, see Robert W. Crandall, "Has Reagan Dropped the Ball?" *Regulation,* vol. 5 (September–October 1981), pp. 15–18.

standards for new automobiles. These proposals were so controversial that proponents of the changes worked actively to limit amendments to the stationary-source provisions of the act. As a result, the meager pressure for change in stationary-source policy was easily turned aside in 1981–82.

Why was there so little support for changing stationary-source policies? Given the Reagan administration's advocacy of a new federalism and the increased use of cost-benefit analysis, general concern over lagging investment and productivity growth, and the excessive costs of the new-source performance standards (for utilities) in the Sun Belt, one might have expected an administration bill that advocated: (1) the use of cost-benefit analysis for setting ambient air quality standards; (2) a movement toward economic incentives, perhaps with greater authority to the states for design, implementation, and enforcement of the policy; (3) elimination of at least the percentage-reduction aspect of new source performance standards, if not the total abolition of separate new-source standards; and (4) elimination of most of the prevention of significant deterioration (PSD) program. The Ninety-seventh Congress retired with virtually no serious movement toward reform in any of these areas. A number of groups, including the administration, offered proposals for changing the Clean Air Act. But these proposals hardly scratched the surface of the problems.

Proposals to Amend the Clean Air Act

As the reauthorization deadline approached, most debate over amendments to the Clean Air Act centered on the automotive standards because of the deepening crisis in Detroit. The stationary-source issues were given a lower priority despite obvious opportunities to reduce the regulatory burden on industry without compromising environmental quality. In part this might have reflected the lack of a concerted effort by industry to press for legislative changes. The proposals advanced by the major participants in the Clean Air Act debate were far from revolutionary.

The Business Position

One might have expected the business community to view 1981 as an opportune time to seek far-reaching changes in the Clean Air Act. Yet business groups advocated little substantive change. Perhaps the most thorough analyses and detailed positions were developed by the Business Roundtable.[6] Its recommendations amounted to far less than an overhaul of the act. The Roundtable advocated:

—a change in the definition of *adverse health effects* (in setting ambient air quality standards) to exclude temporary personal discomfort;

—the consideration of "economic values" and "other public interests" in determining the degree of risk that is reasonable in setting ambient standards;

—establishment of an independent science advisory committee to review Environmental Protection Agency determinations in setting primary standards;

—a cost-benefit test for secondary standards but not for primary standards;

—elimination of class II and class III PSD areas;

—substitution of new-source performance standards (NSPS) for case-by-case best available control technology (BACT) standards for new sources in class I PSD areas;

—a possible exception for even the class I PSD areas for "energy and economic" considerations;

—simplified permit review and state implementation plan (SIP) processes;

—uniform NSPS wherever possible;

—conditions for waiving offset requirements where "no offset is reasonably available";

—a redefinition of *major source* in nonattainment areas as one emitting 100 tons per year; and

—a delay in any action on acid precipitation until the EPA or other federal agencies complete more research.

Nowhere is there a suggestion that the NSPS percentage-reduction requirement be abandoned. The Business Roundtable even advocated continuation of technology-based NSPS despite the obvious inefficiency of this approach. The Roundtable seems unwilling to advocate a cost-benefit test where health is involved.

The Roundtable position is hardly one of substantial relaxation or reform of the act. Large firms may have become comfortable with the federal-state standard-setting approach. Alternatively, the bias against new sources may benefit enough Roundtable members that a position

---

6. *The Business Roundtable Air Quality Project: Executive Summary* (New York: Business Roundtable, 1980).

against new-source performance standards in general and percentage reduction in particular is impossible. Whatever the explanation, this group of large firms does not appear to favor substituting market incentives for command-control regulation.

The Heritage Foundation Report

In late 1980 the Heritage Foundation prepared a number of reports that were designed to provide an incoming Republican administration with blueprints for policy changes in numerous areas.[7] The report on the EPA advocated the following changes in the Clean Air Act:

—substitution of source-by-source standards for uniform requirements in regulating fuel-burning sources;

—permission for the states to extend variances from regulations for up to five years;

—use of "rolling averages" for computing emissions;

—periodic review of air quality control region (AQCR) boundaries;

—a balancing of societal costs and benefits in setting ambient air quality standards;

—outside review of EPA criteria documents that are used in setting ambient air quality standards;

—restoration of "quality-of-life" review and imposition of cost-benefit or risk-benefit analysis for all new proposals;

—extensions of compliance deadlines for facilities voluntarily switching to coal;

—the setting of secondary ambient standards by the states instead of the EPA;

—protection of existing complying sources from changes in standards for up to ten years;

—use of financial incentives to encourage retirement of *environmentally inefficient* facilities;

—retention of BACT for all PSD areas but elimination of the remaining requirements for PSD class II and class III areas;

—unspecified methods for obviating offsets, lowest achievable emission rate (LAER), and BACT where they impede growth and energy development.

7. Heritage Foundation, *Mandate for Leadership: Project Team Report for the Environmental Protection Agency* (HF, 1980), pp. 38–41.

The Heritage report identifies a major problem with the act—its bias against growth—but it does not directly address the source of this problem. Waiving certain new-source provisions when they impede growth or energy development might lead to universal exemptions. But what would take the place of the clumsy approach to new sources in the act? Encouraging the early retirement of *environmentally inefficient* sources might create biases in the other direction. With owners of these sources scrambling for federal financing of closures and exemptions for new sources, one wonders what environmental program would result.

The interesting aspect of the Heritage recommendations is the tilt toward more cost-benefit analysis in setting ambient standards and the shift of responsibility for at least the secondary standards to the states. The report suggests a balancing of "the societal costs of securing additional reductions in pollutant concentrations against the incremental benefits to the public that can reasonably be anticipated" instead of the absolutist health-protection criterion now required for primary ambient standards.[8]

The National Commission on Air Quality

Given a set of difficult political issues, Congress often fashions a compromise and then delegates to an outside "independent" body the task of studying the problem further. The 1977 Clean Air Act Amendments make classic use of this technique, establishing the National Commission on Air Quality (NCAQ) to investigate a range of issues upon which Congress chose not to act. The commission's inquiry was completed in 1980 and its final report published in March 1981.[9] The NCAQ report conveys the impression that air pollution policies are basically sound but poorly administered. Its 109 recommendations are largely minor revisions of existing policies and encouragement to the states and to the EPA to improve their management of the program. The more important proposals were that

—the national ambient air quality standard-setting process remain virtually unchanged;

—state implementation plans be continued with more efficient EPA review and approval;

8. Ibid., p. A-5.

9. National Commission on Air Quality, *To Breathe Clean Air* (Government Printing Office, 1981), pp. 55–66.

—new-source performance standards be retained;

—case-by-case BACT standards be used in both nonattainment and PSD areas;

—PSD class I areas and certain PSD class II areas be retained;

—the reasonably available control technology standards be continued for nonattainment areas, and civil penalties and noncompliance penalties be retained with greater EPA discretion in using them;

—interstate pollution abatement provisions of the act be strengthened; and

—a pollution fee be an option in lieu of offsets.

Economic considerations and economic incentives are relegated to the end of the list of recommendations and account for only 6 of the 109 specific recommendations. Of these six, two would require the EPA to study the employment dislocations caused by air pollution policy, one recommends tax-exempt bonds for pollution control equipment, and one suggests that an existing policy be continued (the bubble policy). The remaining two would require states to consider cost-effectiveness and to consider economic incentive approaches that would lead to improved economic efficiency.

The authors of the report do not realize the breadth of possibilities for economic incentives. If such tools were substituted for existing policy instruments, most other recommendations on stationary-source policy would have to be abandoned. The NCAQ report does not consider one of its most significant proposals an "economic incentive" when in fact it represents a major step toward the use of a market. The proposal—to allow fees to substitute for offsets—is the most far-reaching economic incentive contained in its report.

The Reagan Administration

After several months of attempting to draft a revision of the Clean Air Act, the Reagan administration simply announced a set of principles that would guide its support of alternative legislative proposals.[10] These include:

—continuation of federal ambient standard-setting with no cost-benefit analysis in setting health-related standards;

—except in park and wilderness areas, the use of *uniform technology-based* standards instead of the current PSD policy;

10. Statement of EPA administrator Anne M. Gorsuch, August 5, 1981.

—adjustment of deadlines for achieving ambient standards;

—relaxation of automobile standards; and

—elimination of the percentage-reduction standard for new fossil-fuel-burning sources in favor of uniform emission standards.

The administration strategists appear to ignore the basic problem with technology-based standards: inefficiency and a bias against growth. Support for federally mandated uniform technology-based standards is curious for a conservative administration seeking to relieve the private sector of the burden of unreasonable regulation. Nor is the administration able to muster support for a cost-benefit test in setting ambient standards. However, to the administration's credit it is willing to support elimination of the percentage-reduction requirement for new coal-fired utility and industrial boilers despite the lack of political support for such a change.

Assessment of the Proposals

Although these proposals do not represent all positions being argued before Congress on clean air policy for stationary sources, they are fairly representative of a wide range of interests. How do they measure up in terms of the major reform categories?

Ambient Standards

The ambient-standard-setting process is confusing and confused. The more important standards, from a health perspective, have not been revised. The EPA has not been able to revise the standards for particulates, sulfur dioxide, or carbon monoxide, in part because of the difficulty of grappling with the act's absolutist requirements.

None of these proposals suggests a direct substitution of a cost-benefit test for the current primary ambient-standard criterion. The Heritage Foundation would focus on "actual" health effects and require some balancing of prospective benefits and costs. The Business Roundtable would include economic values in the consideration of the degree of risk that is reasonable, but the administration and the National Commission on Air Quality advocate no change in the criteria for setting primary standards.

Only the Heritage Foundation report appears to suggest cost-benefit analysis as a tool that might apply to even the ambient-standard-setting process. Yet without such an approach, setting primary standards has become a political exercise with few guidelines. The image of regulators trading dollars for human health remains a powerfully emotional obstacle to sensible reform in health-safety regulation.

Federal Point-Source Regulation

Reading the proposals from various groups hardly gives the impression that the EPA has already begun to move away from the detailed approach of setting each point-source standard. Offsets, bubbles, and netting in building new facilities have allowed firms to trade among sources. This trading will undoubtedly increase in the next few years even if the EPA and Congress make no further changes in policy. Thus far, transactions costs and regulatory uncertainty have impeded transfers, since neither buyers nor sellers have had much information on the identity of other market participants, and no one could be sure what the SIP revision process might entail.

Surprisingly, neither the Heritage Foundation nor the administration, which might be expected to abhor detailed federal regulation of business, shows any interest in substituting economic incentives for detailed point-source standards. The Business Roundtable advocates more intraplant offsets through a wider definition of source for nonattainment areas—a proposal already adopted by the EPA but reversed by the courts. The NCAQ would allow a fee to substitute for an offset, although it does not suggest this proposal to improve the functioning of offset markets or to relieve firms of new-source standards. Only the Heritage Foundation advocates some transfer of regulatory responsibilities to the states; even this proposal is only for the secondary ambient standards.

In the political environment of 1981–82 only Congressman Henry Waxman of California was willing to advocate formal procedures to accelerate the development of a market. In H.R. 5555, he proposed a system of controlled trading for sulfur oxides. Firms would be able to buy and sell emission reductions from five regional banks. This banking system would have the advantage of a geographic scope not permitted by the current state-based systems since it would be part of a program aimed at reducing acid deposits, not local sulfur dioxide problems.

Otherwise, most proposals to reform the Clean Air Act leave the point-source standard-setting process largely intact. Their proponents appear either unaware of or uninterested in the inefficiencies created by such an approach. Except for some attention to monitoring issues, most of these proposals fail to address the effectiveness issue. No one seems concerned with the considerable evidence that has accumulated on the inability of the EPA and the states to monitor individual sources. Nor is anyone apparently convinced that resources would be well spent in these endeavors instead of on drafting and enforcing thousands of detailed point-source standards.

New-Source Standards

Perhaps the most incredible political aspect of the discussion of Clean Air Act reform is the inability of the major proponents and antagonists to support proposals to repeal the inefficient new-source performance standards for fossil-fuel-fired boilers. Nor is there much interest in eliminating the new-source bias simply by basing all standards on the same criteria or by allowing full trading between new and old sources.

The administration has proposed the elimination of the percentage-reduction requirement, but it stands alone in this battle. The Business Roundtable narrowly skirts the issue by asserting: ''The Act's numerous definitions of control technology (e.g., NSPS, BACT, LAER) are unnecessary to achieve environmental objectives but add substantial costs to emission control programs.'' Unfortunately, it then recommends uniform NSPS, apparently assenting to the current percentage-reduction standard.

No one seems to advocate a substitution of economic rationality for the current approach to new sources. The Heritage Foundation recommends some unspecified change in regulation whenever the new-source requirements impede growth and energy development. At least its report identifies a major problem with the act; most other proposals do not recognize this problem. The administration, for instance, would use uniform technology-based standards despite the evidence that this approach will discourage new sources.

One can only conclude that the environmentalists' conviction that technology forcing is a good idea combines with certain industrial interests' desire to slow new competition. There is little constituency for altering this bias against new sources.

PSD Policy

A ray of hope appears in at least one area. The administration, the Business Roundtable, the Heritage Foundation, and even the NCAQ seem to agree that the current PSD policy represents overkill. Most would eliminate the class II and class III areas, but all would continue uniform technology-based standards in the attainment areas. Standards would be at least as stringent in these clean areas as in dirtier areas of the country. This amounts to accepting a theory that the value of an increment of pollution abatement is independent of the degree of pollution in the area. How this can square with the health-threshold approach in the primary ambient-standard-setting process is difficult to comprehend.

Although it appears likely that some reduction in the scope of nondeterioration policy will eventually occur, legislators and reformers alike seem reluctant to relax the PSD policy much. On the one hand, they may fear a backlash from the public reflecting concern that valuable national treasures are being desecrated even though the impact of new growth in many areas may involve only slight loss of scenic vistas. On the other hand, the pressure from the acutely distressed northern industrial states ought to be greater in the 1980s than in 1977, when the PSD amendments were passed. Pashigian has demonstrated that the political support for PSD policy comes not from Wyoming, Arizona, and New Mexico but from the urbanized northern areas of the country worried about industrial migration to the Sun Belt.[11]

Summary

The safest prediction for near-term air pollution policies is one of little change, particularly for industrial sources. The naive observer might think that with Republicans in virtual control in Washington and with industrial sectors in greater difficulty than at any time since the Great Depression there might be attempts to weaken the Clean Air Act. More seasoned political observers know that most public policies represent a

11. B. Peter Pashigian, "Environmental Regulation: Whose Self-Interests Are Being Protected?" (University of Chicago, Graduate School of Business, 1982).

political equilibrium that is often difficult to alter without fundamental changes in economic or social conditions.

Many industries, particularly those in the northern industrial areas, may benefit from the antigrowth bias in the Clean Air Act. They might wish to see their own standards quietly relaxed, but they would not want a restructuring of the act. Nor would they like to see the entire system of environmental controls disrupted in favor of a more efficient system of fully tradable rights or emission taxes. Efficiency is a concept that might be important to social planners, but the uncertainty and the wealth transfers that might result from any change are sufficiently frightening to regulated firms for them to suffer gladly the system they understand.

X

A Practical Solution
to the Control Problem:
A Two-Part Tariff

With its development of offsets and bubbles the Environmental Protection Agency has begun to move from the detailed, inefficient approach to regulating individual point sources as envisioned in the Clean Air Act.[1] The evolution toward a system of marketable rights has been impeded by a number of technical and legal problems. Little attention has been given to the integration of a penalty system with the evolving system of marketable rights. In this concluding chapter I propose an integration of enforcement penalties and marketable rights that may appear quite different from current policy. With a few legislative changes and a shift in administrative emphasis, the current system could easily be transformed into this more efficient approach.

The Two-Part Tariff: Quantities and Prices

The evolution in air pollution policy from mandated government standards to transferable emission reductions through bubbles or offsets has continued despite the disquieting effects of changes in administration, political haggles with interest groups and Congress, and adverse court decisions. At the same time simply refining the standard-setting process and creating new categories of mandated standards is neither workable nor efficient. The evolution toward marketable rights is essentially rescuing the EPA and Congress from the bureaucratic nightmare of implementing and enforcing increasingly complicated technology-based standards.

The central feature of a system of transferable pollution rights is that it divorces the distribution issues from the allocation problem. If the

1. See chapter 5.

initial beneficiary of a favorable standard may trade his rights under this standard to a less-favored polluter, the political constraints on efficient policy are substantially eased. It would be naive to think that government can engage in the wholesale reversal of property rights by consulting only efficiency criteria. Pollution standards will inevitably reflect the political strengths of individual polluters, industries, and even geographic regions. However, if these political decisions affect only the initial distribution of pollution rights, not their eventual use, the political process need not be a major impediment to efficient pollution control. Marketable permits allow this separation.

Once the separation of the distribution of the initial rights and their eventual use is firmly embodied in air pollution policy, regulators can be freed from the arduous task of justifying thousands of pollution standards by invoking reasonably available or best available engineering justifications for their final judgments. Lengthy rule making and endless court battles can be avoided by treating the distribution issue as basically one of equity and politics. States can be allowed to distribute the initial rights for each pollutant once the aggregate goal for an airshed (or a finer geographic division) is established. Whether an electric utility or a glass manufacturer receives the right to emit the marginal ton of sulfur dioxide in a given area can be decided in any manner politically acceptable to local constituents. The final arrangement need not be constrained by the requirement that the firm granted the standard use it.

The separation of the initial distribution from final use of emission rights may also free the federal and state environmental regulators from worrying about increments for future economic growth. New firms seeking to build polluting facilities could simply be required to purchase rights (offsets) for any prospective pollution from the current owners of emission rights. The government need not keep any reserve for future growth, although it could if it were politically necessary.

If moving toward a system of transferable rights relieves the EPA and the states from interminable engineering studies and court challenges, it would allow these agencies to address the weak links of the current regulatory chain: monitoring and enforcement. These functions are neglected to the detriment of the entire air pollution program. The movement toward a combined standards-fee system would allow the EPA simultaneously to relieve itself of considerable administrative burdens and obtain a meaningful civil penalty system for excess pollution.

The standards-fee system is a two-part tariff under which polluters obtain penalty-free emission rights of a specified quantity and are subject to civil penalties for emissions exceeding these rights. The rights would be tradable and the tax rate would be the same for all polluters of the same pollutant in a given area. This two-part tariff would differ from the current system in that there would be no engineering standards and there would be a single-penalty rate (for each pollutant in each area) rather than a delayed-compliance fee that varied across firms.

Establishing the Two-Part Fee: The Initial Distribution

A critical step in moving toward a more rational policy of pollution control is to establish the property rights more permanently. The method of distributing the reduced rights to pollute should be simplifed in order to end the years of bickering over the appropriate technology-based standards. This is not a trivial task; it has already been complicated by years of litigation and imperfect enforcement.

The EPA appears to be moving toward a system of tradable emission-reduction credits. While such a system could easily be used in setting up the two-part tariff, many of the agency's problems would remain. How does it calculate the credit? Is that based on a firm's recent emission levels or on standards that may never have been fully enforced? How does it deal with plants that have limited economic life? How does it treat plants that have already closed? Any hard-and-fast rule on these questions involving the baseline or the zero-penalty pollution level will inevitably encounter strong political opposition from some polluters; such pressure will often succeed. After all, noncompliance reflects to some extent the political skill and power of various polluters.

Given these problems, the use of any formal rule for moving from the current standards to the initial distribution of rights is likely to fail. For instance, using reasonably available control technology (RACT) or some fraction of RACT as the baseline will affect many firms adversely, particularly if they are not in compliance. To improve the effectiveness and efficiency of air pollution policy, it might be desirable to make some concessions to political reality in order to begin the process.

It is particularly important that polluters be given greater certainty in their ownership of emission rights. Otherwise, the market for tradable rights is not likely to work well. Firms are not going to bid for rights that might be reclaimed by a government that changes its mind about the optimal quantity of emissions. If it is desired to reduce emissions over time, rights could be tapered, declining with time. For instance, the right to emit 1.0 ton of sulfur dioxide in 1983 might decline to 0.95 ton in 1984. Alternatively, the federal or state governments could simply repurchase rights from polluters out of general tax revenues.

It is important to stress the difference between the approach outlined in this chapter and current policy as each affects the search for further progress in reducing emissions. Under current policy much of the burden for additional reductions falls on new sources—either through offset transactions at a ratio greater than 1:1 or through stringent technology-based standards. The proposal advanced here would end the distinction between new and existing sources; the bias against new sources would be eliminated. The quantity of emissions allowed at a zero fee could be reduced over time, but there is no reason to impose this reduction only on new sources. As long as these rights are tradable, the reductions would not be applied to any identifiable group of polluters.

The Two-Part Tariff: The Penalty Rate

Once the initial distribution of rights or the baseline emissions are determined for all major sources of each pollutant, the state and federal authorities would subject excess emissions to a fixed fee or noncompliance penalty per excess unit of each pollutant. This fee might be varied by air quality control region (AQCR) if maximum efficiency were desired for localized pollutants, or it might be set at some less efficient national level. Since the penalty rate is a tax, Congress might find it necessary or prudent to legislate it directly.

Choosing the optimal fee is not a simple task. If it is consistently used as a means of enforcing compliance with the distributions of rights, it will serve as the actual rationing device for emissions. With imperfect monitoring and enforcement mechanisms under even the best of circumstances, the penalty rate should be set higher than incremental control costs at the efficient level of emissions if it is to induce firms to hold their emissions to the standard. If the rate is set too high, it becomes punitive, and firms never exceed their initial zero-priced allocations. If it is set too low, firms will exceed their limit of zero-priced emissions.

Figure 10-1 displays the effects of alternative civil penalty rates. The planner's problem is to determine the quantity of emissions and the magnitude of the penalty rate. With the same notation as in chapter 4,

Figure 10-1. *The Two-Part Emission Fee*

Dollars per ton

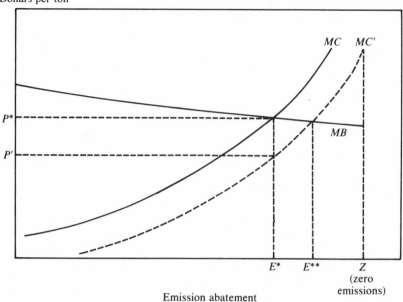

Emission abatement

Dollars per ton

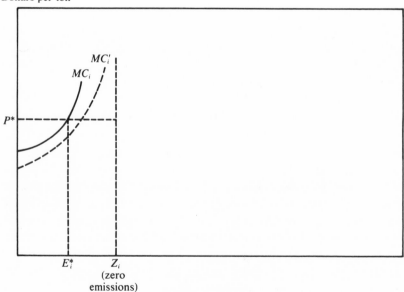

Emission abatement

total emissions are found by equating MB (the incremental benefits of control) with MC (the incremental costs). Total permissible emissions are therefore $Z - E^*$, if there are no transport problems or local hot spots. The ith firm's share of these rights is determined (politically) to be $Z_i - E_i^*$.

The first part of the two-part tariff for the ith firm is a zero penalty rate for emitting up to $Z_i - E_i^*$. This firm pays nothing to the government for these emissions, but its opportunity cost of using them is P^*, assuming that all other firms are in equilibrium, because it could sell them to others and receive P^* per ton per period in return.

The penalty rate must be set so that the expected cost of exceeding the $Z_i - E_i^*$ level of emissions conferred by the rights package is equal to P^*. The difference between the rate established and P^* depends on the probability of avoiding the penalty for violations. Too low a penalty would encourage firms to increase emissions beyond $Z - E^*$.

A two-part tariff of this variety cannot induce emission reductions beyond E^* unless the zero-priced rights are less than $Z - E^*$. This is one of the major drawbacks of any marketable permit scheme. A simple pollution tax is superior to the marketable rights scheme, including this two-part tariff variant, because it provides a continuous incentive for reducing emissions to less than $Z - E^*$ if control costs prove lower than planners estimate. For instance, if all firms (such as the one in the bottom panel of figure 10-1) discover that their marginal abatement costs fall to MC', the annual rental value of emission rights will fall to P'; but unless the environmental planning agency revokes some of the $Z - E^*$ rights, the amount of pollution will not be reduced under a two-part tariff. However, under a constant pollution tax of P^*, total emissions would fall $E^{**} - E^*$. On the other hand, if control costs are higher than planners have anticipated, firms will pay the penalty P^* per unit of excess emissions and increase emissions accordingly.

Providing an incentive for reductions of pollution beyond E^* if control costs prove to be lower than MC is relatively straightforward. The government could make the pollution tax refundable for all emission reductions beyond E_i^* for each firm. If firms reduced their emissions beyond E^*, the government would actually pay polluters more in fees than it collected. Alternatively, planners could provide less than $Z - E^*$ in zero-priced rights, thereby allowing the penalty rate to serve as the rationing device over a wide range of control costs.

Adjusting the Initial Allocation

It is difficult to imagine a smooth and easy transition to an emission rights system such as the one discussed in this chapter. Even without the political problems of implementation, one can easily predict a number of possible complications.

First, many pollutants are emitted by both stationary and mobile sources. Unless Congress included vehicles in an emission rights program, the allocation of hydrocarbon and nitrogen oxide emissions to stationary sources would have to accommodate changes in vehicular emissions. Changes in traffic patterns, local growth patterns, the age distribution of the vehicle stock, and congressionally mandated new-car standards make it unlikely that planners could establish stationary-source emission rights with finality.

Second, the initial plan for distributing emission rights might prove faulty, underconstraining certain pollutants. An adjustment in the zero-priced emission rights might be required to maintain satisfactory air quality. Moreover, trading in pollutants that create distinct local air quality problems from plumes that do not disperse rapidly might have to be constrained. A system of offset trading rather than emission trading might be required to maintain air quality at all receptor points.[2]

Finally, the air quality goals might change with time. New evidence on the health effects of selected pollutants might appear. The public might begin to place a higher value on visibility. Alternatively, local residents might find that the trade-off between air quality and industrial output in the region had generated too great a loss in private income.

A completely flexible policy of responding to these changes would amount to a retrogression toward the current system. If rights are to be bought and sold, some certainty must be attached to them. It would therefore seem desirable to accommodate unforeseen circumstances by selling additional emission rights or repurchasing them as required to meet an ambient air quality goal, but only at specified intervals of several years. Such purchases and sales by government would have the attractive feature of informing the public about the cost of maintaining clean air.

2. See the discussion in chapter 5. See also Alan Krupnick, Wallace Oates, and Eric Van De Verg, "On Marketable Air Pollution Permits: The Case for a System of Pollution Offsets," Economics Working Paper (University of Maryland, 1982).

At present, the costs of policy changes are borne by private firms as they adjust to the latest technology-based standards. With a rights repurchase the government would find itself using taxpayers' monies to purchase clean air. However, if the government chose to sell additional rights, it would give taxpayers potential relief from taxes or additional government services. In either case the trade-off between other goods or services and clean air would become much more visible.

Adjusting the Penalty Rate

A major criticism of pollution taxes has always been the uncertainty created by such taxes when they are established on the basis of imperfect information.[3] If tax authorities (or Congress) must adjust them periodically to reflect changed perceptions of costs or benefits, considerable uncertainty is created. This in turn generates political opposition to the entire pollution control program. Of course, changing standards from best available technology (BAT) to best conventional technology (BCT) or from best available control technology (BACT) to lowest achievable emission rate (LAER) undoubtedly has much the same effect.

An easy solution to the uncertainty problem for penalty rates is to set them at prohibitive levels. This would give firms strong inducement to remain within their zero-fee emission rights allocations, assuming that there is an enforcement program. On the other hand, it is unlikely that a high penalty fee would be politically feasible, and it might even be unconstitutional.

One of the attractive attributes of a penalty rate set reasonably close to the expected marginal benefits of emission reductions is that it could provide useful information. If firms regularly exceeded their zero-priced emission rights and paid the fee for these excess emissions, they would be signaling that their incremental control costs exceeded the penalty rate for emissions beyond the original allocation. This would generate pollution tax revenues from the second part of the tariff—the penalty rate—and probably create pressure for an increase in zero-priced emission rights. But if the price of emission rights fell substantially below the penalty rate, it would suggest that incremental control costs at the initial rights allocation were lower than environmental authorities had planned

---

3. See William Drayton, Jr., "Comment," in Ann F. Friedlaender, ed., *Approaches to Controlling Air Pollution* (MIT Press, 1978), pp. 199–219.

and that the penalty rate and emission allocations should be reduced. With a prohibitive penalty rate such signals would not be as clear.

With imperfect enforcement Congress or environmental authorities would have difficulty finding an optimal penalty rate. It is not inconceivable that changes in the rate would be accompanied by pleas for special exemptions for troubled industries, small businesses, or large campaign contributors. No one doubts that such influences affect the general tax code. They would inevitably affect the setting of pollution fees.

Barriers to the Two-Part Tariff

Were the current civil penalty system actually used, a version of a two-part tariff might be in place today. Unfortunately, the numerous barriers to trading the emission rights implicit in current standards and the complexity of the current penalty system have prevented this evolution. To change the current system so that it more closely resembles the proposed two-part tariff, a number of changes would have to be made.

—All engineering standards such as LAER, BACT, new-source performance standards (NSPS), and RACT would have to be abandoned.

—The assignment of standards (rights) would have to be made more certain and conferred for a reasonably long period.

—Specific rules on the generic and spatial dimensions of pollutant trades would have to be established within each AQCR.

—If governments intend to allow increases in emissions in various AQCRs over time, these intentions should be spelled out as soon as possible to allow traders in marketable rights some basis for planning.

—The existing civil penalty should be scrapped in favor of a penalty that does not differ among firms discharging the same pollutant in the same area.

—A point-source monitoring system, probably using random audit procedures, would have to be established.

None of these changes would be easy to legislate in view of the emotional and ideological traditions embodied in the current policy. Technology forcing, the notion that controls reflect the industry's ability to pay, and concepts of managed growth would have to be abandoned. Finally, improving the monitoring capability of the states and the EPA has the political ring of a more intrusive government, even though the underlying goal of moving to tradable rights is evidence of the desire for a less intrusive policy.

Alternative to the Two-Part Tariff

Given the enormous gaps in knowledge concerning the identity of polluters, the amount that they emit, the diffusion of pollutants in the atmosphere, and even the damage created by various pollutants, one can hardly talk of "optimal" air pollution control policies. The discussion in chapter 4 focused on the social costs of policy errors under alternative control regimes for good reason. The lesson from that exercise was that prices rather than regulatory standards should in most cases ration pollution. The proposed tariff uses a penalty to enforce emission rights, but its use as a rationing device is severely limited. Nevertheless, this may be as close to a pollution tax as it is possible to come.

There are other alternatives to the present cumbersome, inefficient policy. One could simply abandon the attempt to control ambient air quality and resort to uniform technology-based standards. Or one could simply develop tradable emission-*reduction* credits rather than emission rights. Finally, and least likely, it is possible to institute pollution taxes with offsets in other business taxes to ameliorate the enormous initial impact of such a program.

Uniform Technology Standards

A superficially equitable approach to environmental policy would be universal reliance on uniform control technology standards. Each industry or process could be assigned a specific best available control standard by EPA technocrats. These standards would not vary with the quality of local air or with local economic conditions. This is the direction taken in regulating water pollution since 1972. Standards are set for each industry under the best practical technology, BAT, or BCT.

Given the differences in control costs across plants in the same industry and differences in local environmental quality, the uniform technology approach can hardly be recommended as efficient. As the experience with the water program demonstrates, this approach is likely to generate a proliferation of standards as regulators respond to pleas that subindustries within each industry deserve their own standards.[4]

4. Robert A. Leone and John E. Jackson, "The Political Economy of Federal Regulatory Activity," Working Paper HBS 78-6 (Harvard University, Graduate School

As a result, initiation of the standards requires years of rule making. Changes in the regulations are likely to be difficult to obtain even though technology changes. With so many different standards, enforcement becomes much more difficult.

The considerable differences in air quality across the country make uniform technology-based standards seem extremely inefficient for reducing air pollution. Attempting to solve the problems of Los Angeles, Pittsburgh, and Boise with the same standards for utilities or for dry-cleaning plants would be obvious folly. Either Boise would pay for more pollution reduction than it could conceivably want, or much of the Los Angeles problem would remain. If progress is to be made against air pollution at a reasonable cost, the goal must be to reduce emissions in accordance with local ambient conditions, not according to engineering studies of the best technology.

Transferable Emission Reduction Assessments

David Foster of the EPA has suggested a market for transferable emission reduction assessments (TERA) that addresses both the efficiency and the apparent equity arguments.[5] Existing sources would have to reduce emissions of each criteria pollutant by a given percentage. They could do this by one of several methods: (1) direct reduction of emissions at their sources through various technological or fuel-switching practices; (2) purchase of reductions from other sources of the same pollutant in the same area; (3) purchase of pollution reduction through a broker; or (4) payment to local governments of a fee calculated to enable the government to purchase the reduction from some other source. The fee would be somewhat less than the noncompliance penalty because it would not contain a premium incorporating the expected value of nondetection of a violation. Foster's system negates the political opposition to offsets, which is based on the purported unavailability of offsets in many areas. The National Commission on Air Quality has endorsed this approach; its endorsement suggests that such economic incentives are gaining political appeal.[6]

---

of Business Administration, March 13, 1978); and Forest Arnold and others, "Federal Regulation: A Statistical Analysis," Discussion Paper D-94 (Resources for the Future, June 1982).

5. David Foster, "Transferable Emission Reduction Assessments (TERA)," report prepared for the U.S. Environmental Protection Agency (March 30, 1979).

6. National Commission on Air Quality, *To Breathe Clean Air* (Government Printing Office, 1981).

The TERA proposal does not address the problem of enforcement. It simply provides an alternative mechanism for reducing emissions over time through tradable permits. Without a satisfactory penalty system, the problem of noncompliance that bedevils the current approach would remain. Foster's fee in lieu of an offset is analogous to the penalty rate for the second part of the two-part tariff. If no other enforcement incentives exist, however, this lower penalty is unlikely to be a rationing device as firms find that not reducing emissions and incurring a less than certain imposition of the fee are less expensive than purchasing offsets.

The Pollution Tax

Without some method for adjusting the enormous initial impacts of the imposition of a straightforward one-part pollution tax, such an idea has no possibility of acceptance in the political marketplace.

The major practical problem with emission taxes is the unequal distribution of the burden across firms and industries. Table 10-1 provides EPA estimates of the share of the two major stationary-source emissions—total suspended particulates and sulfur dioxide—accounted for by seven major industries. These data include emissions from combustion in electrical utilities and from industrial processes in the manufacturing industries. The seven account for less than 25 percent of all industrial production but generate an estimated 83 percent of sulfur dioxide and 27 percent of particulate emissions. If an emission tax as low as $0.50 per kilogram for particulates and $0.60 per kilogram for sulfur dioxide were imposed, the annual tax collection from these industries alone at their 1980 emission rates would be $12.8 billion a year. The tax rates could be much higher if the new-source standards for steel mills and electric utilities were the guiding values in selecting the stringency of abatement. The tax on sulfur dioxide could be as high as $1.09 per kilogram and on particulates as high as $5.93 per kilogram (in 1979 dollars). These rates would increase interest in abatement since the prospective tax payments from these industries alone would be more than $30 billion. Even after applying stricter abatement practices, however, these firms would undoubtedly face enormous annual emission taxes.

If emission taxes are to have any chance of political acceptance, a two-part tariff must be imposed on existing polluters. The complete reversal of rights implicit in a single-rate tax scheme would be too disruptive for the major polluting industries and would certainly be

Table 10-1. *Emissions of Sulfur Dioxide and Particulates from Seven Industries, 1980*
Billions of grams per year

Industry	Sulfur dioxide	Particulates
Electric utilities	15,920	840
Iron and steel	190	390
Petroleum refining	690	50
Nonferrous metals	1,840	130
Cement	590	490
Pulp and paper	70	80
Chemicals	260	150
Total, 7 industries	19,560	2,130
Total, all sources	23,700	7,800
Share of these 7 industries in total (percent)	83	27

Source: Environmental Protection Agency, *National Air Pollutant Emission Estimates, 1940–1980* (EPA, 1982).

opposed with considerable vigor. The present standard-setting process at least gives the major polluters a quantum of pollution rights at no cost and allows them to argue for more. The obvious alternative is to grandfather a certain level of pollution rights at a zero tax and to charge the efficient tax for the remaining emissions.

Conclusions

In this book I have reviewed in some detail the extremely complex federal policy of controlling air pollution from stationary sources. Evidence on the effectiveness and efficiency of this policy is sketchy at best, but it is sufficient to create concern about the adequacy of current policy. Fortunately, the difficulties in administering the complex provisions of the Clean Air Act have prodded the EPA in the right direction. Continued progress, however, requires some changes that cannot be accomplished without new legislation. Given the political determinants of clean air policy, such changes will not be easy to legislate.

Below are summarized the most important conclusions of this study.
—Current policies for abating most air pollutants cannot be proved to have worked well because of inadequate monitoring data.
—Enforcement of air pollution standards is extremely poor because of inadequate monitoring facilities and a poorly designed civil penalty system.

—Virtually all studies of the cost of complying with current emission standards conclude that the current strategy for controlling air pollution is far more costly than necessary. The potential saving could easily amount to 30 percent of current control costs.

—The bias against new sources is quite pervasive, deriving from the design of new-source standards and lax enforcement against existing sources of the same pollutants.

—The use of pollution taxes rather than standards would improve the efficiency of air pollution policy. While transferable rights are better than mandatory standards, they are inferior to pollution taxes for most pollution problems.

—The EPA has moved steadily toward a system of transferable pollution rights (or emission-reduction credits) through its offset and bubble policies, but a system of fully marketable pollution rights is still far from being implemented. Nevertheless, the beginning of such a system is in place, and it should have salutary effects on the efficiency of air pollution control.

—The delayed-compliance penalty is unworkable and does not contribute to the efficiency of air pollution policy.

—Political forces from the northern industrial areas of the country have affected the design of environmental policies in general and air pollution policies in particular that are biased against new growth.

—The current approach to setting the primary ambient air standards is unworkable because the protection of human health with an adequate or ample margin of safety is impossible without clear thresholds in the dose-response relationship for the criteria pollutants.

If progress toward a rational system of controlling emissions from industrial and utility sources is to continue, a number of changes, such as the following, should be made in the Clean Air Act.

—All new-source performance standards should be abolished. New sources should be treated no differently from existing sources. They should be required to buy pollution rights (offsets or transferable emission credits) for any emissions that they generate, but their emission levels should not be prescribed by government.

—The delayed-compliance penalty should be modified by setting it at a fixed rate per excess unit of emission for each criteria pollutant. Ideally the penalty should vary across air quality control regions, but this complexity may be difficult to introduce.

—The prevention of significant deterioration (PSD) policy should be altered to allow industry to migrate to the growing sections of the country, particularly if these areas have cleaner and more healthful air than the declining northern and northeastern states.

—Tradable emission rights should be conferred with some degree of permanence to allow rational investment planning. Variations in the total permitted level of emissions can be accomplished through appropriate structuring of these rights or through government purchase and sale of the rights.

—A major improvement in monitoring techniques is required, particularly in random monitoring procedures for policing individual polluters. A large increase in resources for monitoring ambient air quality and individual point sources is urgently needed.

—The criteria for setting primary ambient standards should be changed to allow the comparison of compliance costs and welfare benefits at the margin. The EPA should be instructed to pursue control of the most harmful emissions before expending its bureaucratic resources on less urgent problems.

Changing the criteria for setting ambient standards is likely to generate heated, emotional opposition. It should certainly be given a lower priority than improving emissions and air quality monitoring, abolishing new-source performance standards, severely curtailing the scope of PSD policy, and reforming the delayed-compliance penalty. None of these changes will be accomplished easily. In the interim the EPA should move aggressively to implement its tradable rights policies to the maximum extent permitted by the Clean Air Act.

Derivation of EPA Formulas
for Calculating Delayed-Compliance Penalties

These are the calculations required by the Environmental Protection Agency to determine delayed-compliance fees. The definitions of the variables follow.[1]

Pollution Control Cash Flows

To compute the savings from delaying pollution control investment requires that the cash flows be estimated over a thirty-year fixed time horizon. The simplest approach is to calculate the present value of cash flows in the initial cycle of N months and use that value as a basis for all other replacement cycles. The derivation described below uses such an approach.

Initial Cycle of Equipment

The first category is the cash flow resulting from the initial investment of equity:

(1) $$EI = II^*Q.$$

From this amount must be subtracted the effect of the investment tax credit whose cash flow is

(2) $$ITC = II^*t_{ITC}.$$

The initial cash flow at the beginning of the cycle is found by subtracting equation 2 from equation 1:

(3) $$INITIAL_0 = EI - ITC$$
$$= II^*Q - II^*t_{ITC}$$
$$= II^*(Q - t_{ITC}).$$

---

1. This appendix is condensed from *Federal Register,* vol. 45 (July 28, 1980), pp. 50141–55. All variables followed by an asterisk are expressed as decimal fractions in the formulas for use in the model. Definitions of the variables are given at the end of this appendix.

171

The second category of cash flow is the capital-related flow that occurs over the depreciable life of the equipment. It is made up of depreciation and the flows associated with financing the equipment. The effect of depreciation is to reduce the firm's tax liability. The depreciation cash flow in month m is

(4) $$DEP_m = II^* d_m^* t_{TR}.$$

As the equipment is depreciated, the book value of the equipment declines. The book value of the equipment at the beginning of month m is

(5) $$(BOOK\ VALUE)_m = II^* \left(1 - \sum_{k=0}^{m-1} d_k \right).$$

The remainder of the annual capital-related cash flow consists of principal repayments and financing charges (interest and dividends) on the debt and preferred stock issued to finance the equipment purchase. The amount of the initial investment financed by debt is

(6) $$DEBT\ SHARE = II^* B.$$

Debt is repaid monthly in proportion to the depreciation of the asset—at the end of each month the fraction of the principal repaid is the same as the depreciation of the original book value of the investment:

(7) $$PRIN_m = d_m^* II^* B.$$

Interest is paid at the end of each month on the principal outstanding at the beginning of month m:

(8) $$(INTEREST\ CHARGE)_m = R_{INT}^* (PRINCIPAL\ OUTSTANDING)_m.$$

Since interest is tax deductible, only the after-tax effects should be considered in calculating the cash flow. The interest payment net cash flow in month m thus becomes

(9) $$INT_m = R_{INT}^* (PRINCIPAL\ OUTSTANDING)_m^* (1 - t_{TR}).$$

The principal outstanding is the original amount borrowed, $II^* B$, less the amount repaid before the beginning of the month:

(10) $$(AMOUNT\ REPAID)_m = \sum_{k=0}^{m-1} II^* d_k^* B.$$

The principal outstanding at the beginning of month m is the amount initially borrowed less the amount repaid by the end of month $m - 1$:

$$(11) \quad (PRINCIPAL\ OUTSTANDING)_m = II^*B - \sum_{k=0}^{m-1} II^*d_k^*B.$$

Combining equations 9 and 11 yields the formula for the interest-related cash flow in month m:

$$(12) \quad INT_m = R_{INT}^* II^*B^*(1 - t_{TR})^* \left(1 - \sum_{k=0}^{m-1} d_k\right).$$

The portion of the investment financed by preferred stock is

$$(13) \quad PREFERRED\ SHARE = II^*F.$$

The preferred stock too is redeemed as the asset is depreciated. At the end of each month, the fraction of the preferred stock redeemed is the same as the depreciation of the original book value of the investment. Redemption in month m is

$$(14) \quad PREF_m = d_m^* II^*F.$$

Dividends on preferred stock are paid at the end of each month on the amount of stock outstanding at the beginning of the month:

$$(15) \quad DIV_m = R_{DIV}^*(PREFERRED\ OUTSTANDING)_m.$$

These dividends are not tax deductible. The preferred outstanding is the original amount issued, II^*F, less the amount redeemed before the beginning of the month. The latter is

$$(16) \quad (AMOUNT\ REDEEMED)_m = \sum_{k=0}^{m-1} II^*d_k^*F.$$

The amount of preferred outstanding at the beginning of month m is equal to the amount originally issued less the amount redeemed:

$$(17) \quad (PREFERRED\ OUTSTANDING)_m = II^*F - \sum_{k=0}^{m-1} II^*d_k^*F.$$

The preferred dividend paid at the end of month m is found by combining equations 15 and 17:

$$(18) \quad DIV_m = R_{DIV}^* II^*F^* \left(1 - \sum_{k=0}^{m-1} d_k\right).$$

The total monthly capital-related charges for each month m of the initial cycle are

(19) $MONTHLY\ CAPITAL\ RELATED_m$
$$= -DEP_m + PRIN_m + INT_m + PREF_m + DIV_m.$$

The final category of cash flow is that associated with monthly operating and maintenance expenditures, which grow each month at the monthly inflation rate. The resulting cash flow is

(20) $O\&M_1 = M_0^*(1 - t_{TR})^*(1 + i);$
$$O\&M_2 = O\&M_1^*(1 + i) = M_0^*(1 - t_{TR})^*(1 + i)^2;$$
$$O\&M_3 = O\&M_2^*(1 + i) = M_0^*(1 - t_{TR})^*(1 + i)^3.$$

In general, the monthly $O\&M$ expense in month m is

(21) $O\&M_m = M_0^*(1 - t_{TR})^*(1 + i)^m.$

Future Cycles of Equipment

These calculations must be expanded to include the value of any future replacement cycles that might occur in the thirty-year time horizon. This can be accomplished by recognizing that the costs incurred in any given future cycle are identical to those incurred in the corresponding year of the original cycle except that the costs have increased by the inflation rate. For example, the replacement of equipment after N months gives rise to an initial equity investment equal to

(22) $INITIAL_N = INITIAL_0^*(1 + i)^N.$

In general, the initial equity investment at the end of month m will be equal to the investment made N months ago inflated at a monthly inflation rate, i. The initial capital expense at the end of month m is therefore equal to

(22a) $INITIAL_m = INITIAL_{m-N}^*(1 + i)^N.$

This can also be generalized as

(22b) $INITIAL_{(j-1)N} = INITIAL_0^*(1 + i)^{(j-1)N}$

for the jth cycle.

Similarly, the capital-related charges in month m will be

(23) $MONTHLY\ CAPITAL\ RELATED_m$
$$= MONTHLY\ CAPITAL\ RELATED_{m-N}^*(1 + i)^N.$$

Finally, the $O\&M$ expense in month m will be

$$(24) \qquad O\&M_m = O\&M^*_{m-N}(1 + i)^N.$$

The cash flow for each month m is the sum of these three values:

$$(25) \quad MCF_m = INITIAL_m$$
$$+ MONTHLY\ CAPITAL\ RELATED_m + O\&M_m.$$

Salvage Value of Equipment at End of Time Horizon

At the end of the thirty-year time horizon the cash flows cease. However, the firm realizes tax benefits from the deduction of any remaining depreciation and must repay all outstanding debt and preferred stock. The salvage value of the equipment will be zero because it is assumed that technological or regulatory change will render the equipment obsolete at the end of the time horizon.

The additional depreciation cash flow in the final month is the tax shield from a write-off of the remaining book value of the equipment. The book value of the equipment at the beginning of each month m is

$$(26) \qquad (BOOK\ VALUE)_m = (BOOK\ VALUE)^*_{m-N}(1 + i)^N.$$

Therefore, the final tax write-off in month 360 is:

$$(27) \qquad DEP_{FINAL} = t^*_{TR}(BOOK\ VALUE)_{360} - DEP_{360}.$$

To estimate the debt principal outstanding at the end of month 360, the principal outstanding at the beginning of month m is estimated first:

$$(28) \quad (PRINCIPAL\ OUTSTANDING)_m$$
$$= (PRINCIPAL\ OUTSTANDING)^*_{m-N}(1 + i)^N.$$

The final principal outstanding at the end of month 360 will be the principal outstanding at the beginning of month 360 less the principal repaid during month 360:

$$(29) \quad PRIN_{FINAL} = (PRINCIPAL\ OUTSTANDING)_{360} - PRIN_{360}.$$

Finally, the outstanding preferred stock will be repaid at the end of month 360. The preferred stock outstanding at the beginning of month m is

$$(30) \quad (PREFERRED\ OUTSTANDING)_m$$
$$= (PREFERRED\ OUTSTANDING)^*_{m-N}(1 + i)^N.$$

The final preferred stock outstanding at the end of month 360 will be the preferred stock outstanding at the beginning of month 360 less the preferred stock repaid during month 360:

(31) $PREF_{FINAL} = (PREFERRED\ OUTSTANDING)_{360} - PREF_{360}.$

The sum of these final cash flows at the end of the thirty-year time horizon is

(32) $CF_{FINAL} = -DEP_{FINAL} + PRIN_{FINAL} + PREF_{FINAL}.$

Discounting the Cash Flows

The present value of the cash flows in each month will be

(33) $$PV_{MCF_m} = \frac{MCF_m}{(1 + e)^m}.$$

The sum of the present value of the cash flows for each month plus the final cash flow incurred at the end of the time horizon represents the cost to the firm of on-time compliance:

(34) $$PV_{PCE} = \sum_{m=0}^{360} PV_{MCF_m} + \frac{CF_{FINAL}}{(1 + e)^{360}}$$

$$= \sum_{m=0}^{360} \frac{MCF_m}{(1 + e)^m} + \frac{CF_{FINAL}}{(1 + e)^{360}}.$$

The Value of Delay

The quantity just calculated is the present value, as of the day on which compliance should have been achieved, of the firm's pollution control cash flows if it had not delayed. If compliance is delayed, the cash flows each month will be delayed and inflation will increase the magnitude of these cash flows. The cash flows incurred each month m over the thirty-year horizon if the firm delays L months will be

(35) $MCF'_m = MCF'^*_{m-L}(1 + i)^L \quad \text{for } m > L.$

As in the on-time compliance calculation, any remaining book value may be written off in the final month of the horizon. The outstanding debt and preferred stock must also be repaid. This final cash flow is

$$(36) \quad CF'_{FINAL} = [-t^*_{TR}(BOOK\ VALUE)_{360-L} + DEP_{360-L}$$
$$+ (PRINCIPAL\ OUTSTANDING)_{360-L} - PRIN_{360-L}$$
$$+ (PREFERRED\ OUTSTANDING)_{360-L}$$
$$- PREF_{360-L}]^*(1 + i)^L.$$

The present value of delay alternative is the sum of each of the cash flows in equations 35 and 36 discounted by the rate of return on equity:

$$(37) \quad PV_{DELAY} = \sum_{m=0}^{360} \frac{MCF'_m}{(1 + e)^m} + \frac{CF'_{FINAL}}{(1 + e)^{360}}$$

$$= \sum_{m=0}^{360} \frac{MCF_{m-L}(1 + i)^L}{(1 + e)^m} + \frac{CF'_{FINAL}}{(1 + e)^{360}}.$$

The savings from delay is thus given by the difference between the present values of on-time compliance and delayed compliance:

$$(38) \quad SAVINGS = PV_{PCE} - PV_{DELAY}.$$

The savings from delay has two components. The first is the value of forgone $O\&M$ expenditures:

$$(39) \quad SAVINGS_{O\&M} = \sum_{m=1}^{L} \frac{O\&M_m}{(1 + e)^m}.$$

The second component is the value of delaying all capital-related cash flows. The capital component of the savings is the remainder of savings:

$$(40) \quad SAVINGS_{CAP} = SAVINGS - SAVINGS_{O\&M}.$$

Conversion of Savings into Monthly Equivalents

To convert the savings from noncompliance into a series of penalty payments, it is necessary to express savings as a series of equivalent monthly amounts. Let S_j be the savings equivalent at the beginning of month j. The requirement that the series escalate with inflation implies that

$$(41) \quad \begin{aligned} S_2 &= S^*_1(1 + i); \\ S_3 &= S^*_2(1 + i) = S^*_1(1 + i)^2; \\ S_j &= S^*_{j-1}(1 + i) = S^*_1(1 + i)^{j-1}. \end{aligned}$$

The present value of each of these terms is calculated by discounting:

(42) $$PV_{S_j} = \frac{S_j}{(1 + e)^{j-1}}.$$

Combining with equation 41 yields

(43) $$PV_{S_j} = \frac{S_1^*(1 + i)^{j-1}}{(1 + e)^{j-1}}.$$

The present value of L monthly savings equivalents must be equal to the savings from delay. Thus,

(44) $$SAVINGS = \sum_{j=1}^{L} PV_{S_j} = \sum_{j=1}^{L} S_1^* \left(\frac{1 + i}{1 + e}\right)^{j-1}$$

or

$$S_1 = \frac{SAVINGS}{\displaystyle\sum_{j=1}^{L} \left(\frac{1 + i}{1 + e}\right)^{j-1}}.$$

This represents the first term in the series. All terms after the first month can be computed by multiplying S_1 by the quantity $(1 + i)$ raised to the appropriate power. For example, the savings equivalent at the beginning of month k would be

(45) $$S_k = S_1^*(1 + i)^{k-1}.$$

The present value of these monthly savings equivalents is equal to the present value of the costs avoided during the period of noncompliance.

Effect of Precompliance Expenditures

The series of savings equivalents just developed is based on the assumption that the firm installing pollution control equipment will pay for it when installation is completed and operation begins. In reality, substantial precompliance expenditures will often be required before final installation is completed. In calling for the imposition of a non-compliance penalty, Congress explicitly required that these precompliance expenditures be accounted for in the penalty calculation. The adjustments needed to incorporate the effect of precompliance expenditures are described below. The procedure is begun by dividing the savings equivalent into its capital and its operating and maintenance components. The adjustment of the capital component of the penalty is described, followed by a description of the procedure for adjusting the operations and maintenance component of the penalty.

Adjustment of Capital Components

The method used to account for precompliance capital expenditures is to adjust the capital component of a month's savings equivalent by multiplying it by a factor representing the proportion of the capital investment still to be made before the beginning of that month. The computational procedure starts by rewriting formula 44 using formulas 39 and 40:

$$(46) \qquad S_1 = S_1^C + S_1^M.$$

The superscript C refers to the capital component of the savings equivalent and M refers to the operating and maintenance component. Equation 45 for the capital component can then be rewritten as

$$(47) \qquad S_k^C = S_1^{C*}(1 + i)^{k-1}.$$

If X_k^C is the fraction of the initial investment made before the beginning of month k, then

$$(48) \qquad A_k^C = (1 - X_k^C)^* S_k^C.$$

Adjustment of Operation and Maintenance Component

The operating and maintenance component of the savings must be adjusted to a value that is net of any actual $O\&M$ expenditures made during the period of noncompliance. The adjustment of the operating and maintenance component, A^M, is equal to the present value of the operating and maintenance component of $SAVINGS_{O\&M}$ less the present value of any precompliance $O\&M$ expenditures made during the period of noncompliance. Thus,

$$(49) \qquad A^M = SAVINGS_{O\&M} - \sum_{k=1}^{L} \frac{P_k^M}{(1 + e)^k}.$$

Calculation of Quarterly Penalties

The act requires that the noncompliance penalty payments be made quarterly and that all payments be of equal value. The EPA interprets this requirement to mean equality in real rather than nominal terms.

Consequently, the series of payments must increase with inflation. This can be done by converting the monthly values of the capital component of the savings computed above into their present value equivalent, adding the present value of the $O\&M$ component of the savings, and then converting that present value into a new series of escalating quarterly payments. Then the present value is

$$(50) \qquad PV_{ADJUSTED\ SERIES} = A^M + \sum_{k=1}^{L} \frac{A_k^C}{(1 + e)^{k-1}}.$$

The series of escalating payments must have this same present value. Thus, if P_q is the payment to be made at the beginning of quarter q, the following equality must exist:

$$(51) \quad A^M + \sum_{k=1}^{L} \frac{A_k^C}{(1 + e)^{k-1}} = P_1 + \frac{P_2}{(1 + e')} + \cdots + \frac{P_T}{(1 + e')^{T-1}}.$$

However, since $P_q = P_{q-1}^*(1 + i)$,

$$(52) \qquad A^M + \sum_{k=1}^{L} \frac{A_k^C}{(1 + e)^{k-1}} = P_1^* \sum_{q=1}^{T} \left(\frac{1 + i'}{1 + e'}\right)^{q-1}$$

or

$$P_1 = \frac{A^M + \sum_{k=1}^{L} \dfrac{A_k^C}{(1 + e)^{k-1}}}{\sum_{q=1}^{T} \left(\dfrac{1 + i'}{1 + e'}\right)^{q-1}}$$

and

$$(53) \qquad P_q = P_{q-1}^*(1 + i') = P_1^*(1 + i')^{q-1}.$$

Postcompliance Settlement

The original penalty computation is based on the firm's costs had compliance not been delayed. If compliance is delayed, inflation will result in the actual expenditures being somewhat larger. This inflation-induced variation is already accounted for in the formulation described above. However, simple estimation error may also contribute to the difference and it is this error that the postcompliance settlement is intended to remedy.

The settlement amount is the cumulative overpayment or underpayment at the end of the noncompliance period plus interest on each month's outstanding balance (the cumulative overpayment or underpayment at the end of each month). The formula for computing the settlement payment is as follows:

$$\Xi_1 = \Delta_1^* r$$

and

$$\Xi_2 = (\Delta_2 + \Xi_1)^* r.$$

In general,

(54) $$\Xi_k = (\Delta_k + \Xi_{k-1})^* r.$$

The total postcompliance settlement as of the date of compliance is

(55) $$\Xi = \Xi_L.$$

The total postcompliance settlement as of the day of compliance is then adjusted to reflect delay in the actual settlement payment. The final settlement amount is

(56) $$Z = \Xi^*(1 + r)^D.$$

Definition of Symbols

All variables denoted with an asterisk (*) are expressed as decimal fractions in the formulas for use in the model.

A_k^C	Monthly equivalent of capital component of savings adjusted for precompliance expenditures
A^M	O&M component of savings adjusted for precompliance expenditures
B	Fraction of debt in owner's capital structure (book value)*
CF_{FINAL}	Cash flow at end of thirty-year time horizon if compliance is not delayed
CF'_{FINAL}	Cash flow at end of thirty-year time horizon if compliance is delayed
D	Number of months between date of compliance and payment of postcompliance settlement

DEP_{FINAL}	Tax shield from write-off of remaining book value of equipment at end of thirty-year time horizon
DEP_m	Net after-tax cash flow in month m resulting from depreciation of initial investment
DEP_{360}	Depreciation claimed in month 360
DIV_m	Dividend payment in month m on preferred stock used to finance the initial investment
D_j	Fraction of original asset value depreciated in year $j*$
d_m	Fraction of original asset value depreciated in month $m*$
Δ_k	Difference between penalty paid in month k and amount computed based on revised figures for capital and $O\&M$ costs
E	Discount rate*
EI	Amount of cash provided by equity investors to finance initial investment
e	Monthly equivalent of discount rate $E*$
e'	Quarterly equivalent of discount rate $E*$
F	Fraction of preferred stock (at book value) in owner's capital structure*
I	Annual rate of inflation for pollution control expenditures*
II	Initial investment in pollution control equipment; amount that will be capitalized on firm's books and amortized over life of equipment
$INITIAL$	Initial equity investment at beginning of a replacement cycle
INT_m	Interest payment cash flow (after effect of taxes) in month m on debt used to finance initial investment
ITC	Dollar amount of investment tax credit
i	Monthly equivalent of annual inflation rate $I*$
i'	Quarterly equivalent of annual inflation rate $I*$
j, k, m	Indexes, usually indicating year or month in which a cash flow occurs
L	Number of months the firm is expected to be out of compliance
M_0	Monthly operating and maintenance expense in current dollars as of beginning of period of noncompliance
MCF_m	Cash flow in month m if compliance is not delayed

MCF'_m	Cash flow in month m if compliance is delayed
$MONTHLY$ $CAPITAL$ $RELATED_m$	Capital-related cash flows in month m
N	Useful life of pollution control equipment, in months
$O\&M_m$	Net operating and maintenance cash flow in month m
P_k^M	Precompliance operating and maintenance expenditure incurred in month k
P_q	Penalty payment to be made at beginning of quarter q
$PREF_{FINAL}$	Repayment of outstanding preferred stock at end of thirty-year time horizon
$PREF_m$	Prepayment of reallocation of preferred stock in month m
$PREF_{360}$	Preferred stock repaid in month 360
$PRIN_{FINAL}$	Repayment of outstanding debt at end of thirty-year time horizon
$PRIN_m$	Repayment of reallocation of debt in month m
PV	Present value of cash flow
PV_{DELAY}	Present value of costs of original and all future cycles of pollution control equipment if compliance is delayed, as of day compliance should have been achieved
PV_{MCF_m}	Present value of cash flow occurring in month m
PV_{PCE}	Present value of all cash flows resulting from purchase and operation of original and all future replacement cycles of pollution control equipment over thirty-year time horizon
Q	Fraction of common equity (at book value) in owner's capital structure*
q	Index indicating quarter in which penalty payment is made
R_{DIV}	Monthly dividend rate on preferred stock*
R_{INT}	Monthly rate of interest on long-term debt*
r	Monthly rate of interest to be paid on postcompliance settlement amounts*
$SAVINGS$	Savings from delaying compliance
$SAVINGS_{CAP}$	Savings from delaying capital-related cash flows
$SAVINGS_{O\&M}$	Savings from forgone $O\&M$ expenditures during period of delay
S_k^C	Monthly equivalent of capital component of savings

S_k	Monthly equivalent of savings
t_{ITC}	Adjusted investment tax credit rate*
t_{TR}	Marginal income tax rate*
Z	Actual settlement to be paid (or refunded) on day of settlement
Ξ_k	Cumulative overpayment or underpayment at end of month k, including interest

Votes on Bills Rated by the League of Conservation Voters to Derive Results in Table 7-3

Environmental Votes, House of Representatives

1975

H.R. 25	Surface Mining Control and Reclamation Act of 1975 (LCV 2)
H.R. 25	Surface Mining Control and Reclamation Act of 1975 (Spellman amendment) (LCV 3)
H.R. 5899	Supplemental Appropriations, Fiscal Year 1975 (LCV 4)
H.R. 25	Surface Mining Control and Reclamation Act of 1975 (override veto) (LCV 5)
H.R. 8122	Public Works Appropriations, Fiscal Year 1976 (LCV 9)
H.R. 8122	Public Works Appropriations (Steelman amendment) (LCV 10)
H.R. 8773	Interior Appropriations, Fiscal Year 1976 (LCV 11)
H.R. 8070	Housing, Space, and Veterans' Appropriations (LCV 14)
H.R. 8841	Pesticide Control Act Amendments (LCV 15)
H.R. 8631	Price-Anderson Act Amendments (LCV 17)

1976

H.R. 11455	Indiana Dunes National Lakeshore Amendments (LCV 1)
H.R. 22345	Land and Water Conservation Fund (LCV 3)
H.R. 9560	Water Pollution Control Act Amendments—Wetlands (LCV 6)
H.R. 14236	Public Works–ERDA Appropriations (LCV 8)
H.R. 13777	Public Land Policy—Mining Withdrawals (LCV 11)
H.R. 9719	National Park Taxes (LCV 14)
H.R. 13372	Amendments to the Wild and Scenic Rivers Act—New River (LCV 15)
H.R. 14230	Toxic Substances Control Act—Toxic Chemicals (LCV 17)
H.R. 10498	Clean Air Act Amendments—Nondegradation (LCV 18)
S. 2371	National Parks Mining (LCV 19)
S. 2371	Death Valley Mining (LCV 20)
H.R. 10498	Clean Air Act Amendments—Auto Emissions (LCV 21)

1977

H.R. 2	Strip Mining (Baucus amendment) (LCV 2)
H.R. 6161	Clean Air Act (Breaux-Emery amendment) (LCV 4)
H.R. 6161	Clean Air Act (Preyer substitute for Dingell amendment) (LCV 5)
H.R. 6161	Clean Air Act (Dingell amendment) (LCV 6)
H.R. 6970	Tuna/Porpoise Protection (LCV 7)
H.R. 6804	Federal Energy Department (LCV 8)
H.R. 7557	Noise/SST—Transportation Appropriations, Fiscal Year 1978 (LCV 9)
H.R. 8444	National Energy Policy (LCV 12)
S. 393	Montana Wilderness Study (LCV 19)

1978

H.R. 12936	Environmental Protection Agency Funding (Brown amendment) (LCV 11)
H. Con. Res. 559	Pollution and Health Regulations (LCV 12)
H.R. 12441	Toxic Substances Control Act (LCV 13)
H.R. 4544	Black Lung Benefits (LCV 14)
H.R. 12929	Occupational Safety and Health (LCV 15)
H.R. 39	Alaska Lands Act (Young amendment) (LCV 19)
H.R. 39	Alaska Lands Act (Meeds amendment) (LCV 20)
H.R. 3813	Redwood Park Extension Act (LCV 21)
H.R. 3813	Boundary Waters Canoe Area (LCV 22)
H.R. 3454	Endangered American Wilderness Act (LCV 23)
H.R. 14101	Endangered Species Act (LCV 27)
H.R. 12932	National Environmental Policy Act (LCV 28)
H.R. 12536	Delaware River National Parks Additions (LCV 29)

1979

H.R. 39	Alaska Lands Act (Udall-Anderson amendment) (LCV 1)
H.R. 4388	Endangered Species Act—Tellico Dam (LCV 3)
H.R. 3546	Pesticides (LCV 4)
H.R. 3546	Pesticides (congressional veto of EPA regulation) (LCV 5)
H.R. 4394	Groundwater Contamination and Acid Rain (LCV 6)
H.R. 3509	Safe Drinking Water Amendments (LCV 8)
H.R. 4985	Energy Mobilization Board (allowing EMB to waive environmental regulations) (LCV 12)

H.R. 4985   Energy Mobilization Board (Eckhardt amendment) (LCV 13)

1980

S. 1308   Energy Mobilization Board (LCV 4)
H.R. 7631   National Commission on Air Quality (LCV 9)
H.R. 7020   Cleaning Up Toxic Chemicals (LCV 10)
S. 2009   Idaho Wilderness (LCV 13)
S. 2009   Idaho Wilderness (final version) (LCV 14)
H.R. 7380   Big Sur Coast Area Act (LCV 15)
H.R. 2609   Colorado River Desalting Plant (LCV 21)

Environmental Votes, Senate

1975–76

S. 7   Surface Mining Control and Reclamation Act of 1975—Strip Mining (LCV 1)
S. 7   Surface Mining Control and Reclamation Act of 1975—Strip Mining (McClure amendment) (LCV 2)
S. 7   Surface Mining Control and Reclamation Act of 1975—Strip Mining (Mathias amendment) (LCV 3)
H.R. 9852   Flood Plain Development (LCV 14)
S. 961   200-Mile Fishery Zone Limit Act (LCV 15)
S. 2371   Mining in National Park System Act (LCV 16)
S. 3015   Airport and Airway Development Act—Concorde (SST) Landings (LCV 17)
S. 3149   Toxic Substances Control Act (LCV 18)
. . .   Public Works Authorizations for Jobs—Sewage Treatment Funds (Muskie amendment) (LCV 19)
S. 2555   Rangelands Improvement Act (LCV 20)
S. 2150   Solid Waste Disposal Authorization (LCV 23)
S. 3219   Clean Air Act Amendments (LCV 24)
S. 3219   Clean Air Act Amendments (Moss amendment) (LCV 25)
S. 3219   Clean Air Act Amendments (Hart amendment) (LCV 26)
S. 3219   Clean Air Act Amendments—Aerosol Sprays (LCV 27)
S. 3091   National Forests Management Act (LCV 29)
H.R. 13372   Wild and Scenic River Act Amendments (LCV 30)
S. 2710   Federal Water Pollution Control Act Amendments of 1976—Wetlands Protection (LCV 31)

1977–78

S. 252	Clean Air Act Amendments (Griffin amendment) (LCV 1)
S. 252	Clean Air Act Amendments (Baker substitute for Riegle-Griffin amendment) (LCV 2)
S. 252	Clean Air Act Amendments (Stevens amendment) (LCV 3)
S. 1952	Water Pollution Control Act Amendments (Nelson amendment) (LCV 4)
S. 1952	Water Pollution Control Act Amendments—Clean Water Enforcement (LCV 5)
S. 1952	Clean Water Act of 1977 (Bentsen amendment) (LCV 9)
H.R. 12932	National Environmental Policy Act Exemption (LCV 11)
S. 1976	Redwood Park Extension (Hayakawa amendment) (LCV 13)
S. 2899	Endangered Species Act (Stennis amendment) (LCV 14)
S. 2899	Endangered Species Act (LCV 15)
S. 7	Surface Mining Control and Reclamation Act of 1977 (LCV 22)
S. 7	Surface Mining Control and Reclamation Act of 1977 (Johnston amendment) (LCV 23)
S. 7	Surface Mining Control and Reclamation Act of 1977 (Bumpers amendment) (LCV 24)
S. 7	Surface Mining Control and Reclamation Act of 1977 (Danforth amendment) (LCV 25)
S. 717	Mine Safety (Schmitt amendment) (LCV 26)
S. 717	Mine Safety (McClure amendment) (LCV 27)
S. 9	Outer Continental Shelf Lands Act—Offshore Oil Drilling (LCV 29)
S. 9	Outer Continental Shelf Lands Act—Offshore Oil Drilling (Bartlett amendment) (LCV 28)
H.R. 5263	Energy Policy Act—Oil Shale (LCV 30)

1979–80

H.R. 39	Alaska Lands Act (Jackson amendment to table Hart-Chafee amendment) (LCV 1)
H.R. 39	Alaska Lands Act (Jackson-Hatfield substitute for Hart-Chafee amendment) (LCV 2)
H.R. 39	Alaska Lands Act (Byrd cloture amendment) (LCV 3)
H.R. 39	Alaska Lands Act (Melcher amendment) (LCV 4)
S. 2009	River of No Return—Salmon River in Idaho (LCV 5)
S. 14	Acre Limitations Increased from 1902 Reclamation Act (LCV 12)
S. 2470	Coal Conversion Bill—Clean Air (LCV 13)
S. 1477	Pollution Regulations (Culver motion to kill Bumpers amendment) (LCV 14)
S. Con. Res. 86	Pollution Control Regulations (Chiles amendment) (LCV 15)

H.R. 3904	Workplace Environment OSHA (Boren amendment) (LCV 16)
S. 1403	Surface Mining Amendments of 1979 (LCV 23)
S. 1403	Surface Mining Amendments of 1979 (identical Byrd bill submitted one year later) (LCV 24)
H.R. 1197	Surface Mining Amendments of 1979 (Bumpers amendment) (LCV 25)

Table B-1. *Senate Votes Rated by the League of Conservation Voters, 1975–80*[a]

Percent

State	All votes			Purely environmental votes		
	1975–76	*1977–78*	*1979–80*	*1975–76*	*1977–78*	*1979–80*
Alabama	19	24	20	22	33	23
	32	40	31	39	40	57
Alaska	41	43	28	33	62	20
	22	15	5	38	15	-1
Arizona	6	8	5	12	2	21
	0	43	34	4	56	39
Arkansas	54	79	58	71	85	82
	22	88	33	36	100	46
California	84	85	78	92	95	83
	74	12	33	75	15	23
Colorado	72	93	73	73	95	82
	71	69	27	71	85	-2
Connecticut	81	78	74	87	85	96
	65	72	87	80	67	89
Delaware	84	44	65	89	45	57
	52	92	71	64	98	91
Florida	49	51	33	50	73	49
	39	39	65	44	72	69
Georgia	29	30	10	33	38	26
	26	36	40	39	42	54
Hawaii	18	54	33	46	79	60
	49	67	51	25	80	57
Idaho	64	64	45	71	73	83
	3	16	6	6	20	-1
Illinois	49	62	77	58	73	31
	56	81	66	57	87	98
Indiana	60	75	63	72	83	67
	31	24	30	35	20	23
Iowa	89	96	85	93	91	96
	85	94	41	89	94	36

(Continued)

Table B-1 *(continued)*

Percent

State	All votes			Purely environmental votes		
	1975–76	1977–78	1979–80	1975–76	1977–78	1979–80
Kansas	11	20	49	23	26	46
	32	36	48	44	46	41
Kentucky	32	41	19	44	38	44
	36	30	33	40	46	49
Louisiana	22	12	7	34	40	16
	25	26	13	24	15	16
Maine	65	76	82	76	94	77
	67	81	69	62	84	100
Maryland	32	68	62	50	70	66
	76	86	85	88	95	99
Massachusetts	84	96	77	93	99	41
	87	89	82	94	98	97
Michigan	7	71	96	17	76	100
	85	19	80	69	22	92
Minnesota	66	80	67	79	94	62
	76	80	75	86	99	85
Mississippi	18	23	0	37	37	−6
	5	23	19	10	37	16
Missouri	33	62	46	48	73	57
	19	32	48	27	37	46
Montana	77	51	44	90	98	53
	74	96	78	76	67	100
Nebraska	3	51	33	4	60	54
	0	7	33	−3	0	54
Nevada	26	36	23	23	48	23
	0	16	16	3	15	−1
New Hampshire	83	78	72	92	88	83
	61	86	27	70	90	8
New Jersey	86	72	82	98	90	92
	81	79	75	86	90	99
New Mexico	11	26	23	17	27	32
	30	18	27	41	20	−2
New York	39	76	65	53	83	85
	74	65	71	93	73	92
North Carolina	10	18	23	6	10	0
	22	41	8	29	22	16
North Dakota	50	11	0	56	15	−2
	10	45	33	11	50	39
Ohio	43	76	53	52	80	77
	26	78	71	30	85	92
Oklahoma	2	16	1	−1	0	6
	19	0	6	28	9	15
Oregon	51	61	43	61	73	27
	65	41	75	78	52	62

Table B-1 (*continued*)

Percent

State	All votes			Purely environmental votes		
	1975–76	1977–78	1979–80	1975–76	1977–78	1979–80
Pennsylvania	74	35	44	86	83	44
	40	66	67	44	50	49
Rhode Island	65	90	65	81	95	71
	74	62	87	83	62	77
South Carolina	42	11	27	40	15	32
	6	57	44	11	65	71
South Dakota	90	83	65	90	85	51
	76	79	65	80	87	72
Tennessee	26	32	25	40	54	7
	9	47	23	11	67	46
Texas	18	0	11	29	0	−3
	4	41	31	−1	50	57
Utah	3	11	13	4	15	0
	40	7	17	37	10	0
Vermont	79	74	71	86	98	77
	59	94	90	72	87	87
Virginia	39	35	16	39	30	−1
	6	1	27	10	9	31
Washington	53	65	47	67	85	85
	49	71	33	64	80	62
West Virginia	39	56	23	44	65	39
	39	51	49	44	65	58
Wisconsin	87	91	93	83	95	100
	87	84	87	83	95	100
Wyoming	7	21	28	6	20	31
	28	18	45	29	25	34

Source: League of Conservation Voters, *How Congress Voted on Critical Environmental Issues* (Washington, D.C.: LCV), annual editions. Figures are rounded.
a. Ratings are for each senator from each state.

Table B-2. *League of Conservation Voters Average Rating of Votes, by State, in House of Representatives, 1975–80*

Percent

State	1975	1976	1977	1978	1979	1980
Alabama	22	24	20	28	21	24
Alaska	21	0	0	8	16	6
Arizona	23	26	29	22	25	25
Arkansas	20	31	30	27	31	23
California	56	60	53	50	53	51
Colorado	56	57	48	52	47	53
Connecticut	63	63	60	60	72	63
Delaware	77	36	59	47	50	65
Florida	47	43	45	42	39	36
Georgia	26	18	31	39	30	42
Hawaii	67	57	53	52	50	42
Idaho	23	1	7	16	9	6
Illinois	43	48	43	49	41	45
Indiana	63	62	56	55	50	48
Iowa	65	70	56	65	53	64
Kansas	38	31	38	46	19	40
Kentucky	39	45	30	40	25	32
Louisiana	28	16	18	16	19	30
Maine	72	70	63	75	54	67
Maryland	64	68	66	66	61	64
Massachusetts	79	80	82	82	82	81
Michigan	60	54	60	63	60	61
Minnesota	59	62	49	48	53	58
Mississippi	15	13	5	13	15	17
Missouri	42	44	40	42	41	41
Montana	75	62	55	47	51	56
Nebraska	39	26	39	47	47	50
Nevada	54	24	35	23	28	50
New Hampshire	50	63	43	54	44	47
New Jersey	72	74	70	72	69	72
New Mexico	11	14	9	8	10	32
New York	69	69	67	65	68	60
North Carolina	37	29	36	41	30	43
North Dakota	22	21	20	24	14	27
Ohio	45	49	44	44	45	45
Oklahoma	8	21	14	13	31	30
Oregon	62	61	58	64	57	63
Pennsylvania	51	49	50	55	48	52
Rhode Island	77	55	73	59	70	63
South Carolina	34	36	40	48	35	37
South Dakota	43	28	9	28	46	52
Tennessee	37	29	35	41	30	35
Texas	27	26	25	28	29	26
Utah	36	32	26	10	14	29
Vermont	91	70	85	84	89	91
Virginia	30	26	31	31	25	28
Washington	50	66	43	50	54	59
West Virginia	51	51	40	60	42	35
Wisconsin	75	75	67	72	67	63
Wyoming	67	64	41	42	28	12

Source: Same as table B-1. Figures are rounded.

Table B-3. *League of Conservation Voters Average Rating of Votes on Purely Environmental Issues, by State, in House of Representatives, 1975–80*

Percent

State	1975	1976	1977	1978	1979	1980
Alabama	11	34	28	37	24	35
Alaska	10	9	0	0	17	19
Arizona	28	43	29	19	28	26
Arkansas	18	44	35	33	47	37
California	57	57	56	59	59	65
Colorado	57	58	46	60	63	64
Connecticut	59	73	60	72	77	75
Delaware	78	52	61	54	88	57
Florida	39	54	27	52	46	53
Georgia	25	24	37	44	40	40
Hawaii	49	61	48	71	55	64
Idaho	27	9	6	6	10	−2
Illinois	41	24	45	56	42	54
Indiana	59	70	57	61	51	54
Iowa	67	70	56	76	66	66
Kansas	33	37	41	52	12	37
Kentucky	27	49	31	50	20	47
Louisiana	26	22	28	24	16	44
Maine	80	83	42	65	60	69
Maryland	57	72	65	72	61	79
Massachusetts	75	89	87	91	89	90
Michigan	68	61	59	71	56	70
Minnesota	59	73	48	54	53	61
Mississippi	17	15	5	11	10	15
Missouri	31	47	46	47	40	53
Montana	71	67	55	47	54	57
Nebraska	40	51	44	51	60	66
Nevada	55	48	38	14	20	49
New Hampshire	50	75	19	44	52	57
New Jersey	68	82	80	87	75	81
New Mexico	10	13	21	23	19	36
New York	63	75	71	76	68	69
North Carolina	25	40	31	50	36	57
North Dakota	10	33	25	15	20	66
Ohio	42	29	47	58	50	49
Oklahoma	12	21	19	20	28	32
Oregon	55	56	56	69	60	76
Pennsylvania	48	63	53	67	44	57
Rhode Island	63	69	62	84	80	88
South Carolina	22	39	34	51	34	53
South Dakota	36	39	2	29	52	58
Tennessee	27	28	42	43	43	43
Texas	35	36	30	39	26	34
Utah	42	49	19	19	11	35
Vermont	88	83	79	85	100	99
Virginia	29	26	32	33	27	29
Washington	46	77	33	58	67	79
West Virginia	43	60	47	81	31	59
Wisconsin	76	83	69	87	78	67
Wyoming	60	64	46	78	50	−1

Source: Same as table B-1. Figures are rounded.

Table B-4. *Independent Variables*[a]

State	INCOME	INCOME-GROWTH	NATLANDS	AIRPOLLUTION SO₂	TSP	O₃	WATER-QUALITY
				SO_2	TSP	O_3	
Alabama	5,758	4.41	0.02	0.69	14.78	28.22	87.28
Alaska	10,440	4.84	0.97	0.00	0.00	0.00	n.a.
Arizona	6,862	4.05	0.38	14.10	44.50	27.65	90.10
Arkansas	5,651	4.92	0.08	0.00	0.00	15.14	83.20
California	8,597	3.69	0.41	0.83	56.38	90.96	91.00
Colorado	7,985	4.14	0.36	4.58	55.21	53.80	95.95
Connecticut	9,302	3.74	0.00	0.00	25.15	100.00	92.80
Delaware	8,129	3.30	0.02	0.00	0.00	67.72	87.16
Florida	6,685	3.96	0.09	3.87	0.00	58.46	85.90
Georgia	6,387	4.50	0.04	0.00	0.53	37.84	87.97
Hawaii	8,041	4.38	0.06	87.09	6.97	0.00	n.a.
Idaho	6,543	4.05	0.61	4.57	6.72	0.00	97.00
Illinois	8,604	3.76	0.01	1.48	32.37	84.51	84.97
Indiana	7,454	4.08	0.01	22.86	14.53	44.15	87.40
Iowa	7,672	4.38	0.00	1.69	11.73	0.00	87.19
Kansas	8,201	4.34	0.00	0.00	3.68	21.45	87.16
Kentucky	6,015	4.44	0.03	23.21	30.49	33.21	83.83
Louisiana	6,581	4.48	0.03	0.00	0.00	59.86	83.80
Maine	5,878	3.76	0.01	6.29	0.00	62.71	97.60
Maryland	8,316	4.06	0.01	0.00	16.78	81.53	83.17
Massachusetts	7,739	3.75	0.01	0.00	5.54	100.00	84.49
Michigan	8,244	4.14	0.09	1.87	18.28	90.11	94.51
Minnesota	7,954	4.45	0.07	49.38	48.23	0.00	84.91
Mississippi	5,081	5.00	0.04	0.00	1.22	0.00	85.90
Missouri	7,150	3.91	0.04	0.00	24.11	53.35	81.91
Montana	6,861	3.75	0.29	10.26	10.86	0.00	87.55
Nebraska	7,694	4.31	0.01	0.00	33.38	0.00	76.00
Nevada	8,629	3.66	0.81	1.73	43.56	28.43	94.87
New Hampshire	7,182	3.96	0.12	2.00	2.00	85.96	90.40
New Jersey	8,580	3.71	0.01	0.00	0.00	99.88	88.24
New Mexico	6,128	3.68	0.29	3.10	20.93	31.72	92.80
New York	7,841	3.41	0.00	2.98	3.65	86.67	86.62
North Carolina	6,207	4.58	0.05	0.00	0.00	6.78	88.15
North Dakota	7,416	4.73	0.04	0.00	0.00	0.00	85.93
Ohio	7,624	3.89	0.01	29.53	35.87	91.82	85.18
Oklahoma	7,074	4.45	0.01	0.00	17.64	17.11	85.90
Oregon	7,515	4.06	0.52	0.00	5.08	28.89	98.80
Pennsylvania	7,237	3.73	0.02	15.39	18.09	100.00	89.32
Rhode Island	7,086	3.86	0.00	0.00	29.85	100.00	87.55
South Carolina	5,665	4.78	0.04	0.00	5.12	28.07	87.55
South Dakota	6,556	4.33	0.06	0.00	5.37	100.00	85.39
Tennessee	6,101	4.49	0.05	0.48	19.37	53.29	89.20
Texas	7,624	4.45	0.01	0.00	17.46	45.61	83.80
Utah	6,234	3.68	0.59	43.87	33.48	51.87	93.70
Vermont	6,075	3.99	0.05	0.00	0.00	0.00	91.54
Virginia	7,362	4.51	0.08	0.00	0.00	53.91	87.16
Washington	8,316	4.12	0.26	0.00	27.92	27.15	88.75
West Virginia	5,883	4.35	0.06	1.06	10.65	0.00	74.95
Wisconsin	7,586	4.07	0.05	16.87	15.32	48.89	85.30
Wyoming	9,007	4.64	0.47	0.00	4.56	0.00	99.52

Source: Same as table B-1.
n.a. Not available.
a. See table 7-2 for explanation of variables.

Index

Acid rain, 14

Ackerman, Bruce A., 39n, 61n, 120, 121n, 123n

Adams, William C., 139n

Administrative Procedures Act, 10

Air pollution policy: benefits and costs, 9, 55–57; capital outlays, 32–33, 43; economic incentives versus qualitative standards, 58, 63; inefficiencies, 3, 32, 33, 57, 59; marketable rights system, 72–77; measuring success of, 16, 17. *See also* Air pollution standards; Ambient air quality standards; Benefits, control; Costs, control; New-source performance standards; Pollution tax; Reforms, air pollution policy

Air pollution standards: compliance certification, 29–30; control costs, 67–68; incremental costs, 34–35, 37; maximization of welfare, 58, 63–65; pollution tax as alternative, 167–68; TERA as alternative, 166–67; uniform technology standards as alternative, 165–66. *See also* Ambient air quality standards; New-source performance standards

Air quality: data, 1, 4, 16, 26–28; emissions data and, 25–26; monitoring, 17, 19, 26–31, 168, 170

Air Quality Act of *1967*, 7, 125

Air quality control regions (AQCRs), 7; incremental control costs, 39; marketable rights, 92–93; monitoring sites, 27; primary standards, 9–10; SIPs, 10–11; variation in air quality, 17

Alabama Power v. *Costle*, 12

Ambient air quality standards: criteria for setting, 133–35; for exceedances of criteria pollutants, 137–38; primary versus secondary, 8–9, 131–32; proposed changes, 151–52, 169; regional uniformity, 136–37; setting of primary, 138–43, 169

Anderson, Peter H., 30n

Anderson, Robert C., 52n, 54n, 142

Anne M. Gorsuch et al. v. *Natural Resources Defense Council, Inc., et al.,* 12n, 13n, 85n

ASARCO v. *EPA*, 12, 85

Atkinson, Scott E., 49

Automobiles: emission standards for new, 1, 5, 6, 7, 14, 15; mandatory inspection and maintenance system, 10

Bailey, Martin J., 53n

Banking emissions, system of, 86; proposed changes, 152; resistance to, 88

Bardach, Eugene, 98n

Basala, Allen C., 43n

Battelle Laboratories, 60n; study for steel industry, 45; study of control costs, 34, 35, 40

Baumol, William J., 59n

Benefits, control, 52–53, 60; costs versus, 2, 9, 55–57; maximization of, 61; from reductions in particulates and sulfates, 54; uncertainty in measuring, 59, 63

Best available control technology (BACT): case-by-case review of, 13, 86; LAER and, 12; for new facilities, 88, 89; proposed changes in, 147, 148, 150; for PSD areas, 11; steel industry, 47

Best available retrofit technology (BART), 13

Best available technology (BAT), 60–61, 72

Best practicable technology (BPT), 70

Bubble policy, 73, 83–84; effect on pollution abatement, 95–96; proposed liberalization of, 98; resistance to, 88; steel industry support for, 45

Buoni, C., 34n, 60n

Burch, J. E., 34n, 60n

Bureau of the Census, 48n, 112n, 130n; on manufacturing sector, 40; on pollution control cost, 51; on emissions, 23, 25

Burrows, Edward, 45, 47

Burton, E., 49n

Business Roundtable, 147, 151, 152, 153, 154

Business sector: expenditures for air pollution control, 33; proposed amendments to Clean Air Act, 146–48

California: air pollution program, 50; marketable rights trading, 95–96